CIMA

MANAGEMENT

PAPER E2

ENTERPRISE MANAGEMENT

PRACTICE & REVISION KIT

In this Kit we:

- Discuss the **best strategies** for revising and taking your E2 exam

- Show you how to be well prepared for the **2013 exams**

- Give you **lots of great guidance** on tackling questions

- Demonstrate how you can **build your own exams**

- Provide you with **three** mock exams

FOR EXAMS IN 2013

BPP
LEARNING MEDIA

ii

First edition 2010
Fourth edition January 2013

ISBN 9781 4453 6615 9
Previous ISBN 9781 4453 8088 9
e-ISBN 9781 4453 9278 3

British Library Cataloguing-in-Publication Data
A catalogue record for this book is available from the British
Library

Published by

BPP Learning Media Ltd
BPP House, Aldine Place
142-144 Uxbridge Road
London W12 8AA

www.bpp.com/learningmedia

Printed in the United Kingdom by Polestar Wheatons

Hennock Road
Marsh Barton
Exeter
EX2 8RP

Your learning materials, published by BPP Learning
Media Ltd, are printed on paper obtained from traceable
sustainable sources.

The contents of this book are intended as a guide and not
professional advice. Although every effort has been made to
ensure that the contents of this book are correct at the time
of going to press, BPP Learning Media makes no warranty
that the information in this book is accurate or complete and
accept no liability for any loss or damage suffered by any
person acting or refraining from acting as a result of the
material in this book.

We are grateful to the Chartered Institute of Management
Accountants for permission to reproduce past examination
questions. The suggested solutions in the exam answer bank
have been prepared by BPP Learning Media Ltd

BPP
LEARNING MEDIA

Contents

Question index

The headings in this checklist/index indicate the main topics of questions, but questions often cover several different topics.

Questions set under the old syllabus's *Integrated Management (IM) exam* are included because their style and content are similar to those that appear in the Paper E2 exam.

Part C: Strategic Management and assessing the competitive environment

Planning your question practice
Our guidance from page xxii shows you how to organise your question practice, either by attempting questions from each syllabus area or by **building your own exams** – tackling questions as a series of practice exams.

BPP
LEARNING MEDIA

Topic index

Listed below are the key Paper E2 syllabus topics and the numbers of the questions in this Kit covering those topics.

If you need to concentrate your practice and revision on certain topics or if you want to attempt all available questions that refer to a particular subject you will find this index useful.

Syllabus topic	Question numbers
Competitor analysis	61, 63, 72
Conflict and negotiation	2, 20, 21, 23
Controlling projects	37, 47
Corporate appraisal	68, 73
Corporate governance	6, 13, 14
Critical path analysis	27, 28, 29, 30
Critical success factors	54
Culture	7, 8, 9, 53, 72
Environmental analysis	49, 60, 64, 67, 69, 71, 72, 73
Ethics and corporate social responsibility	12, 15
Finance function	18, 25, 26
Health and safety	16, 17
Management and leadership	1, 4 ,5, 11
Management ideas and theories	24
Mission, objectives and strategy	48, 50, 51, 52, 57
Outsourcing	58, 65, 66
Project lifecycle	46
Project management techniques	34, 35, 41, 42, 44
Project planning and initiation	32, 33, 39, 43, 45
Project risk	31, 38, 42
Project stakeholders and responsibilities	36, 40, 43, 44
Staff development and motivation	3, 10, 19, 22
Stakeholders	59
Strategic approaches	55, 56, 62, 70, 73, 74

Using your BPP Learning Media Practice and Revision Kit

Tackling revision and the exam

You can significantly improve your chances of passing by tackling revision and the exam in the right ways. Our advice is based on feedback from CIMA. We focus on Paper E2; we discuss revising the syllabus, what to do (and what not to do) in the exam, how to approach different types of question and ways of obtaining easy marks.

Selecting questions

We provide signposts to help you plan your revision.

*   A full **question index**

*   A **topic index**, listing all the questions that cover key topics, so that you can locate the questions that provide practice on these topics, and see the different ways in which they might be examined

*   **BPP's question plan**, highlighting the most important questions

*   **Build your own exams**, showing you how you can practise questions in a series of exams

Making the most of question practice

We realise that you need more than questions and model answers to get the most from your question practice.

*   Our **Top tips** provide essential advice on tackling questions and presenting answers

*   We show you how you can pick up **Easy marks** on questions, as picking up all readily available marks can make the difference between passing and failing

*   We include **marking guides** to show you what the examiner rewards

*   We summarise **Examiner's comments** to show you how students coped with the questions

*   We refer to the **BPP 2012 Study Text** for detailed coverage of the topics covered in each question

Attempting mock exams

There are three mock exams that provide practice at coping with the pressures of the exam day. We strongly recommend that you attempt them under exam conditions as they reflect the question styles and syllabus coverage of the exam. To help you get the most out of doing these exams, we provide guidance on how you should have approached the whole exam.

Our other products

BPP Learning Media also offers these products for practising and revising the E2 exam:

Passcards	Summarising what you should know in visual, easy to remember, form
Success CDs	Covering the vital elements of the E2 syllabus in less than 90 minutes and also containing exam hints to help you fine tune your strategy
i-Pass	Providing computer-based testing in a variety of formats, ideal for self-assessment
Interactive Passcards	Allowing you to learn actively with a clear visual format summarising what you must know

You can purchase these products by visiting www.bpp.com/learningmedia

BPP LEARNING MEDIA

Revising E2

The E2 exam

General comments

All questions are compulsory, so you will need to revise **all areas of the syllabus**

Bear in mind that any area of the syllabus can be tested in **either section of the paper**. Again, this means that you must have enough knowledge of all areas of the syllabus. **Therefore question spotting is difficult and not advised.** The nature of the paper suggests that the examiner will draw widely upon all of its relevant aspects.

The examiner for E2 stated that overall performance of candidates on the May 2010 first diet of Enterprise Management was not as good as that of the previous examinations for the Integrated Management syllabus. To do well on this paper, candidates need to study the whole syllabus and to pay attention to the question requirements and the mark allocation for each answer so that they don't run out of time.

Our experience of preparing students for this type of exam suggests that to pass Paper E2 you will need to develop a number of **key skills**. Think about what the examiner said in her report as you read through our key skills guidance. We list these skills here.

1   **Planning** your answer to ensure **relevance** and **completeness**. When you sketch your answer plan, think about **what** the examiner wants and how you will answer this. Then make short notes covering the points you will put in your answer.

2   Understanding and applying **the CIMA active verbs**. The most likely learning verbs to be used in E2 are **explain**, **identify** and **apply**. You need to understand what these mean and practice answering questions which use them. Refer to 'What the examiner means' to ensure you are clear on their exact meaning. Look at answers to questions in the kit and see how these are structured. In particular **do not stick to bullet points** and **be prepared to comment and explain**.

3   **Knowledge of the syllabus** is essential for both sections of the exam.

     You may have a good memory or just be lucky in exams! It is more than likely, however, at this stage in your exam career that you use mindmaps, mnemonics or some other memory aid to help you learn.

4   Knowing **how** and **when** to **use theory** in your answer. You may know a lot of theory but you also need to make sure you only **apply** it if this is relevant to the question.

5   Producing an answer that is more than a general analysis, ie is **tailored** to the particular organisation in the exam question.

     Answers at this level must contain a balance of practical and theoretical points as well as relate to the particular organisation and its specific issues.

Question practice

Your revision time should be spent learning the material and practising questions. Use our advice on **key skills** to extract the maximum benefit from question practice.

It is vital to practise both types of question. You may feel that Section B questions are important as they are worth 25 marks each. Make sure, however, that you don't neglect Section A question practice. These are compulsory and you can't guess the answers.

Page (xxii) gives you a **question plan** and you must attempt all of the boxed questions to give yourself a good chance of passing the exam.

If you find that you are struggling in the early stages of your revision with some questions, then don't be afraid to look at the answers and use them as a revision tool. You can then go back to the Passcards or Study Text and highlight the areas that you need to revise further. In the later stages of revision and when you are attempting the mock exams, you should avoid looking at the answers. The **mock exams** in particular should be attempted **under exam conditions** to give you a fair idea of how well you are progressing.

Develop time management skills

Examiners have routinely identified time management as being a problem. It is particularly important, therefore, that you practise all types of question, only allowing yourself the time you will be given in the exam.

Develop business awareness

Candidates with good business awareness can score well in a number of areas.

- Reading articles in CIMA's *Financial Management* magazine and the business press will help you understand the practical application of many of the theories covered throughout the syllabus.

- Being aware of the work of different departments in your own organisation (or others you know about) will help you discuss the practical management issues involved in running a business.

This kind of awareness will not only give you ideas on which to model your solutions to the business/management problems passed in exam scenarios. It will also help you to think practically and realistically about the solutions you propose – which is what real-world management is all about.

Develop your exam technique

Another good reason to practise past and exam-style questions is to get into good habits for the exam, in terms of:

- How to make best use of your reading time
- How to ensure that you obey the examiner's instructions
- How to analyse the precise requirements of each question – and stick to them in your answers

We will give some guidance on tackling each of the E2 question types, a bit further on.

Passing the E2 exam

Displaying the right qualities

The examiner will expect you to display the following qualities.

Qualities required	
Depth of knowledge	Make sure that you write enough to show your depth of knowledge. One line bullet points don't generate sufficient depth.
Application skills	You must be able to **apply** relevant theories, models and frameworks to the scenario given. This means that you will need to use your knowledge to find solutions. It will not be enough to quote a standard solution and state, for example, 'Porter's five forces are relevant here'. You will need to look at the scenario and say **why** they are relevant for that particular company.
Requirements focus	You must focus on the question requirements rather than writing down everything you know about a particular topic. This is known as brain dumping! You must ask yourself if you can relate what you are saying to the scenario in some way. If you can, it is worth doing.
Good planning	Prepare answer plans for all parts of Section B questions before you start answering them. This will ensure the answer is relevant and there is no duplication between different parts. There are several ways of planning. You can make notes on the exam paper and number them in the order you are going to write about them. You can use mind maps. You can also try brainstorming. This is writing down key words and how they relate to the scenario.

Avoiding weaknesses

The examiner for the previous syllabus commented on weaknesses that occurred in many students' answers at every sitting. These comments are relevant to your E2 Paper, as essentially the same approach is needed.

Try to avoid these pitfalls:

- **Inadequate preparation**. Make sure you have covered all areas of the syllabus and practised all types of questions.

- **Lack of theoretical knowledge**. Again, this means having adequate knowledge of all areas of the syllabus.

- **Lack of depth of knowledge**. As mentioned above, make sure you explain fully what you mean, to demonstrate your depth of knowledge.

- **Repetition of scenario material**. The examiner wants to you discuss items in the scenario but doesn't want chunks of the scenario to be copied onto the answer paper.

- **Lack of time management**. It is important to stick to the time limit for each question. Move onto the next question when the time is up.

- **Focusing on to a single word in the question**. Make sure you satisfy the full question requirement. Don't just read the work 'appraisal' for example, and write all you know about appraisals.

- **Quoting theories that aren't relevant to the scenario**. You won't score any marks for discussing a theory which is not relevant to the scenario.

- **Lack of application**. The examiner wants you to apply the issues being examined to the scenario in the question.

Using the reading time

During the 20 minutes reading time you are allowed to write on the exam paper but not in your exam answer book.

We recommend that you spend the reading time:

*   Working out the main points for Section A questions
*   Planning answers to longer Section B questions

The reading time should be used to analyse the question requirement carefully; look at the whole question and break down the question requirement.

Choosing which questions to answer first

There are no strict rules on which questions you should answer first. All questions are compulsory. It is probably a good idea to start with the Section A questions because these are more straightforward. **You must stick to the time plan of 1.8 minutes per mark**. This means you should have finished Section A and B half way through the exam time. You could do Section C questions first if you prefer essay style questions but again, make sure you stick to the time plan.

Approach to questions

Most questions will involve a scenario. Many students find these difficult to deal with. If you have this problem, try the approach outlined below.

STEP ① Read the requirements first to identify the knowledge areas being tested and see if there are links between them. This helps with focusing on what's important in the scenario. Ensure you can define technical terms used so that you know what the question is about.

STEP ② Identify the action verbs in the requirement because this conveys the level of skill you need to exhibit (eg define, illustrate, evaluate require quite different skills. See *What the examiner means* list on page xxi).

STEP ③ Identify the parts to the question. For example a requirement with 'and' implies two parts to the question that may be linked.

STEP ④ Check mark allocation of each section. This shows you the depth anticipated and helps allocate time

STEP ⑤ Read scenario/preamble and put key points under headings related to requirements (eg by marginal notes, highlighting or jotting down on page).

STEP ⑥ Scribble a plan answer (just a few words jotted untidily under the key requirements not a summary that someone else could write the answer from. Perhaps a brainstorm or spider diagram/mindmap).

STEP ⑦ Write answer.

Discussion questions

Remember that **depth of discussion** is also important. Discussions will often consist of paragraphs containing 2-3 sentences. Each paragraph should:

*   **Make a point**
*   **Explain the point** (you must demonstrate **why** the point is important)
*   **Illustrate the point** (with material or analysis from the scenario, perhaps an example from real life)

Gaining the easy marks

There are likely to be easier marks available for stating the risks you've spotted in the scenario, also for defining key topics in general terms when the question doesn't require you to link these definitions in with the scenario. The examiner has stated that on some papers you may see an essay question that doesn't link into a scenario and this type of question may well be easier than other scenario-linked questions on that paper.

Often the easier marks will be in the first part(s) of the question. If they are in subsequent parts, we would not recommend that you do these parts first, as question requirements and hence answers will generally have a logical flow to them. However you must give yourself enough time on these parts, and not get bogged down in the more difficult question parts.

There will also be some easy marks available for answering using an appropriate format, for example a report.

BPP
LEARNING MEDIA

The exam paper

Format of the paper

		Number of marks
Section A:	Five compulsory questions each worth 10 marks.	50
Section B:	Two compulsory questions each worth 25 marks.	50
		100

Time allowed: 3 hours

CIMA guidance

Good answers demonstrate knowledge and show understanding in the application thereof. Reading the scenario should give you clues on what issues or tools to use.

Weaker answers tend to repeat book knowledge without applying it to the question set. Candidates who fail reveal a lack of knowledge or depth in their understanding.

The key to passing this paper is to understand the theories and principles in the syllabus and show you can apply these to whatever situation presents itself in the exam.

Numerical content

This paper can be wholly written. Any numbers are likely to be included in question on project planning tools.

Breadth of question coverage

Questions in **all** sections are likely to cover at least two out of three syllabus areas. The Section A shorter questions will be used to test the **breadth of the syllabus**. Section B questions will be scenario-based and reflect topical management issues. Students will need to apply knowledge often across syllabus areas in one question.

November 2012

Section A

1   Corporate social responsibility
2   Appraisal process
3   Stakeholder management
4   Managing conflict
5   Negotiation

Section B

6   Critical path analysis
7   Porter's value chain; competitor analysis

This paper is Mock Exam 3.

September 2012 (re-sit exam paper)

Section A

1   Product portfolios, BCG matrix
2   Levels of strategy
3   Competitive advantage and rivalry
4   Project stakeholders
5   Organisational culture

Section B

6   PRINCE2
7   The finance function

Examiner's comments

The overall performance of candidates on this paper was lower than in the comparable re-sit diet in March 2012. Relatively few candidates gained high scoring marks with the majority of candidates scoring between 50 and 60 per cent. Only a few candidates managed to gain a mark in excess of 70%.

This relatively poor performance seems to have been due to two main failings on the part of the candidates. First a significant number of candidates prepared answers to questions that had been set for the main diet in May 2012 in the expectation that the questions would be pretty much the same for the September re-sit diet. Some candidates even went so far as to make reference to the case scenarios used in the May exam. This kind of preparation is obviously a mistake.

The second reason for the poor performance of candidates was a failure to read the questions thoroughly. The outcome of this lack of care was that candidates spent considerable time on writing an answer that brought them little if any benefit and used up precious time that could have been employed more profitably on another part of the paper.

Question 3 on the bases of competitive advantage and the reasons for competitive rivalry seemed to cause problems for a large majority of candidates. By contrast Question 4 on the distinction between project owners and project sponsors and the relationships between the project manager and the other major stakeholders was generally well answered.

Of the remaining Questions 1.2.5 and 7(a) were generally well answered while Q6(a) requiring the application of PRINCE2 methodology and 7(b) requiring knowledge of factors that contribute to the effectiveness of a multidisciplinary management team were generally badly answered.

This paper is Mock Exam 2.

May 2012

Section A

1   Market size, share and groth
2   Project stakeholders
3   Positioning approach to strategy
4   Culture
5   Levels of strategy

Section B

6   Shared servicing
7   Project lifecycle

Examiner's comments

The pass rate for this examination was in line with that of the previous main May/November examinations. A particular feature of overall performance this time was the noticeable gap between high scoring candidates at the top end of the scale and very poor performances at the lower end. This examination saw a much larger number of candidates than usual scoring over 70% while at the other end of the scale there were candidates who achieved only a few marks. A significant number of candidates appeared to have done little if any preparation for the examination.

Time management appeared to be a problem for some candidates with some of their Section A answers more detailed and lengthy than Section B answers; the superficial nature of the Section B answers indicating that these candidates had run out of time and thus sacrificed the opportunity to gain marks in the 25 mark questions of Section B. It was also noticeable in this session that a higher proportion of candidates than usual had been unable to complete all seven questions, again indicating a lack of good time management or lack of breadth of knowledge of the syllabus.

A noticeable trend in recent examinations is that more and more candidates are not bothering to tick the boxes indicating which questions they have attempted. Candidates should note that this is an essential requirement to ensure that all their answers are marked and their marks credited to their overall score.

In Section A, Q2, Q3 and Q5 posed few problems with many candidates gaining a pass mark or more, but Q1 and Q4 did seem to create difficulties for a sizable number of candidates.

March 2012 (re-sit exam paper)

Section A

1   Transaction costs and asset specificity
2   Project risk management
3   Delegation
4   Health and safety
5   Corporate governance

Section B

6   Project initiation
7   Formal/rational approach to strategy

Examiner's comments

The number of candidates who passed this examination was greater than in previous examinations although there was little difference in the average marks gained. Many candidates scored in the low fifties whereas in previous examinations there has been a much wider spread of marks.

In terms of performance on individual questions, only Question 1 on transaction cost theory produced overall low scores. This is surprising since it is an area that has been tested on a number of previous occasions. Candidates appeared to have most difficulty on part (b) that dealt with asset specificity and its role in outsourcing decisions. This would seem to be an area which candidates should familiarise themselves for future examinations.

The remaining questions in Section A of the paper were fairly well answered in that most candidates were able to gain a pass mark, though only a minority produced very good answers.

In general, the Section B answers were also well answered although some answers to Question 7 on the formal/rational approach to strategy development suggested a lack of preparation by some candidates. Question 6 on what should be included in a project initiation document and how problems threatening success of a particular project should be overcome produced some very good answers but also some very poor ones. The poorer answers appeared to stem partly from a lack of preparation of the subject area and partly from a lack of planning about how to set out the answer.

Candidates would be well advised in future to give some thought as to how best structure their answers to the longer (25 mark) questions before commencing to write their answers.

November 2011

Section A

1   Sources of power
2   Controlling projects
3   Transaction cost theory
4   CIMA's Code of Ethics
5   Disciplinary procedures

Section B

6   Approaches to strategy: rational model and emergent strategies
7   Project management: dealing with slippage and managing project teams

Examiner's comments

The overall performance of candidates in this diet was lower than that in recent diets. There appears to be two main reasons for this:

Firstly, many candidates had simply not prepared adequately enough to give themselves a good chance of success. Too many of them relied on their general knowledge of the subject area and as a result never came near to passing the examination. This was most evident in the case of Q4 where many candidates seemed not to have studied the CIMA Code of Ethics and therefore scored few if any marks for the question.

The second reason for poor performance was due to the fact that a significant number of candidates did not exercise sufficient care in reading the question set before writing their answer. This weakness in their examination technique was most evident in their response to questions 6(b) and 7(a).

Question 6(b) asked candidates to

'Discuss the strategic management models\frameworks that R could use in undertaking his analysis of the strategic position of VRC Company'

Unfortunately candidates who skimped on a careful reading of the question jumped to the conclusion that only one model/framework was required and so only discussed one model/framework instead of a number of frameworks. This single mistake contributed to the loss of many marks.

Question 7(a) asked candidates to

'Analyse the strategies available to J Company to address the issue of time, cost and quality in the website project.'

In this case a very large number of candidates appear to have misunderstood the word 'strategies' in the context of the question and so instead of concentrating on the actions necessary to get the project back on track focussed instead on how project tools such as WBS, Gantt Charts and the like could provide information as a basis for action. Consequently they gained only a few of the total marks available for this part of the question

September 2011(re-sit exam paper)

Section A

1   Style of management and leadership
2   Porter's Diamond and national competitive advantage
3   Characteristics and appropriateness of a matrix structure
4   Competitor analysis and information required
5   Competitor advantage and the resource-based view

Section B

6   Project management methodology; project sponsor
7   Sources of conflict; effective meetings

Examiner's comments

The overall performance in the September examination was poorer than that of candidates for previous diets. A much greater number of candidates than usual scraped through the examination with just over fifty marks. The main reasons for this seem to be twofold. First, many candidates appeared to have a superficial knowledge of theoretical models/frameworks and secondly a significant number were unable to apply the models to the issues raised in the scenario questions. The net result of these weaknesses was for candidates to obtain just four or five marks for a 10 mark question and a marginal pass in the 25 mark questions. Several candidates only managed to pass the examination because they were able to gain a respectable score of marks on the part (b) sections of questions 6 and 7. It is noteworthy that neither Q6 (b) nor Q7 (b) required the application of a theoretical model.

Of the candidates who performed well in the examination only a very small minority gained marks in excess of 70%. This contrasts with previous diets in which a good number of candidates scored over 70% and a significant number gained marks in excess of 80%.

In terms of performance on individual questions, candidates in general did relatively well on Q4 and on the part (b) sections of Q6 and Q7, but performed relatively badly on questions 1,2,3,5,6(a) and 7(a).

May 2011

Section A

1 Porter's Five Forces model
2 Work Breakdown Structure and Gantt charts
3 Management and leadership styles
4 Resource-based approach to strategy
5 Competitive intelligence information

Section B

6 Project management: project vs business as usual; role of project manager
7 Training for better communication; staff appraisal system

Examiner's comments

The overall performance in this Enterprise Management paper was generally poorer than in recent papers.

The main reason for poor performance was a lack of adequate preparation. A significant number of candidates appeared not to have done even the most basic preparation and consequently scored marks of less than 20%. This was particularly evident for Question Four where many candidates scored no more than four marks and this was despite the fact that an article, together with a specimen question and answer, had appeared in Financial Management just prior to the examination.

A second reason for poor performance was due to a lack of care in reading the question set. This was notably the case with Question Five in which many candidates interpreted the question to be asking about the types and sources of information in the wider macro external environment rather than types and sources of competitive intelligence information. Consequently, they produced a PEST or Five Forces analysis rather than an answer specifically focusing on competitive information as required.

Similarly, a significant number of candidates misinterpreted Question Six (a) and so instead of distinguishing the characteristics of the website project from business as usual work, produced answers which discussed the difference between an online store and a retail store.

A third reason for low marks was the tendency to cite theory without application. This was evident for Question Three where candidates often demonstrated a grasp of management style theory but failed to apply this to the case set out in the scenario of the question. To some extent this was also the case for Question One, where some candidates seemed unable to link the Five Forces model to the context of the question.

Well prepared candidates, as always, did well in the examination and their hard work was rewarded with a clear pass. Once again, a number of candidates attained marks in the high seventies and a couple of candidates scored 80%.

March 2011 (re-sit exam paper)

Section A

1 Benefits of having a clear mission
2 Levels of strategy – how functional areas support the other levels
3 Characteristics of a role culture; change to a task culture
4 Critical path analysis
5 Analysis of external environment

Section B

6 Managing conflict; negotiation
7 Project planning; project management tools and techniques

Examiner's comments

The overall performance for this session of Enterprise Management was the best achieved by candidates since the new syllabus commenced in 2010.

There were fewer really excellent papers than in November 2012, with only one candidate achieving over 80%. However, several other candidates scored in excess of 70% which is a very good performance indeed on a question paper of seven compulsory questions.

For the candidates who, unfortunately, did not manage to pass this examination, question two on the role of functional strategy and question six (a) on conflict handling strategies appeared to cause the most difficulty. In both cases, candidates appeared to lack knowledge of the relevant theoretical concepts and so struggled in their attempt to answer the question. The only solution to this kind of problem is to ensure careful preparation of the whole syllabus. There is no hiding place in an examination paper in which all questions are compulsory.

Other general reasons for poor performance included poor time allocation, though this was less prevalent than in previous papers, and misinterpretation of question requirements.

November 2010

Section A

1   Task oriented management; demotivated staff
2   Appropriateness of a matrix structure
3   Process and benefits of mentoring
4   Purpose of corporate appraisal (SWOT) and what it would involve
5   Types and sources of conflict

Section B

6   Porter's Diamond and competitive advantage; analysis of external environment
7   Project management software; stakeholders

Examiner's comments

The examiner commented that performance in November 2010 was better than in May 2010. Candidates in general were better prepared for the paper and most managed their allocation of time across the seven compulsory questions rather better than in the May diet. Another reason for the higher pass rate was that candidates performed relatively well on the two final 25 mark questions.

The range of marks between that of better candidates and that of the less well prepared was much the same as that in previous diets, but rather more candidates produced really excellent papers with marks exceeding 80 per cent.

Once again however, candidates scoring low marks did so because of lack of depth of knowledge and poor preparation. For others the major weakness was in poor time management. In particular the length of several of the section A answers provided by some candidates were out of proportion to the marks available and this affected the candidates' ability to give sufficient time to answer section B questions.

Another reason for loss of marks can be attributed to a lack of care in the reading of the question set. This was particularly the case for Q6 *(a)* in which answers often related to the wrong companies and the wrong country. This problem arose because some candidates did not read the scenario with sufficient care.

Too many candidates wasted time simply repeating material directly from the scenarios rather than addressing the specific requirements of the questions set and describing theories without applying them to explain why problems had arisen and how problems might be solved.

May 2010

Section A

1 Competitor analysis: importance; high/low market growth and market share.
2 Organisational culture: cultural change with organisation's growth.
3 Critical path analysis.
4 Social responsibility: points for a presentation.
5 Strategic business unit and link to functional strategies.

Section B

6 Project plan; project stakeholders; project manager skills.
7 Problems with outsourcing; approach to negotiations.

Examiner's comments

The examiner was disappointed with candidates' performance as compared with examinations set under the previous syllabus. The range of marks between that of better candidates and that of the less well prepared was also wider than that in previous diets. Several candidates gained marks of over 80 per cent while at the lower end too many candidates obtained marks of less than 30 per cent.

The main reason for poor performance seems to lie in lack of preparation. Too many candidates did not possess the requisite theory and knowledge necessary to answer the full range of questions adequately. This meant that although they often scored well on two or three questions they were unable to pass because they had not assimilated the breadth of knowledge to perform well across the paper. In many cases such candidates fell back on common sense explanations or simply regurgitated elements of the case scenario with no theoretical underpinning.

A sizable number of candidates performed less well than they might have done because they did not read the question sufficiently carefully and then spent valuable time writing material that brought them no marks. In other cases it was clear that candidates ran out of time, either because they lacked knowledge of what to write or sometimes because they spent too long on answering a particular question and so had insufficient time to give to their later answer.

Specimen exam paper

Section A

1 Porter's Five Forces model applied to analyse competition in a foreign country.
2 Work breakdown structure and Gantt charts.
3 Stakeholder groups affected by a takeover bid.
4 Formal rational approach to strategy.
5 Corporate governance issues and autocratic management.

Section B

6 Characteristics of a project; role of project manager.
7 Conflict between departments; effective team leadership.

What the examiner means

The table below has been prepared by CIMA to help you interpret exam questions.

Learning objective	Verbs used	Definition
1 Knowledge		
What you are expected to know	• List • State • Define	• Make a list of • Express, fully or clearly, the details of/facts of • Give the exact meaning of
2 Comprehension		
What you are expected to understand	• Describe • Distinguish • Explain • Identify • Illustrate	• Communicate the key features of • Highlight the differences between • Make clear or intelligible/state the meaning or purpose of • Recognise, establish or select after consideration • Use an example to describe or explain something
3 Application		
How you are expected to apply your knowledge	• Apply • Calculate/compute • Demonstrate • Prepare • Reconcile • Solve • Tabulate	• Put to practical use • Ascertain or reckon mathematically • Prove the certainty or exhibit by practical means • Make or get ready for use • Make or prove consistent/compatible • Find an answer to • Arrange in a table
4 Analysis		
How you are expected to analyse the detail of what you have learned	• Analyse • Categorise • Compare and contrast • Construct • Discuss • Interpret • Prioritise • Produce	• Examine in detail the structure of • Place into a defined class or division • Show the similarities and/or differences between • Build up or complete • Examine in detail by argument • Translate into intelligible or familiar terms • Place in order of priority or sequence for action • Create or bring into existence
5 Evaluation		
How you are expected to use your learning to evaluate, make decisions or recommendations	• Advise • Evaluate • Recommend	• Counsel, inform or notify • Appraise or assess the value of • Propose a course of action

Planning your question practice

We have already stressed that question practice should be right at the centre of your revision. Whilst you will spend some time looking at your notes and the Paper E2 Passcards, you should spend the majority of your revision time practising questions.

We recommend two ways in which you can practise questions.

- Use **BPP Learning Media's question plan** to work systematically through the syllabus and attempt key and other questions on a section-by-section basis

- **Build your own exams** – attempt the questions as a series of practice exams

These ways are suggestions and simply following them is no guarantee of success. You or your college may prefer an alternative but equally valid approach.

BPP's question plan

The plan below requires you to devote a **minimum of 35 hours** to revision of Paper E2. Any time you can spend over and above this should only increase your chances of success.

STEP ① **Review your notes** and the chapter summaries in the Paper E2 **Passcards** for each section of the syllabus.

STEP ② **Answer the key questions** for that section. These questions have boxes round the question number in the table below and you should answer them in full. Even if you are short of time you must attempt these questions if you want to pass the exam. You should complete your answers without referring to our solutions.

STEP ③ **Attempt the other questions** in that section. For some questions we have suggested that you prepare **answer plans or do the calculations** rather than full solutions. Planning an answer means that you should spend about 40% of the time allowance for the questions brainstorming the question and drawing up a list of points to be included in the answer.

STEP ④ **Attempt Mock exams 1, 2 and 3** under strict exam conditions.

Syllabus section	2012 Passcards chapters	Questions in this Kit	Comments	Done ☑
Management of relationships	1-5			
Management functions	1	3	A good test of your knowledge of discipline from the November 2011 exam .	☐
		1	Answer this question in full.	☐
Control systems	2	16	Health and safety policy is covered in this short question.	☐
	2	17	A test of both your knowledge of health and safety and your ability to apply it from the March 2012 exam.	☐
	2	12	A good question from May 2010 for testing your knowledge of social responsibility.	☐
Groups and teams	2	6(b)	Part (b) of this question from the May 2012 exam covers team building	☐
Conflict and discipline	3	Mock 1 q4	A good test of your knowledge of disciplinary procedures and also why discipline is a good idea.	☐
		23	A comprehensive question from the Specimen Paper on conflict and leadership.	☐
	3	18	These two short questions get you to think clearly about what the finance function does and how it fits into the organisation.	☐
Management skills	1	20	This question from November 2010 asks you to compare and contrast the different types and sources of conflict.	☐
Culture	5	8	A useful May 2010 question on how culture changes as the company grows.	☐
Project management	6 to 9			
	6	31	This question brings together two topics within project management. These are project management and risk management. Make sure you understand how these are linked.	☐
	6	43	This May 2010 question tests your understanding of project management. Use the information in the question to illustrate your points.	☐
	6,7	39	This question gives good general coverage of the nature of project management and the roles of those involved in projects.	☐
Project management tools and techniques	8	30-35	Do all these questions – networks get easier with practice. You need to be able to draw a basic network quickly and accurately. The logic of dependencies and interactions must be carefully analysed and the critical path arithmetic completed. Prepare full answers.	☐

Syllabus section	2012 Passcards chapters	Questions in this Kit	Comments	Done ☑
	8	41	A question covering a specialist area, project management software. Remember to make clear points about stakeholders too in part (b).	☐
Strategic management	10-13			
Approaching strategy	10	74	This longer question from the March 2012 exam is a good test of the rational/formal approach to strategy. Answer in full.	☐
Goals of the organisation	11	54	Make sure you understand what Critical Success Factors are and how these affect strategy when answering this previous syllabus May 2006 exam question.	☐
	11	57	Prepare a full answer to this question from November 2005 which tests mission and objectives.	☐
	2	6	This question from March 2012 is a good test of your knowledge of corporate governance. Answer it in full.	☐
	2	48	Prepare an answer plan for this question.	☐
		65	Use this shorter past exam question to revise transaction cost theory and its application.	☐
National culture	5, 12			
		53	This question requires you to apply your knowledge of national and corporate culture. Answer in full	☐
Competitor analysis		61	A short question asking about the importance of competitor analysis (Part (a)) and market share and market growth (Part (b)). This is from May 2010.	☐
Porter's Diamond	12		Answer this question in full	☐
		64		☐
Competitive advantage	13	70(b)	Part (b) only considers different approaches to competitive advantage. Do this part in full.	☐
				☐

Build your own exams

Having revised your notes and the BPP Passcards, you can attempt the questions in the Kit as a series of practice exams, making them up yourself or using the mock exams that we have listed below.

	Practice exams						May 2012
	1	2	3	4	5	6	7
Section A							
1	4	3	1	10	2	8	7
2	9	23	16	19	6	10	36
3	18	15	17	13	20	14	49
4	28	40	29	35	27	25	52
5	50	49	45	48	43	51	55
Section B							
6	36	21	39	22	40	23	26
7	70	42	71	37	72	38	46

Whichever practice exams you use, you must attempt **Mock exams 1, 2 and 3** at the end of your revision.

QUESTIONS

Management of relationships

Questions 1 to 32 cover the management of relationships, the subject of Part A of the BPP Study Text for Paper E2.

Section A questions: Management of relationships

1 Dr Strong   18 mins

The C Pharmaceutical Company is in a state of crisis. The development of new drugs and treatments on which the vary survival of the organisation depends has slowed dramatically in recent years. An investigation into the operation of the organisation's research and development (R&D) unit has revealed that the slow rate of innovation has much to do with the way the department has been managed.

The head of the unit, Dr Strong, regards it as his duty not to exceed the unit's budget allocation and has introduced strict controls to avoid this happening. Members of the R&D unit are set clear targets with time limits and expected to be working in the laboratory or office on a 9-5 basis every working day. This system of control is not to the liking of research staff and several of the most innovative members have left. The morale of the remaining staff is very low and further resignations are expected.

Required

Analyse why the problems in the R&D unit of the C Pharmaceutical Company might have developed. Recommend what actions could be taken to encourage creativity and innovation.   **(10 marks)**

2 Conflict in organisations   18 mins

Conflict in organisations is often considered to be inevitable and can have positive as well as negative outcomes.

Required

(a)   Identify and explain three key sources of conflict in organisations.   **(5 marks)**
(b)   Explain the win-win approach to resolving conflict and contrast this approach with win-lose and lose-lose approaches.   **(5 marks)**

(Total = 10 marks)

The following data are given for questions 4 and 5 below

The T Aerospace Company is in the early stages of planning the development of its latest commercial jet, the 007. The aircraft industry is a fiercely competitive one, dominated by a few large global players who operate at the forefront of technology. In this industry, competitors quickly copy any advance in technology or new management technique that might provide them with a competitive edge. Some of the T Aerospace Company's competitors have adopted team working as a means of speeding up their development and production processes.

The T Aerospace Company is thus considering the adoption of team working in its operations, but some of the traditionalists in the company are doubtful. They are concerned that the benefits of work specialisation will be lost. Some of the managers have had negative experiences with team working and so have strong reservations about the proposed changes.

3   Disciplinary procedures   18 mins

T, a member of the finance team, has been constantly arriving late to work and in recent months he has consistently made significant errors in his work. A number of colleagues have complained to Pm, their line manager, about T's aggressive behavior towards them and V, a junior administrator, has suggested that T has bullied her.

P knows he must take action to deal with the situation.

Required

Explain to P what is involved in the process of taking disciplinary action.   **(10 marks)**

4   Source of power   18 mins

TF Company is about to embark on a restructuring programme which will mean significant changes to the roles and responsibilities of staff in the Finance Department. It is anticipated that there will be some resistance to the proposed changes, so the Board of TF Company has asked KK, a senior manager in the department, to lead the changes. The board has chosen KK because she is generally well liked and respected by her colleagues. She is also held in high regard for her expert knowledge and her interest in, and support she fives to, all those who work for her.

Required   French + Raven

Describe the different sources of power KK possesses /and/ which could help her to manage the changes in the Finance Department.   **(10 marks)**

5   Benefits of delegation   18 mins

YT is the Finance Manager of SBM Magazine Publishing Company. He has recently had his appraisal and was expecting that he would get a good review, since he felt that he had met all of his targets for the year, although at a personal cost of working exceptionally long hours. YT was therefore surprised when his line manager, RP, suggested to him that he was not using his staff effectively and should be delegating more work to his team. Whilst RP commented that YT had achieved the department's objectives, he suggested that delegating more would be mutually beneficial to YT and his team as well as being in the long term interests of the company.

Required

Explain the benefits of delegation from the point of view of YT, the Finance Manager, and also his team.

(10 marks)

6   Corporate governance issues   18 mins

M has recently joined the board of X Company, a major listed confectionary manufacturer. The company was established as a family business over a century ago and members of the founding family still occupy many of the senior board positions. When directors are due to retire they are usually replaced by other family members. The Board is reluctant to make any external appointments, M being an exception.

M has noted that there are seven executive board members and only two non-executive members. On doing some homework about each of the directors, M discovered that all of the directors were from similar backgrounds.

At the first board meeting after M's appointment, the board papers for discussion were handed out at the start of the meeting. The agenda included discussion of a major contamination issue that had occurred in one of the manufacturing plants but when this point was to be discussed at the meeting it was discovered that the board papers for discussion had been omitted. One of the major institutional investors had expressed concern over the incident. At the subsequent board meeting the executive chairman commented that the company had outperformed in its sector in the past year and that the shareholders should therefore trust him to run the company as he sees fit.

Required

Analyse the corporate governance issues facing X Company. **(10 marks)**

7 Strong culture — 18 mins

The Board of PCC Company, which operates in the investment and risk management industry, has determined that in order to 'take the company to the next stage of its growth' there will need to be significant changes in its internal operations and in the way staff work. The Managing Director feels that whilst the company has built a strong organisational culture, this is now becoming a barrier to realising the company's future aspirations, particularly since future developments may involve a merger with another company.

Required

Explain how the organisational culture of PCC Company might influence, both positively and negatively, its performance. **(10 marks)**

8 CT (5/10) — 18 mins

CT established her business, KCC, specialising in making handmade cakes, six years ago. Initially CT worked from her home, developing new recipes and cake designs. The business thrived on the creative talents of CT and her staff. In fact, the business became more successful than CT could have hoped for with a number of upmarket supermarkets now stocking her products.

Six years on, CT is reflecting on her success. She does feel that things have changed significantly since the early days when her business was run from her home kitchen. To satisfy increasing demand, three years ago she bought a factory for the production of her cakes, and in the last year she has opened five shops to sell the company's products.

KCC currently employs over 450 staff and the company has significantly changed compared to when it was first established. It now has a formal functional structure and the culture has more of the feel of a large bureaucratic organisation. CT feels that she has lost the passion and enthusiasm she once had for her business and feels that far too much of her time is spent on management issues rather than creating designs for cakes. She has a senior management team made up of the managers looking after different functional areas of the business. They make decisions about the running of the business, but seem to be focused on achieving efficiencies, control and bottom line performance, and have little interest in the creative side of the business. CT used to be on first name terms with her staff, but this is no longer the case. She was particularly saddened when she overheard an employee comment that he just felt he was a robot on a production line rather than a craft worker and that his ideas for new cake designs do not get heard.

Required

Distinguish between the characteristics of KCC's culture when it was first set up and the culture the company is likely to have now. **(10 marks)**

9 Role culture (3/11) — 18 mins

S Company has for many years been a long standing household name, designing and manufacturing electrical appliances for use in the kitchen. It has developed a strong culture over the years which can be best typified as a role culture. However, this culture is now acting as a barrier to the company's ability to adapt to become more flexible so that it is able to respond quickly to changes in the environment and initiatives taken by its competitors in product design.

In particular, the company is falling behind its new competitors when it comes to innovations in new product development and design. Effective new product development requires staff to work together across functional boundaries but this is becoming hard to achieve in S Company where people now fiercely protect their functional specialism and will only work on the tasks specified in their job descriptions.

Required

(a) **Describe** the key characteristics of a role culture, explaining why this type of culture is no longer appropriate for S Company. **(6 marks)**

(b) **Recommend**, with reasons, the type of culture to which S Company now needs to change. **(4 marks)**

(Total = 10 marks)

10 Task oriented management (11/10) — 18 mins

TS Consultants has been asked to investigate the issues underlying the underperformance and low staff morale of the Finance Department in YR Hospital.

The consultants have access to various sources of information such as the recent staff satisfaction survey which shows that staff morale in the department is low. In addition, statistics from the HR Department reveals that both absenteeism and staff turnover are exceptionally high in the Finance Department. There have also been many complaints from other areas of the hospital about both the management and staff working in the department. However, staff enjoy competitive salaries and other excellent working conditions such as free car parking, a subsidised canteen and access to sports facilities.

[handwritten: Hygeine Factors] [handwritten: Herzberg – Hygeine – motivation]

The consultants have run some focus groups with members of staff working in the department to try to gather more information to help them better understand the causes of underperformance and low staff morale. The findings suggest that there appears to be very much a "them and us" culture between management and staff, with the managers in the department exerting power based on their position and status. Staff say that they are only allowed to undertake the specific activities included in their narrow job descriptions and feel unable to fully contribute as a result of the chain of command in the Finance Department. Staff also say that they are not involved in decisions regarding the department's activities, and many say they have not had any training. They mentioned that there are very few career progression opportunities because of this. They feel their contributions are not recognised by management and that they never receive feedback on their performance. Staff characterise the leadership and management of the department as task-focused, with tight controls and close supervision.

Having undertaken the review, the consultants are preparing the recommendations on how to improve the poor performance and low staff morale.

Required

[handwritten: See from both sides] [handwritten: Tangible recommendations needed.]

With reference to theory, **discuss** the recommendations TS Consultants could make to help improve performance and staff morale in the Finance Department of YR Hospital. **(10 marks)**

[handwritten: shift in mgmt style needed → currently dictatorial]

11 TR (5/11) — 18 mins

TR has recently been promoted to his first management position. In the past, he very much enjoyed working as part of a team, but is having some difficulty in adapting to his new role as leader of a team. In his recent appraisal he has acknowledged that his style of management is not effective in all instances. In particular, he feels that he has not been very flexible in dealing with some of the issues that he has faced. He has identified that he would benefit from leadership training to help him better understand the alternative styles of management that he could adopt to help him develop to become more effective in his role.

Required

Explain to TR, with reference to theory, the different management / leadership styles he could adopt to help him to become more effective in his role. **(10 marks)**

12   PW (5/10)   18 mins

PW has been asked by her local management accountants' forum to present a paper at the annual conference on the subject of social responsibility. She has been asked to do this as her company has recently won a national award for its socially responsible initiatives including its success in recycling methods, community based projects and reducing its carbon footprint.

PW has decided that her presentation should start by setting out what is meant by the concept of social responsibility since she feels there are often misconceptions surrounding the term. She also wants to emphasise through her presentation the key benefits that companies can gain from developing strategies which are socially responsible. PW is aware that there will be some cynics in the audience who view socially responsible business driven strategies as unrealistic, that they conflict with the achievement of healthy profits and detract from creating shareholder value.

Required

Discuss the points that PW should include in her presentation on social responsibility.   **(10 marks)**

13   Megamart   18 mins

MegaMart plc is a medium sized retailer of fashion goods with some 200 outlets spread throughout the UK. A publicly quoted company on the London Stock Market, it has pursued a growth strategy based on the aggressive acquisition of a number of smaller retail groups. This growth has gone down well with shareholders, but a significant slowdown in retail sales has resulted in falling profits, dividends and, as a consequence, its share price. MegaMart had been the creation of one man, Rex Lord, a high profile entrepreneur, convinced that his unique experience of the retail business gained through a lifetime working in the sector was sufficient to guide the company through its current misfortunes. His dominance of the company was secured through his role as both Chairman and Chief Executive of the company. His control of his board of directors was almost total and his style of management such that his decisions were rarely challenged at board level. He felt no need for any non-executive directors drawn from outside the company to be on the board. Shareholders were already asking questions on his exuberant lifestyle and lavish entertainment, at company expense, which regularly made the headlines in the popular press. Rex's high profile personal life also was regularly exposed to public scrutiny and media attention.

As a result of the downturn in the company's fortunes some of his acquisitions have been looked at more closely and there are, as yet, unsubstantiated claims that MegaMart's share price had been maintained through premature disclosure of proposed acquisitions and evidence of insider trading. Rex had amassed a personal fortune through the acquisitions, share options and above average performance related bonuses, which had on occasion been questioned at the Shareholders' Annual General Meeting. His idiosyncratic and arrogant style of management had been associated with a reluctance to accept criticism from any quarter and to pay little attention to communicating with shareholders.

Recently, there has been concern expressed in the financial press that the auditors appointed by MegaMart, some twenty years ago, were also providing consultancy services on his acquisition strategy and on methods used to finance the deals.

Required

Explain the corporate governance issues raised by the management style of Rex Lord.   **(10 marks)**

14 SP Company (Specimen Paper)   18 mins

E is Chairman and Managing Director of SP Company which he started 10 years ago, specialising in the manufacture of kitchen cabinets. The company has been very successful and through a series of acquisitions has diversified into the manufacturing of a range of household furniture and currently employs around 2,000 people. SP is now a public quoted listed company, and whilst E is no longer the majority shareholder, he remains a major force in the company. He still acts as if he is the owner manager and his management style is very autocratic, illustrated by his unwillingness to involve other Board members in decisions concerning the future strategic direction of the company.

F, the Finance Director, has become increasingly concerned about the decisions being made by E and the fact that he has put pressure on her to participate in some illegal accounting practices. This included covering up the substantial remuneration package which E has awarded to himself. F is also aware that E has accepted bribes from foreign suppliers and of insider dealing relating to a number of the acquisitions.

F has discussed her concerns with other members of the Board including the Marketing Director, Production Director and HR Director. However, they seem willing to overlook the wrongdoings of E and never challenge the decisions made by him. The opportunity to do so is limited since the Board meets on an irregular and infrequent basis with no external representatives.

Required

Discuss the corporate governance issues facing SP Company.   **(10 marks)**

15 Code of Ethics   18 mins

The Head of Insurance at JKL Bank has been considering how to make efficiencies in the operation of the Car Insurance Business Unit. One option under consideration is to outsource the Customer Contact Centre (CCC) for its car insurance business. The work of the CCC currently involves dealing with customer telephone enquiries on issues such as insurance claims, policy changes, renewals and premium/payment information.

To help him make a decision on whether or not to proceed, the Head of Insurance has asked for an evaluation of the proposed outsourcing of the CCC.

Required

Explain how transaction cost theory could help the Head of Insurance on deciding whether or not to outsource the Car Insurance Business Unit's Customer Contact Centre.   **(10 marks)**

16 Health and safety policy   18 mins

Whilst Z Company has a policy and a code of conduct on health and safety, the results from a recent survey suggest that many senior managers are not aware of their responsibilities for health and safety in the workplace.

The Board has nominated H, the finance director, to deliver a seminar to help senior managers appreciate the importance of health and safety at work. He is currently considering what he should include in the seminar.

Required

Explain the key areas that H should cover in the health and safety seminar.   **(10 marks)**

17 Health and safety
18 mins

Z works for HS Company and has been asked to undertake an assessment of any health and safety issues that may be potential hazards in the department which she manages. Z's response was that she did not see the need to undertake the assessment as her department only had computers and a photocopier and she did not see what hazards they could cause. Z felt that her time would be better spent delivering company objectives as that would be more cost beneficial.

Required

(a) **Describe** the types of hazards that might be found Z's department. **(4 marks)**

(b) **Illustrate** the benefits to a company from having a robust health and safety procedure. **(6 marks)**

(Total marks = 10 marks)

18 Finance function
18 mins

The finance director of MiniMart Co has recently reorganised the finance department following a number of years of growth within the business, which now includes a number of overseas operations. The company now has separate treasury and financial control departments. The finance director is also considering the use of the balanced scorecard approach in appraising the effectiveness of the finance function.

(a) **Distinguish** the finance function from the treasury function, identifying any areas of interaction between the two functions. Explain the advantages to MiniMart Co of having separate treasury and financial control departments. **(6 marks)**

(b) **Explain** the ways in which the balanced scorecard approach could be used in appraising the finance function. **(4 marks)**

(Total = 10 marks)

19 Mentoring (11/10)
18 mins

JB has recently joined the Finance Department of P Company as a trainee management accountant. As part of the Company's induction, she has been offered a mentor. However, since JB has not had any previous experience of mentoring, she is unconvinced of the benefits. She has asked LC, the facilitator of the induction session, to explain what is involved in the process of mentoring and how it might be a benefit to her as a new member of staff.

Required

Explain the points that LC should make concerning the process and the benefits of mentoring for new members of staff. **(10 marks)**

20 LS Company (11/10)
18 mins

The data on sales performance in LS Company has shown a significant downward trend over the last year. The Marketing and Sales Department is blaming the Finance Department for the poor performance, since it was the pressure from the Finance Department that led the Marketing and Sales Department to increase the product price. The Marketing and Sales Department staff say that, in current market conditions, this was inappropriate and was the main reason for the loss of market share. They feel that the Finance Department staff are short sighted, too focused on costs in pricing decisions and do not appreciate that there are other factors that should be considered in product price setting. However, the Finance Department thinks that the Marketing and Sales Department has been complacent and has not had an aggressive marketing and sales strategy in place. Perhaps not surprisingly, communications and cooperation between the staff in the two departments is at an all time low and in meetings there is constant in-fighting and disagreements.

To make matters worse, a consequence of the drop in sales has been that the senior management is proposing that there will need to be job losses in the Production Department. The trade union which represents the production workers is now threatening to take industrial action.

Required

Compare and contrast the different types and sources of conflict occurring in LS Company.   **(10 marks)**

Section B Questions: Management of relationships

21 ZEZ Company (3/11)	45 mins

ZEZ Company is in the business of designing and printing bottle labels for soft drinks distributors. The company is, at present, facing very difficult times as recessionary economic conditions have had a negative impact on the demand for its customers' products, which in turn is having a knock-on effect on the demand for ZEZ Company's labels. As a result, the senior management team has been investigating how the company can become more efficient to ensure its future survival.

Redundancies across the company have recently been announced. In addition, the current operating conditions mean that there will be some significant changes made to the contractual terms and conditions for management and administration staff working in the various functional departments, along with a restructuring of operations.

Of immediate concern to the senior management is the threat made by the trade unions to take industrial action to protect jobs and also the contractual terms and conditions of their members.

Required

(a)   **Discuss** the different conflict handling strategies that could be used in managing the conflict in ZEZ Company.   **(13 marks)**

(b)   **Explain** the different stages of negotiation that should take place to ensure the negotiation process between senior management and the trade union representatives is effective.   **(12 marks)**

(Total = 25 marks)

22 FPC Company (5/11)	45 mins

PR has recently joined FPC Company as the new Finance Director. He is required to work towards getting the finance staff to play a fuller role in the company, becoming more integrated into the strategic and business activities of the organisation. However, PR is aware that this will not be an easy task since his impression is that the Finance Department has a very poor reputation in the company, and current relationships between the finance staff and other departments are not good.

Having discussed the poor perception with other department heads, it is clear that the finance staff are generally viewed as being unhelpful. Many of the complaints surround poor communications. A consistent comment made is that messages received from the Finance Department are too complicated and that too much financial jargon is used. Another common observation is that at inter-department meetings, the finance team use 'financial speak' which other members of staff find hard to understand. The finance staff have an obsession with financial indicators, and do not appreciate that there are other factors which inform decisions. It is also felt that too many emails are sent from the Finance Department, and it is often difficult to find the relevant information on some of the financial spreadsheets circulated which are supposed to help in decision making.

PR has noted that many of the staff in the Finance Department are de-motivated. None of them appear to have clear targets and objectives, and they have told him that they have had no feedback on their performance and staff development simply has not existed. PR has established that, whilst there is a company-wide staff performance appraisal system in place, none of the staff in his department have had an appraisal in recent years.

PR has identified a number of immediate actions to improve the performance of the Finance Department. He has decided that all staff in the Finance Department need training to improve their communication skills. He also intends to make sure the company's appraisal system is implemented and that all staff in his department will have an appraisal in the next three months.

Required

(a)   **Discuss** what should be covered in the series of training sessions to help members of staff in the Finance Department improve their communication skills. **(15 marks)**

(b)   **Explain** how implementing FPC Company's staff appraisal system in the Finance Department could help improve the performance of staff. **(10 marks)**

(Total = 25 marks)

23   RM Company (Specimen paper)   45 mins

F is the Chief Executive of RM Company, a manufacturer of ready made meals. The company is facing difficult business conditions as a result of strong competition from supermarket own brand products and consumer demand for variety and new products.

F appreciates that the company needs to improve its performance in bringing new products to market. However, she is aware of the problems the company currently faces in its approach to new product development (NPD). Whilst collaboration is essential to successful NPD, in the past the NPD process in the company has resulted in disagreements and arguments between the various departments.

The marketers complain that the Research and Development (R&D) Department is very slow in responding to their proposals for new recipes and the whole process of R&D takes too long. The Production Department complains that R&D does not consider the implications for the production process when coming up with new recipes and product packaging. The sales team is frustrated with the length of time the whole NPD process takes. It says that the lack of new products puts it at a disadvantage when negotiating with retailers to sell RM Company's products.

The Finance Department is concerned that the investment in NPD does not provide adequate returns, and both the Marketing and R&D Departments are always over budget. However, the other departments see Finance as controlling and sanctioning spend rather than supporting new product development.

F knows that to remain competitive NPD is essential but that changes need to be made to the NPD process in the company. She has decided to establish a cross functional team to work on a new range of luxury ready made meals designed to appeal to the sophisticated end of the market. She has appointed T as head of NPD and given him the particular remit of leading and managing the NPD team.

Required

(a)   **Identify** the nature and sources of conflict between the different departments in RM Company. **(10 marks)**

(b)   **Discuss** what T should do to be effective in leading and managing the NPD team. **(15 marks)**

(Total = 25 marks)

24   Sales targets (IM, 11/06)   45 mins

The Direct Sales and Customer Contact Centre (the Centre) of A Insurance Company deals with vehicle, home and contents insurance products. B, who has been the manager of the Centre for the last three years, has a participative leadership style, involving staff in key decisions about the Centre. Initially she was very successful in achieving high staff morale as evidenced in the results of annual staff surveys for the first two years of her appointment. The Centre scored consistently higher on dimensions such as job satisfaction, communication and co-operation when compared with other parts of the company.

However, twelve months ago B was responsible for introducing a sales target system which involved allocating staff to teams as part of a restructuring programme. Each team is set targets and the results are published on a monthly basis in a league table. The team that is top of the league receives a cash bonus.

B is concerned that the restructuring has had an adverse effect on the performance of the Centre. She is particularly concerned that the results of the most recent staff survey show that communication and co-operation between teams have fallen dramatically. She has also observed animosity between the team leaders. Absenteeism has increase significantly, particularly in team Y. As part of her review of the issues facing the Centre, she has noted the following:

*   Team X is always at the top of the league and, as a result, receives the cash bonus. The team leader of X is highly motivated and team spirit is high. Team members are constantly coming up with ideas on how

to increase sales. The team seems to be very cohesive group and team members regularly organise social events for themselves.

- Team Y never succeeds in meeting its targets. The team leader does not seem bothered by this, and appears more interested in working out how much longer he needs to work before he can retire. Team members have complained to B about the team leader, and two members have resigned. There is a personality clash between the team leader and another member of the team who is viewed by the rest of the team as the 'unofficial' leader.

- Team Z, whilst achieving its targets, is always behind Team X. The team members are an extremely tight knit group, but have become very insular and are no longer responsive to the work needs of other members of staff in the Centre. They appear to have their own agenda.

The restructure of the Centre into teams and the sales target system was dictated by Head Office. Nevertheless, B is determined to take action to resolve the problems she currently faces.

Required

(a) **Discuss** the benefits and problems of introducing sales teams and the sales target system in the 'the Centre' of A Insurance Company. **(13 marks)**

(b) **Explain** the strategies that could be used by B to minimise the problems caused by introducing sales teams and the sales target system in order to improve performance in 'the Centre'. **(12 marks)**

(Total = 25 marks)

25 T4M (5/10)   45 mins

T4M is a mobile phone network provider, with its main headquarters based in B country. Whilst there has been significant industry growth in the last decade, more recently there are signs that this growth has begun to level off. At the same time, competition is intensifying.

The Board of T4M is preparing to take on the strategic challenges of the changing operating environment. As well as assessing the external environment, it has started a major review of its internal capability, with a particular focus on examining how efficiency gains can be achieved across the various business functions.

F, the Finance Director, is deliberating on how he can gain efficiency in his department. His initial assessment has identified a number of transaction activities that he feels could be outsourced, such as the work undertaken by the customer bill payment team, including some aspects of customer service on bill queries and payroll. F is very enthusiastic about this and his thinking has been informed by the fact that he was only recently approached by G2O, a company specialising in this type of service, based in H Country.

If the outsourcing strategy goes ahead, along with other efficiencies the Finance Director has planned, then this would mean a substantial reduction in headcount within the Finance Department, with predicted job losses of around 300 staff. The trade union has already heard about the proposal and the possibility of redundancies. It has made it clear that it will put up a fight against redundancies, on behalf of its members, to keep jobs in T4M.

F will need good negotiation skills since it is likely that he will be involved in a number of negotiation scenarios if the outsourcing strategy is implemented.

Required

(a) **Explain** the benefits and drawbacks associated with T4M's proposal to outsource some of the work currently undertaken in the Finance Department. **(12 marks)**

(b) **Discuss** how F, the Finance Director, should approach negotiations so that they are effective if the outsourcing strategy goes ahead. **(13 marks)**

(Total = 25 marks)

26 TFX Company

45 mins

TFX is a multinational company which manufactures and retails branded designer clothing with business units in a number of different countries globally. Up until now, each of the business units has had its own finance department.

The company recently appointed an external consultancy company to undertake an internal review of the organisational structures to establish if they are 'fit for purpose'. One of the outcomes of the review is the recommendation that the finance function should be transformed, moving to a shared service centre model.

In taking this recommendation forward a number of factors will need to be considered, for instance any possible difficulties of moving to a shared service centre model, and also in which country the shared service centre should be established. The implementation of a shared service centre will also require the formation of new teams of staff.

Required

(a)   **Discuss** the rationale for TFX Company moving to a shared service centre model, including the benefits and any possible disadvantages.   **(13 marks)**

(b)   **Explain** how TFX Company should develop and build the new finance teams, if the move to a shared service centre goes ahead.   **(12 marks)**

(Total = 25 marks)

Project management

Questions 33 to 61 cover project management, the subject of Part B of the BPP Study Text for Paper E2.

Section A Questions: Project management

---

27 Project network | **18 mins**

The following tasks, estimates and precedences have been agreed in a project.

Task ID	Task description	Estimate (in days)	Precedences
A	Write project initiation document	3	
B	Research Site One	4	A
C	Research Site Two	2	A
D	Document requirements – Site One	6	B
E	Document requirements – Site Two	5	C
F	Define non-functional requirements	2	A
G	Define agreed requirements	3	D, E, F
H	Write invitation to tender	4	G

Required

(a) Prepare a project network for this project. **(6 marks)**
(b) Identify which activities are on the critical path of the project. **(1 mark)**
(c) Calculate the estimated elapsed duration of the project. **(1 mark)**

Explain the effect be on the elapsed duration of the project if:

(d) Task C overran by two days. **(1 mark)**
(e) Task B overran by one day. **(1 mark)**

(Total = 10 marks)

---

28 F Bakery (3/11) | **18 mins**

ST is the operations director of F Bakery. He is in the process of putting together a project plan for the introduction of a new production plant that will enable the bakery to expand its product range, moving into high quality cakes and desserts.

ST has identified a number of activities that must be undertaken to set up the new bakery production plant. He now intends to construct a network analysis to assist ST in the planning of the project. This will also enable him to provide an answer for the HR manager who has asked him to provide advice on when she can start the recruitment campaign to select new employees needed to work in the new part of the bakery.

The activities can be broken down as follows.

Activity	Preceding activities	Activity duration in weeks
A	-	12
B	-	10
C	-	6
D	C	26
E	A	9
F	B	14
G*	E,F	10
H	D,G	6

G* = Recruitment campaign

Required

(a)   **Construct** a network diagram showing the critical path for the introduction of the new production plant for the bakery and the overall duration of the project.   **(4 marks)**

(b)   Identify the earliest time the recruitment campaign can start.   **(2 marks)**

(c)   Identify the activities where there is float/slack time in the project, and calculate how much float/slack time there is.   **(4 marks)**

(Total = 10 marks)

29   V (5/10)   18 mins

V has just left her job as a website designer for a large systems design company and is about to start up her own website design business. She will be renting an office which needs to be prepared, and also needs to procure all the necessary equipment before the business can commence operating. She intends to open her business in 12 weeks' time. In her previous role, she often encountered critical path analysis when she was involved in large design projects and she considers that this technique may also be useful to help her to plan the setting up of the new business.

V has devised a list of activities shown below that must be completed before the new business can commence. When drawing up this list she was aware that there was a degree of uncertainty in the timescales for some of the activities. She is concerned that if these uncertainties are not considered at this stage then she may not hit the deadline of opening her new business in 12 weeks' time. (Note: there is no slack shown).

Activity		*Dependency*	*Time (weeks)*
Find rental office	A	-	2
Procure equipment	B	A	1
Prepare office	C	A	3
Recruit staff (2 people)	D	A	4
Delivery and installation of equipment	E	B,C	2
Train staff	F	D,E	2
Design tests on web design system	G	F	1
Test web design system	H	G	1

Required

(a)   Using the above information, construct a network diagram, clearly identifying the critical path, for setting up V's business.   **(4 marks)**

(b)   **Explain** to V the difference between 'contingency/scenario plans' and 'buffering' in the context of helping V plan for the uncertainties in setting up the business.   **(6 marks)**

(Total = 10 marks)

The following data are given for questions 35 and 36

You work for a firm of management accountants that specialises in implementing information systems. The latest assignment is to implement new systems at a small chain of ten shops managed by FRS Co and to integrate these into the systems of a multinational retail organisation (MRO Inc) that has recently acquired them. FRS Co sells a range of wines, spirits and groceries.

Draft implementation plans

The information systems department of MRO Inc had drawn up an outline timetable for the introduction of the new system to FRS Co.

The first draft of this follows.

Task	Description	Planned duration (weeks)	Preceding activities
A	Communication – inform staff at each FRS shop and indicate how it will affect them	1	–
B	Carry out systems audit at each FRS shop	2	A
C	Agree detailed implementation plan with board of directors	1	B
D	Order and receive hardware requirements	4	C
E	Install hardware at all FRS shops	4	D
F	Install software at all FRS shops	2	D
G	Arrange training at premises of MRO Inc	3	D
H	Test systems at all FRS shops	4	E and F
I	Implement changeover at all shops	10	G and H

30   Netcrit   18 mins

Necrit Ltd is about to undertake a project about which the following data is available.

Activity	Preceded by activity	Duration	Workers required
		Days	
A	–	3	6
B	–	5	3
C	B	2	4
D	A	1	4
E	A	6	5
F	D	3	6
G	C, E	3	3

(a)   Calculate the duration of the critical path for this project.   **(4 marks)**

(b)   Calculate the minimum number of staff that will be required on day 6 of the project, assuming the critical path is not extended.   **(6 marks)**

                            (Total = 10 marks)

31   Risk (IM, 11/06)   18 mins

It is often claimed that all project management is risk management since risk is an inherent and inevitable characteristic of most projects. The aim of the project manager is to combat the various hazards to which a project may be exposed.

Required

Explain the concept of risk and the ways in which risk can be managed in a project.   **(10 marks)**

32 Project initiation stage (IM, 5/07) | 18 mins

A number of volunteers were so moved by news coverage reporting on the difficulties facing earthquake victims in F country that they organised a sponsored walk to raise funds for the appeal. Two of the volunteers visited some of the worst hit areas and this prompted them to set up their on charity. Their first major project is to rebuild and provide equipment for a school in one of the villages that has been devastated by the disaster. They hope to have the school up and running in twelve months' time.

A number of people have been enlisted to help with the project, including some local businesses as well as family and friends. The volunteers realise this will be a more complex project than organising a sponsored walk and therefore will require a much more professional approach to ensure that they achieve their objectives. They have limited experience of managing projects and are trying to determine the purpose of the different phases and activities. P, one of the volunteers, has been given the task of finding out about the first stage, initiating the project, and specifically, how to put together a project initiation document.

Required

To help P, **describe** what is involved in the initiation stage of a project and **explain** what should be included in the project initiation document for the school project. **(10 marks)**

33 Matrix structure (11/10) | 18 mins

M is a business that sells custom made computer-based information systems. Each customer order is for a unique system, which will involve experts from many functional areas within M. Each customer expects a high level of individual attention. Some systems take only four to six months to design and produce and cost less than €50,000, whereas other systems cost several million Euros and can take up to three years to complete. Projects are continually being completed and started.

A Management Consultant's review of M's organisational effectiveness has concluded that the matrix structure is the most appropriate for M.

Required

Identify the characteristics of the organisation that make it appropriate for M to have a matrix structure.

(10 marks)

34 WBS and Gantt Charts (Specimen paper) | 18 mins

Required

Explain how the work breakdown structure (WBS) technique and Gantt charts can assist in the project management process. **(10 marks)**

35 Graphical planning techniques (5/11) | 18 mins

Due to the complexity of the tasks involved in many projects, communication of responsibility for those tasks is often helped by means of graphical planning techniques.

Required

(a) **Describe** the techniques of work breakdown structure (WBS) and Gantt charts. **(4 marks)**

(b) **Explain** the importance of **both** WBS **and** Gantt charts in the project communication process. **(6 marks)**

(Total = 10 marks)

36 Project stakeholders   18 mins

At the last board meeting of X Company, the Finance Director showed concern for the lack of planning information available to the company. It was accepted that the company needed better quality information and the board agreed that the company should go ahead with a project to source and implement an integrated enterprise resource planning (ERP) system.

The new system will integrate internal and external information across the entire organisation embracing finance, manufacturing, sales and service and other functions of the business. The system will facilitate the flow of information between all business functions within the organisation and enable real-time connections to outside stakeholders like suppliers and customers. A software supplier is still to be chosen. P, as Project Manager, has been told that his first task is to identify the project stakeholders and to make sure that he is aware of the needs of each stakeholder in respect of the project.

Required

Explain the role played by the main project stakeholders in the sourcing and implementation of the enterprise resource planning (ERP) system.   **(10 marks)**

37 Project control processes   18 mins

Project control processes cannot be overemphasised in their importance to the success of a project. The project manager must continually take a pro-active approach in controlling a project.

Required

Discuss the actions the project manager should take as a project progresses to ensure effective project control.
                                                                  (10 marks)

38 Risk management in projects   18 mins

Risk management is an important aspect of managing a project in order to ensure that the project objectives are completed successfully and with the minimum of undesirable events. The task of managing risk is to ensure that the organisation makes effective use of a risk process that has a series of well defined steps.

Required

(a)   **Describe** the steps that a project manager should include in the process of risk management.   **(6 marks)**

(b)   **Explain** TWO strategies that a project manager might implement to address a project risk.   **(4 marks)**

                                                                  (Total = 10 marks)

Section B questions: Project management

39 Project planning and roles (IM, 5/05) · 45 mins

S Company is a major retailer selling mobile phones. In recent years the Company has opened new outlets and taken on more support staff at the head office. As a result the Company has outgrown its existing headquarters and so the decision has been taken to relocate to a larger purpose-built building.

Although the building work is complete, there are a number of different initiatives associated with the relocation. These include making sure that the premises are ready to move into on time and within budget and setting up a customer service contact team to support the retail outlets dealing with customer enquiries and complaints. In addition, an upgraded office IT support system is to be designed and must be ready for installation in the new premises.

P, the head of facilities management, has decided to establish a project team to ensure that all of the activities associated with the move to the new premises are co-ordinated and within budget. She has the formal role of project sponsor working on behalf of the Board and has appointed D to manage the project.

Required

(a) **Identify** and **explain** the activities that D would need to undertake in the planning phase of the project for re-location. **(15 marks)**

(b) **Compare** and contrast the roles of P, as the project sponsor and D, as the project manager. **(10 marks)**

(Total = 25 marks)

40 P Company (5/11) · 45 mins

P Company manufactures and sells a range of children's clothing through its retail shops and is currently designing a website in order to allow customers to purchase products online. The project is a major investment for P Company and it is seen by the Board of Directors as being a critical strategic development to ensure the continued success of the business in a highly competitive market.

The project team consists of staff from different departments of P Company. This is seen to be important by the Board of Directors, as a number of different business areas in P Company are dependent on the new website going live successfully and on time. The Board of Directors has also appointed G to be the project manager responsible for the development and implementation of this new website. G only joined P Company six months ago as an IT Manager, and she has never previously taken on the role of a project manager. She was chosen by the IT Director to be the project manager on the basis of her strong technical knowledge and experience in website development.

However, G has expressed concerns to the Board of Directors about her appointment as project manager on this strategically important project. She feels that she has a very limited understanding of the roles and responsibilities of a project manager. She is used to the day to day operations of the IT Department and is most comfortable with the technical aspects of the project, but feels that she does not have the range of skills necessary to lead such an important project.

Required

(a) **Distinguish** the characteristics of the website development project in P Company from the characteristics of 'business as usual' work. **(10 marks)**

(b) **Explain** to G the role and responsibilities of the project manager for the new website development project. **(15 marks)**

(Total = 25 marks)

41 Project Management Software

45 mins

As part of M University's ambitious strategy for growth, investment is being made in the development of a student village.

The finance director of M University has been appointed as the project manager and is in the early stages of setting up the project. This will be a complex project involving the construction of new buildings to provide for the growth in student numbers, including living accommodation for students, teaching rooms, a state-of-the-art business and conference facility aimed at attracting corporate clients to work with the University, and sports and recreation facilities. The build will be a collaborative venture funded by the University and investment from two local businesses.

The regional authority currently owns the land that the University wants to acquire to build the student village. The authority, the members of which are directly elected by local residents makes the decision on whether to accept or reject planning proposals made. It was recently reported in the local paper that the local residents are unhappy about the proposal.

The development will mean that staff from two University departments will be relocated to the new site which is two miles away from the main campus. In the first open meeting held by the finance director to communicate the proposals he was net with a hostile reaction from staff, with most of them being very unhappy about moving to the new site.

The finance director knows that this will be a complex project to manage and that project management software will be essential in making his job objective achievable. He is also aware that the project has a number of different stakeholders that he must consider in putting together the project plan.

Required

(a) **Discuss** how project management software might help the finance director and his team successfully carry out the project. **(15 marks)**

(b) Using examples, explain why the finance director should consider the interest of the different stakeholders in the student village project. **(10 marks)**

(Total = 25 marks)

42 Project management (3/11)

45 mins

Over the years, E has had a number of business successes in the building trade and property development. Her latest venture is to build a hotel in YX town. E has already gained the financial backing, identified a suitable site, had an architect draw up plans and received planning permission. She wants the construction work on the hotel to start without delay.

E has appointed P to be the project manager on the basis of his impressive record of managing successful construction projects. However, conflicts are already emerging as E is interfering in the management of the project. She is frustrated by the time P says he needs for the project planning phase, and is irritated by his insistence on formalising the project management process. E is putting pressure on P to cut corners in the first stages of the project, and to get started on the construction of the hotel.

Required

(a) **Discuss** the potential problems that the hotel project could face without good project planning. **(10 marks)**

(b) **Explain** the contribution that different project management tools and techniques could make to help P in planning the hotel project. **(15 marks)**

(Total = 25 marks)

43 COL (5/10)   45 mins

COL is a private college offering online tuition and qualifications to candidates all over the world. The Board of Directors of COL has decided to upgrade its computer system in order to enable COL to offer faster, more flexible delivery of courses and examination materials. It feels that this is necessary due to increasing competition in the delivery of online tuition and qualifications from both private and public colleges throughout the world. The Board of Directors and senior managers of COL have spent several months identifying the objectives for the proposed new system and identifying and discussing a range of project proposals. They have identified a clear requirement for the new online system but recognise that they do not possess the internal expertise they need to undertake such a project.

COL has contracted a local systems development company, SYS, to carry out the project. A project manager, D, has been assigned from SYS to lead the COL project. He will be responsible for all of the key stages of the project management process, beginning with the project plan. He will also be responsible for leading the project team, which will be made up of mainly SYS designers and also a number of IT staff and users from COL. He is also responsible for communication of the project's progress and events to Mrs Y, the senior IT manager at COL.

COL has made it clear that no extra money will be available than that presented in the original budget of $3 million and that any cost overruns will be borne by the contracting company. It has also set a deadline for final delivery of the system of 12 months. Again, there is no flexibility on this deadline.

One of the main enhancements to the updated system required by COL is the security of candidates' details. Unauthorised access to these details or candidates' results is the greatest outcome risk to the new system.

Mrs Y has insisted that staff from COL should play an active role in the systems development project and that communications between COL and SYS should be a key feature of the project management process.

Required

(a) Construct an outline project plan for the upgrade of COL's online system to be presented by D, the project manager, to the key stakeholders of the project. **(15 marks)**

(b) **Describe** the main skills required of the project manager, D, to lead the project team and create customer confidence. **(10 marks)**

(Total = 25 marks)

44 Sporting facility (11/10)   45 mins

V is a regional authority, which is about to invest in a new sporting facility in one of the main towns in the region. The sporting facility will include a large swimming pool, an athletics track and a number of indoor facilities such as a gymnasium and indoor tennis courts. It is hoped that this facility will attract major sporting events to the town and will encourage more local people, particularly school children, to take part in more sporting activities.

The Finance Director of V has been appointed as the project manager and is in the early stages of setting up the project. This will be a complex project involving the construction of a range of new buildings and facilities involving a large number of specialist building contractors and equipment suppliers. The project is a collaborative venture funded by the regional authority and investment from three large local businesses. The Finance Director has been informed by the Board of V that this is a very high profile project for the regional authority and that overspending on this project is not allowed.

It has recently been reported in the local newspaper that the local residents living near to the proposed site for the new sporting facility are not happy with the proposal. This is largely because the proposed site is in a wealthy area on the edge of the town and local residents feel that it would be more appropriate if the new facility was located more centrally.

The new sporting facility would mean that two other smaller sporting facilities in the town, currently owned and run by the regional authority, would be closed down and staff relocated to the new facility. In the first meeting held by the project manager to communicate the proposals to staff, he was met with a hostile reaction, with many of them being very unhappy about moving to the new site.

The Finance Director is aware that it is a complex project and that the use of project management software will be an important tool in making the project objectives achievable. He is also aware that he must consider the needs of the different stakeholders throughout the duration of the project.

Required

(a)   **Explain** how project management software could help the project manager and the project team during the life of the project.   **(12 marks)**

(b)   **Identify** the main stakeholders of the project and recommend appropriate strategies that the project manager could use to manage the different stakeholders' expectations.

(13 marks)

(Total = 25 marks)

[handwritten annotations: Usually between 1 - 3 marks per stakeholder]

[handwritten: stakeholder Analysis]
[handwritten: ① Identify key stakeholders]
[handwritten: ② Categorises them e.g power + interest]
[handwritten: ③ Recommend how to manage/deal with them]

45   Project initiation   45 mins

S Company has been awarded the contract for the refurbishment of a local hotel. The overall timescale for the project has been agreed at 30 weeks (a very fast completion for this sort of project). The timescale is not flexible as the hotel needs to re-open to host the wedding of a very famous and influential music star. In order to meet this deadline the project has no contingency.

All other information about the project is vague as the hotel only produced a brief document outlining the requirements of the project. No definite specification was included in the document with the hotel commenting 'we are not the experts; we will let them tell us what we need; after all they should know.'

B has been assigned as project manager and has focused on selecting the project team which has meant that no detailed plan has yet been produced. When one of the project team members asked about the tools and techniques to be used on the project, B seemed unsure about which ones would be most beneficial and suggested that he was going to rely on project management software. The project team is concerned about the lack of control on the project as there appear to be no project milestones.

Due to the amount of other project work in S Company's order book, some of the core staff have had to be released from the hotel refurbishment project. This has meant that phase one of the project is now two weeks late and the first stage payment from the hotel is therefore also delayed.

It has been brought to B's attention that the hotel would like to add additional activities to the original project specification and wants a meeting to discuss the implications of the changes to the overall project progression. B has asked about the project initiation document which he feels should form the basis for the discussion of the changes. B has been told that the 'brief document' compiled by the hotel is the only document available.

Required

(a)   **Explain** to S Company the purpose of a project initiation document and what should have been included in the document for the hotel refurbishment project.   **(10 marks)**

(b)   **Explain** the problems that are threatening the success of the hotel refurbishment project and the ways in which B can minimise the threats identified.   **(15 marks)**

(Total = 25 marks)

46   Entertainment attraction project   45 mins

Z Company has had to close down its new entertainment attraction after only six months due to its inability to attract its forecast number of visitors. The company is keen to understand more about why this particular attraction failed in order to learn from its mistakes and improve on future projects. The chairman of Z Company has cited a number of problems that were experienced throughout the lifecycle of the new Entertainment Attraction Project. An extract from his report is given below:

•   There was a lack of a detailed plan as to the exact content required by the attraction.

•   The contract was given to a contractor recommended by the Finance Director and consequently no research was undertaken on its suitability.

- Throughout the project there had been an unsuitable management structure and a lack of understanding of the elements of work required to complete the project.

- The targets for the visitor numbers were highly ambitious.

- There had been a major failure to establish sufficiently robust financial management. The cost of the building and its content was 10% over the original budget. (Z Company believes that this is due to a combination of poor cost estimates originally and poor financial control throughout the project).

- Throughout the project there appeared to be an enormous amount of conflict between the various project stakeholders which made it difficult to manage the timeframe. The project manager spent so much time managing this conflict that project meetings were regularly cancelled.

- No one in Z Company appears to be committed to undertaking post-completion reviews.

The chairman understands that there are a number of project management frameworks that would help in identifying the different issues of project management that need to be considered in order to effectively manage a project and deliver the desired outcomes.

Required

(a) **Demonstrate**, with reference to the stages in the project lifecycle, the steps that could have been taken to avoid the problems being experienced in the new Entertainment Attraction Project, as highlighted in the scenario. **(15 marks)**

(b) **Explain** to Z Company the practices associated with continuous project improvement that could be used to help Z Company learn from the mistakes of the new Entertainment Attraction Project. **(10 marks)**

(Total = 25 marks)

47 J Company   45 mins

J Company is a retailer of fashion goods operating in a highly competitive market place. The Board of the company has given the go-ahead to redesign the company's website to make it more convenient for customers to use.

The project is currently at week 12 and there are problems with the functionality of the site and the fact that it is not easy to navigate. The Project manager, CW, has expressed concerns about the rising costs of the project and the time needed to improve the functionality. He estimates that the change to the functionality will delay the project by three weeks. CW understands that improved customer satisfaction (by making the website easy to use) is important. There will also be diminishing returns since the increased levels of customer satisfaction obtained by the change in functionality will be offset by the increased time and cost spent.

The Board has had feedback from the project team members who have complained that there has been a lack of visibility of CW. Team members have said that they were unaware of any deadlines as they had not been shown any plan or schedule of work and this had made it difficult to prioritise tasks and understand how they can contribute to the project.

The Board of J Company has called an emergency meeting with the Project Manager in order to come up with some immediate solutions which address the project slippage. It has been recommended that CW needs guidance on how to improve his management of project teams before he leads any future projects.

Required

(a) **Analyse** the strategies available to J Company to address the issue of time, cost and quality in the website project. **(12 marks)**

(b) **Explain** to CW the factors he should consider to ensure the project teams he manages in future are effective. **(13 marks)**

(Total = 25 marks)

Strategic management and assessing the competitive environment

Questions 62 to 102 cover strategic management and assessing the competitive environment, the subject of Part C of the BPP Study Text for Paper E2.

Section A questions: Strategic management and assessing the competitive environment

48 SBU (5/10)   18 mins

Required

Explain why it is important that the strategies of a strategic business unit (SBU) link to both the overall corporate strategy of a company and to the company's functional strategies.   **(10 marks)**

49 Market size, share and growth   18 mins

When JF persuaded a leading retail supermarket chain to trial her 'home-made' chocolate dessert range she could not have anticipated how well it would sell. Now a year on she has formed her own company, CP Company, in association with YT, who has a long history in the food sector and was himself a former supermarket manager. The company is currently operating out of rented factory premises in order to cope with the increased demand for the company's products from other supermarket chains.

JF is now being put under pressure by the supermarkets to introduce more products at lower prices. This is in the face of competition from other suppliers of similar products. Seeing that JF is unsure of how to respond, YT, drawing on his experience in the sector, suggests that the company undertakes a competitor analysis before making any decision with regard to future strategy. He has suggested that they should collect information in order to have a better understanding of the nature of competition and determine the market size, CP Company's market share and also market growth.

Required

Discuss why it would be helpful for CP company to understand the key concepts of market size, market share and market growth.   **(10 marks)**

50 PV Company (3/11)   18 mins

T has recently been appointed as the new Chief Executive of PV Company which manufactures cosmetics and toiletries. She has spent the first three months meeting with her senior management team, employees and customers of the company to establish how PV is currently perceived by some of its various stakeholders. The discussions with the different groups have revealed that there seems to be a great deal of confusion on what PV Company stands for. It is apparent to T that there are many inconsistencies in the priorities and objectives across the different departments of the company. T has determined that immediate action is needed to establish a clear mission for PV Company.

To start the process, T intends to run a series of events at which the mission will be discussed with different groups of employees. She has asked for your help in preparing for the first workshop session. Specifically, she has asked you to put together a presentation with the aim of helping the various audiences to understand why it would be beneficial for PV Company to have a clear mission.

Required

Discuss the points you would include in the presentation on the benefits of having a clear mission for PV Company.   **(10 marks)**

51   Levels (3/11)   18 mins

Required

Discuss the ways in which the strategies of the functional areas of an organisation should support the other levels of strategy.   **(10 marks)**

52   Levels of strategy   18 mins

J plc manufactures a range of cars. The company is structured on a divisional basis with each division having responsibility for a segment of the market. One of the divisions manufactures the most popular car in J plc's own country and, based on this success, J plc is now looking to expand into new markets. The Finance Director of J plc has made a statement that 'the company needs to consider its strategic growth possibilities and that the emerging economies of Brazil, Russia, India and China (BRIC) might be markets for future consideration and for establishing a manufacturing presence. Competing successfully and delivering effectively in these markets will be important to delivering the promise to shareholders of 5% profit growth over the next two years.'

Required

Explain with reference to the above statement, the different levels of strategy that will exist within J plc, with specific reference to the growth possibilities within the BRIC economies.   **(10 marks)**

53   Fast food culture   18 mins

A very successful multinational fast food company (FFC) from country S has just opened a small group of restaurants in country C, but a range of problems has affected the new venture. Customers have complained about the menus, the seating arrangements and the music that is played. Local residents have protested about the architecture of restaurant buildings, and the restaurant employees have complained about the style and practices of the managers from country S who run the business.

Required

Using your knowledge of national and corporate cultures, **explain** why FFC is experiencing the problems noted in the scenario.   **(10 marks)**

54   T Venture (IM, 5/06)   18 mins

T is seeking investment funds for his new venture to open a chain of fast-food restaurants. Despite the competition in this sector, having undertaken market research amongst his target market, T is convinced that he can succeed with his fast-food concept.

He is currently in the process of putting together a business plan which will outline his strategy to enter the market place. Having recently attended a seminar on what to include in a business plan, T remembers that he will need to determine what the critical success factors (CSFs) for his business are, but he is confused about how these differ from core competences.

Required

(a)   **Explain** why T needs to determine the CSFs as part of the development of his strategy and how they differ from core competences.   **(6 marks)**

(b)   **Identify** what the CSFs might be for T's chain of fast food restaurants.   **(4 marks)**

(Total = 10 marks)

55 AT Company   18 mins

AT Company is a specialist travel company which offers adventure holidays for the independently-minded traveller. AT Company was originally a subsidiary of a larger tour operator. The present owner-manager, K, was able to buy the business when it was sold off by its parent company five years ago. K has been able to make the business into a profit making concern by taking advantage of a growing trend amongst older clients who have the disposable income to seek adventure holidays. The company has also benefited from predicting the increase in the number of young people taking a gap-year prior to going to university, and who want to book adventure holidays as part of their gap-year experience.

There is no doubt that the company's success so far has been a result of its positioning approach to strategy and in particular its ability to differentiate itself from rival companies . However, K is aware that this market has become very competitive. He is concerned about the longer term sustainability of the competitive advantage the company has built up and he has also begun to question the positioning approach to strategy formulation.

Required

(a)   **Explain**, with reference to AT Company, the characteristics of the positioning approach to achieving competitive advantage.   **(6 marks)**

(b)   **Explain** the potential problems AT Company could face in continuing to rely on the positioning approach.   **(4 marks)**

(Total = 10 marks)

56 MT (Specimen Paper)   18 mins

MT is the entrepreneurial owner of S Software Development Company which he set up five years ago with his business partner ZF, who provided the financial backing. Since that time the company has grown. Despite MT not having any clear view on what should happen, strategies have tended to emerge without any formal approach. ZF feels that, whilst still a small business, the company has come to a point in its lifecycle where perhaps a more formal approach to establishing its future strategic direction would be beneficial. However, MT has a different view and argues that the company has been a success to date. He feels that ZF's suggestion to adopt a formal rational approach to strategy development would have more disadvantages than advantages.

Required

Describe the potential advantages and disadvantages of the formal rational approach to strategy development for S Software Development Company.   **(10 marks)**

57 N Airline (IM, 11/05)   18 mins

N Airline operates in the short haul flight industry. Unlike many of its competitors who are constantly seeking to reduce costs, often at the expense of customer service, the foundation of N's business strategy is based on providing a superior quality of service. Its mission is to be market leader, providing unrivalled customer service, in flight comfort and reliability in the short haul airline industry. N Airlines views its customers as central to strategic developments, and values its staff in building success.

Required

(a)   **Distinguish** between the concepts of mission and objectives.   **(4 marks)**

(b)   Using examples, **illustrate** how the mission for N Airline could be translated into strategic objectives.   **(6 marks)**

(Total = 10 marks)

58 Outsourcing costs | 18 mins

Many organisations are making decisions to outsource some of their activities. However, when considering the option to outsource, organisations must consider the transaction costs which may be incurred. These will be influenced to some extent by the specificity of the assets required for the contract.

Required

(a) **Describe** FOUR types of transaction cost which organisations could incur if they use an outside supplier for an input or service. **(4 marks)**

(b) **Explain** what is meant by the term 'asset specificity', providing examples of THREE different types of asset specificity. **(6 marks)**

(Total = 10 marks)

59 OD (Specimen Paper) | 18 mins

OD Company is in the business of designing, manufacturing and retailing outdoor equipment including hiking boots, rucksacks, tents and other associated products. The company's headquarters, including its manufacturing function, is in LM town where it is one of the major employers. It also has a chain of 25 retail shops in Country A.

The company is still owned by its founder J, who has been hugely successful in building up the OD brand, which now has global recognition. J has recently received a takeover bid from ZZ Company, which is based in another country. ZZ Company is particularly interested in buying the brand and design capability of OD Company. If the bid was accepted, then ZZ Company would close down the manufacturing activity in LM town and would outsource this to other parts of the world where production and labour costs are significantly lower. This would mean the loss of over 800 jobs in LM town, and the trade union has already stated it will fight any job cuts.

J is contemplating whether or not he should accept the bid.

Required

Discuss the power and interests of the different stakeholder groups who are likely to be affected by the takeover bid. **(10 marks)**

60 DPW (3/11) | 18 mins

DPW is a very successful home furniture company operating in P Country. It has a good reputation for being customer focused and providing value for money through its effective operations. Following a systematic analysis of its home/domestic market, it is apparent that the market is reaching maturity and to attain further growth and expansion will involve moving into markets abroad. It has identified F Country as a possible target for its first step into internationalisation.

The company now wants to undertake formal analysis to help it to better understand the external environment of F Country.

Required

Describe ONE strategic management model/framework and **explain** how it could be used to help DPW to understand the external environment of F Country. **(Total = 10 marks)**

61 SM (5/10)   18 mins

SM is a consultant who has been asked to work with FX Company, a family owned business, which produces 'home-made' ice cream. Her brief is to undertake an assessment of the company's competitive position. As part of her review she is gathering information from various areas of the business. She has asked the Sales and Marketing Director to provide her with: an overview of the company's competitors; information on whether market growth is high or low; and what FX's market share is. She is surprised by his response that the company does not undertake any competitor analysis and that he has no idea of its market share.

Required

(a)   **Explain** why FX Company should undertake competitor analysis.   **(4 marks)**

(b)   **Discuss** why it is important for FX Company to understand the concepts of high/low market growth and market share when undertaking competitor analysis.   **(6 marks)**

(Total = 10 marks)

62 Digital media products (5/11)   18 mins

Z Company is very successful as market leader in digital media products where it has demonstrated its ability to innovate in new product development and design at a very fast pace, creating new products that its customers had not yet imagined. At a press launch for its latest product, the Chief Executive was asked about the company's impressive performance in recent years. She responded by saying that the company is committed to a resource-based approach to strategic development, with a desire to challenge itself to constantly stretch its capabilities.

Required

Discuss the main characteristics of the resource-based approach to strategic development that the Chief Executive of Z Company referred to at the press launch.   **(10 marks)**

63 Competitor intelligence (5/11)   18 mins

K is a kitchen and bathroom design and installation company which currently has showrooms in one region only of Country T. The company has enjoyed considerable success since it was established five years ago, using high quality products and computer-aided design techniques. This has now encouraged K Company to target other regions of Country T where it hopes to open more showrooms.

Since the company will, as yet, be unknown to potential customers, it recognises that it may be difficult to break into a competitive market in the other regions that are already being served by other well-established local and national companies. In order to help determine whether to pursue the expansion strategy, the owners of K Company have decided to try to collect as much intelligence information as possible on its potential competitors in other regions of Country T.

Required

Describe what would be involved in K Company gathering competitive intelligence information, making reference to the type of information that is needed and the different sources that could be used.   **(10 marks)**

64 Y Corporation | 18 mins

Background

The Y Corporation is based in the United States of America (USA). It was founded in the early part of the last century when Mr Y produced cartoon films. These soon proved very popular as a form of family entertainment and the characters in the films became household names.

The Corporation established a theme park (based around the film characters) in the southern USA, where there was a warm and mainly dry climate. The theme park, known as Y-land, proved to be an immediate success, attracting millions of visitors each year. A whole range of family entertainment flourished, based on the original theme of the cartoon characters. These included shops, restaurants, hotels and amusement rides.

Following the success of Y-land in the USA, the directors of the Corporation established another Y theme park based in Northern Europe. The rationale behind this was that although many Europeans visited Y-land in the USA, the cost of travel made visiting the attraction very expensive. The directors believed that establishing a Y-land in Northern Europe would enable European people to visit the attraction without incurring high travel expenses. Y-land Europe was built in a highly-populated area of Northern Europe which is easily accessible. A factor which differentiates Y-land Europe from the theme park in the USA is that it is located in a region which is frequently affected by rain and it does not enjoy a guaranteed warm climate.

Y-land Europe did not in fact attract the volume of visitors that were expected and almost went bankrupt before receiving a massive cash injection from a wealthy donor who took part shares in the theme park.

Further strategic development

The T Corporation is now considering building another theme park, this time in a tropical area in the Far East. Y-land FE will be part-funded by the host government in the Far East, which will take a 60% share in the park. The Y Corporation will fund the remaining 40%. Profits and losses will be shared in direct proportion to the shareholding of each of the joint venture partners. It is believed that local tourism and related sectors of the entertainment industry will benefit from the development as the theme park will attract more visitors to the region. Similar to the other two Y-land theme parks, the development will include many facilities such as hotels, bars and restaurants as well as the entertainment attractions.

Required

Apply Porter's Diamond Theory (the Competitive Advantage of Nations) to help the directors of the Y Corporation determine whether or not it should proceed with establishing Y-land FE.

It is not necessary to draw a diagram of the Diamond Theory. (10 marks)

65 XTX (IM, 5/09) | 18 mins

XTX Company, established 15 years ago, is in the business of designing, manufacturing and retailing sportswear and training shoes. It currently holds the licence to design the kits for both the national football and rugby teams of H country, where it is based.

Although these licences are potentially highly profitable, the company is currently facing difficult trading times as a result of the economic downturn and rises in manufacturing costs. Its manufacturing overheads are escalating out of control and although D, the Managing Director, has always had a commitment to manufacturing in XTX's home country, he is trying to work through some difficult business decisions about the future strategic development of the company.

He is reflecting on whether it would make business sense to outsource all manufacturing activities and focus on design and retail. He is now considering the possibility of outsourcing all manufacturing activities to country L, where costs are significantly lower. In other words, he is assessing the make or buy decision, which forms the basis of transaction cost theory where organisations choose between hierarchy or market solutions.

Required

Discuss the factors D will need to consider in making his decision on whether or not to outsource the manufacturing activity. Your answer should make reference to transaction cost theory. (10 marks)

66 JKL Bank — 18 mins

The Head of Insurance at JKL Bank has been considering how to make efficiencies in the operation of the Car Insurance Business Unit. One option under consideration is to outsource the Customer Contact Centre (CCC) for its car insurance business. The work of the CCC currently involves dealing with customer telephone enquiries on issues such as insurance claims, policy changes, renewals and premium/payment information.

To help him make a decision on whether or not to proceed, the Head of Insurance has asked for an evaluation of the proposed outsourcing of the CCC.

Required

Explain how transaction cost theory could help the Head of Insurance on deciding whether or not to outsource the Car Insurance Business Unit's Customer Contact Centre. **(10 marks)**

67 CN (Specimen Paper) — 18 mins

CN Company is a manufacturer of confectionery products with a well established position and brand recognition in Country P. The potential for future growth in Country P is, however, limited, with the market reaching saturation. A proposal put forward is that to achieve growth CN Company should move into new markets in other countries, offering its existing product range. One possible method of achieving market entry that has been identified is through a joint venture with a company that is already established in Country K.

The business development team are undertaking a feasibility study to explore the viability of the proposed strategy to sell CN Company's confectionery product range in Country K. As part of the feasibility study there will need to be some assessment of industry competition and the attractiveness of the market in Country K.

Required

Explain how Porter's Five Forces model could be used by the business management team to assess the confectionery industry competition in Country K. **(10 marks)**

68 Corporate appraisal (11/10) — 18 mins

PRC Company, a retailer of baby clothes and toys, has been in existence for 20 years. Its approach to strategy has tended to be informal and emergent rather than planned. However, the company is facing uncertain times and at a recent Board meeting, one of the directors suggested that the company should adopt a more formal approach to how it develops its strategy. He has suggested that the use of strategic management tools and techniques could help and, as a start, has recommended that the company should undertake a corporate appraisal.

Required

Explain the purpose of corporate appraisal (SWOT), **and** what would be involved in PRC Company undertaking a corporate appraisal. **(10 marks)**

69 FF Supermarket (5/11) — 18 mins

The Board of FF Supermarket is examining the company's current market position. As part of the review, the Board has asked for an analysis of industry competition to be undertaken in order to establish the attractiveness of the industry and sources of competition.

Required

Discuss the contribution of Porter's Five Forces model in assessing the attractiveness of the industry in which FF currently operates. **(10 marks)**

Section B questions: Strategic management and assessing the competitive environment

70 F Company (IM, 11/05) — 45 mins

F Company is a medium sized business that manufactures electrical kitchen appliances including food processors, toasters, juicers and coffee makers. In the last twelve months the company has lost market share to its competitors and has underperformed on most of its key performance indicators. Its future survival is threatened as new entrants are stealing market share and the customers are demanding new product and design features.

G, the company's management accountant, suggests that F Company's difficulties are because it has been too complacent, not responding to changing environmental conditions and not having undertaken any formal strategic planning. He is also concerned that different areas of the company appear to be pursuing conflicting objectives.

To help the company develop a sustainable competitive advantage, G proposes that a more formal top down approach to developing business strategy should be adopted. He is also of the view that greater emphasis should be placed on understanding the external environment.

However, at a recent meeting where G outlined the benefits that a more formal approach to planning would bring, he was surprised that P, the HR director, disagreed. P argued that the dynamic environment that F Company operates in means that the formal approach is a waste of management time. She suggested that the company should assess how sustainable competitive advantage can be achieved through using its unique combination of resources, skills and capabilities.

Required

(a) **Explain** the benefits and drawbacks associated with F Company adopting a top down approach to the formulation of business strategy. **(12 marks)**

(b) Compare and contrast the different views held by G and P on how F Company can gain competitive advantage. **(13 marks)**

(Total = 25 marks)

71 Porter's diamond and PEST (11/10) — 45 mins

S Company operates in the consumer electronics industry designing and producing component parts which it assembles into products such as mobile phones, laptops and MP3 players.

To date, it has only sold its products in D Country, its home market, where until recently it was market leader. However, the competitive landscape has changed significantly as companies from PP Country have entered D Country's market, competing aggressively on product innovation, quality and price. Market intelligence gathered by S Company on the new competitors suggests that they are supported in pursuit of their international strategies by sources of national competitive advantage.

Looking to the future, S Company is evaluating its options on how to respond to the increased competition, including how it could better position itself, and what alternative strategies it could pursue. One option under review is to sell its products in new markets. GR, the Sales and Marketing Director, has identified NN Country as a possible market opportunity. As the first step in understanding whether this is a viable option, he has asked his team to undertake an initial assessment of the external environment in NN Country.

Required

(a) With reference to Porter's Diamond model, **explain** the different sources of national competitive advantage that the companies from PP Country may enjoy and which could give them a competitive edge over S Company. **(15 marks)**

(b) Using an appropriate strategic management framework / model, **describe** the information that GR, the Sales and Marketing Director, would require to help him assess the external environment in NN Country. **(10 marks)**

(Total = 25 marks)

72   Strategic models (IM, 5/08)   45 mins

W Company is a fashion retailer which designs and sells its own brand of women's clothes through its chain of shops in F country. However, it is facing tough operating conditions in its home market where strong competition means there is little opportunity for future growth. The Board has taken the strategic decision that expansion can only be achieved through market development abroad.

Initial research has identified L country as offering the potential to be a possible suitable location for W Company to develop a new market. Further information now needs to be collected on the external environment and competition in L country in order to help evaluate the viability of the strategy being proposed.

If the outcomes from the research are positive, W Company intends to find an existing retail chain in L country that it can acquire, rather than set up a new operation through internal development. A senior management team will be sent from W Company to manage the operations in L country. However, the Board is aware that this could create challenges for the managers if there are cultural differences between the two countries.

Required

(a)   Apply appropriate strategic management models/frameworks to **explain** the key external environmental and competitive factors on which information should be collected to help W Company evaluate its proposed strategy to move into L country.   **(13 marks)**

(b)   **Discuss**, with reference to appropriate theory, why the management team from W Company will need to take account of cultural differences when managing the new operation in L country.   **(12 marks)**

(Total = 25 marks)

73   VCR   45 mins

VRC is a family owned business which has been manufacturing racing cycles for over a century. Over the years, the company has been relatively successful, although its growth has tended to happen in what can only be described as an unplanned, ad hoc, and opportunistic way. To some extent the developments have been as a result of personal interests of F, the owner and Managing Director, who was a former road racing cyclist.

Two years ago, R, who is F's son, joined the company. The plan for him to succeed as Managing Director when his father retires. To date he has spent his time working in a various departments to familiarise himself with the operations of the company. More recently, R has taken on a more strategic role and, in particular, is trying to form a view on the longer term future strategic direction the company should take. He acknowledges the company has built up a strong brand but feels this could be used to expand into other product areas.

R has approached a Business Consultant for advice on strategic planning. In the first meeting, the Business Consultant has suggested that the company should adopt a more formal/rational approach to business planning and strategic development.

The Business Consultant has recommended that, as a first step, R should undertake a strategic analysis of the company in order to help R better understand its current position.

Required

(a)   **Distinguish** between the way strategy is current developed in VRC Company and the approach the Business Consultant is recommending.   **(12 marks)**

(b)   **Discuss** the strategic management models\frameworks that R could use in undertaking his analysis of the strategic position of VRC Company.   **(13marks)**

(Total = 25 marks)

74 WFH Trading Company   45 mins

RF and JT are both former international rugby players who, when they retired, formed their own business, WFH Trading Company. The company that they established initially manufactured replica sports shirts and its own branded casual wear bearing their names and unique logo. The main route to market at the outset was through the company's own mail order catalogue. As the business has developed it has diversified into a wide range of related products such as footwear, outdoor clothing and accessories.

To date, the growth of the business has tended to happen opportunistically rather than being a planned approach. However, in recent months it has become clear that the two partners, RF and JT, have quite different views on the future direction that WFH Trading Company should take.

JT feels strongly that, given the stage of the company in its lifecycle, it is now time to take a more formal and planned approach to the business's development. In particular, having recently attended a business seminar on strategies for growth he is suggesting that the company could benefit from undertaking formal planning using the 'rational' approach to strategy development. JT feels that this would help the company evaluate the alternatives for future growth. As part of this process, he is keen to look at new products and routes to market, including the internet and also investing in retail outlets.

RF, however, thinks that it is best to let the strategy and developments for the business emerge. His entrepreneurial spirit leads him to remain unconvinced of the benefits of spending too much time on planning and is reluctant to change from what the company is currently doing which, in his opinion, has proved so successful for them both so far.

Required

(a)   **Explain**, with reference to WFH Trading Company, the main stages involved in the formal/rational approach to strategy development.   **(13 marks)**

(b)   **Evaluate** both the benefits and disadvantages of the formal/rational approach to strategy development for WFH Trading Company.   **(12 marks)**

(Total = 25 marks)

ANSWERS

1 Dr Strong

> **Text references.** Chapter 2.
>
> **Top tips.** This question invites a very wide-ranging answer. Note that it is only worth ten marks and do not let your enthusiasm run away with you! Make sure you understand and apply the CIMA active verbs in the requirement. You must **analyse** and **recommend** in your answer. There are lots of points to make, but you must try even harder than usual to be concise. Note that a mention of *Burns and Stalker* and the organic-mechanistic spectrum is almost mandatory: their book was called *The Management of Innovation*, after all.
>
> **Easy marks.** The characteristics of the organic organisation may well be worth up to half of the total available marks.

Why C Company's problems may have developed

System of management

Dr Strong's system of management clearly does not support the innovatory science that the C Pharmaceutical Company depends on for its commercial success. Dr Strong's system, with its strict financial and personnel discipline, clearly **constrains the creativity** of the R&D unit's scientists.

Mechanistic or bureaucratic system in place

It is widely accepted that a management system based on rules, procedures and routine (that is to say, a **bureaucratic** system) is unsuited to dealing with new problems and rapid developments. *Burns and Stalker* called such a system a **mechanistic** system and contrasted it with an **organic** (or **organismic**) system. The latter emphasises interactive teamwork, collaborative problem solving, respect for individual expertise at all levels and commitment to the overall task. This is likely to be very effective in contexts such as R&D.

However, such an approach is not a licence for random, unstructured activity more or less directed at a vague objective. There is still a need for **control of resources and effort**. In an organic system this is achieved largely by cultural means. There is a network structure of control, with decisions and plans being made after consultation with all parties concerned. The bureaucratic idea of power flowing down from the top of the hierarchy is largely abandoned: prestige and influence can exist anywhere and tend to revolve around expertise.

Actions to encourage creativity and innovation

Replacing Dr Strong

It is probably impossible for Dr Strong to preside over such a system, because of his commitment to the more formal current methods. **He may have to go.** However, scientists generally will find a more collegiate approach familiar and easy to operate. If it is necessary to replace Dr Strong, an important criterion for the selection of a replacement will be experience of operating a more organic system of management.

Teamwork and collaboration

It would then be appropriate to **encourage teamwork and collaboration** within the R&D unit by employing suitable HRM policies. For example, recruitment should emphasise commitment to those ideals, appraisal should be based on actual work done rather than procedures adhered to and remuneration should be include an element of reward for team success. However, none of this should be done at the expense of individual creativity.

Innovation can be encouraged in other ways

(a)   Leaders must create a **vision and a climate of support** that takes a long-term view of R&D. Suitable targets should be set to cover both short and long-term timescales.

(b)   **Risk** must be accepted. Not all programmes may come to fruition, but there must be no recriminations for failure not caused by incompetence.

(c)   A careful watch should be kept on what is going on in the **wider pharmaceutical development world**. This is not so that so that ideas can be copied, but so that R&D staff can learn from others and are stimulated into speculation and experiment. It is also appropriate to keep abreast of emerging requirements for new products.

2 Conflict in organisations

Text references. Conflict is covered in Chapter 2.

Top tips. This question examines understanding of conflict within organisations. Part (a) asks you to identify and explain the key sources of conflict in organisations.

In part (b), you need to deal effectively with the three approaches to resolving conflict referred to in the question. A very general answer about conflict in its broadest sense, not necessarily within organisations and without reference to the specifics of the question, will not be awarded many marks.

Marking scheme

		Marks
(a)	1 marks per valid point made about each source of conflict identified up to a maximum of 4 marks	4
(b)	2 marks for clear description of win-win, 2 marks for contrast with win-lose, 2 marks for contrast with lose-lose	6
		10

(a) <u>Key sources of conflict in organisations</u>

Conflict is the clash of opposing 'forces', including the personalities, interests, opinions or beliefs of individuals and groups. Conflict often arises within and between teams, because of a number of factors.

(i)   **Power and resources** are limited (and sometimes scarce) in the organisation. Individuals and groups **compete** for them, fearing that the more someone else has, the less there is to go around.

(ii) Individuals and teams have their own **goals, interests and priorities** – which may be incompatible.

(iii) There may be differences and incompatibilities of **personality** between individuals, resulting in 'clashes'.

Difference and **competition** by themselves do not lead directly to conflict: they can even be positive forces, helping people to solve problems or to lift their performance. However, they can **escalate** or **deteriorate** into destructive conflict when there is poor or limited communication, status barriers or demands from workload causing pressure in the team.

(b) <u>The win-win approach to resolving conflict and contrast with win-lose and lose-lose</u>

The **win-win model** of conflict resolution states that there are three basic ways in which a conflict or problem can be worked out.

Method	Frequency	Explanation
Win-lose	This is quite common.	One party gets what (s)he wants at the expense of the other party. For example, Department A gets the new photocopier, while Department B keeps the old one (since there were insufficient resources to buy two new ones). However well-justified such a solution is (Department A needed the facilities on the new photocopier more than Department B), there is often lingering resentment on the part of the 'losing' party, which may begin to damage work relations.
Lose-lose	This sounds like a senseless outcome, but actually compromise comes into this category. It is thus very common.	Neither party gets what (s)he really wanted. For example, since Department A and B cannot both have a new photocopier, it is decided that neither department should have one. However 'logical' such a solution is, there is often resentment and dissatisfaction on both sides.
Win-win	This may not be common, but working towards it often brings out the best solution.	Both parties get as close as possible to what they really want.

It is critical to the **win-win approach** to discover **what both parties really** want. The important questions in working towards win-win are:

(i)   What do you want this *for*?

(ii)   What do you think will happen if you *don't* get it?

Win-win is not always possible, it is **working towards it** that counts. The result can be mutual respect and co-operation, enhanced communication, more creative problem-solving.

3   Disciplinary procedures

Text references. Disciplinary procedures are covered in Chapter 1 of your BPP Study Text.

Top tips. This is a straightforward requirement which can be answered by repeating the knowledge you have learnt from your Study Text.

Easy marks. As long as you have studied this area of the syllabus, you should be able to earn plenty of easy marks by repeating the process that you have learnt should be followed in relation to disciplinaries.

Although T's actions are serious, it appears that P is yet to take any action. It is important that P takes action now before the situation gets any worse.

P should follow a process of progressive discipline, which could consist of the following steps:

Informal talk

Talking informally to T may resolve the problem. For example it may be that he is dealing with significant issues in his personal life which are now starting to cause his behaviour at work to change. You can then work with T to find the best way to deal with the situation to prevent the negative impact on his work and colleagues.

An informal oral warning can be given at this stage if it is deemed necessary.

This part of the process does not form part of the formal disciplinary process but you should make sure T clearly understands what is expected of him and what action will be taken if his conduct does not improve.

Warning

If T does not improve following this then a formal warning will need to be issued. This could be either oral or written depending on how serious you believe the case to be.

Oral warnings should include the reason for issuing it, notice that it constitutes the first part of a disciplinary procedure and details of the right of appeal. You should ensure you keep this on file but disregard it after a specified period, such as six months.

Written warnings are appropriate in more serious cases. It should state the improvement required and state that a final written warning will be considered if there is no improvement. You should ensure you keep this on file but disregard it after a specified period, such as twelve months.

If an earlier warning is still current and there is no satisfactory improvement, a final written warning may be appropriate.

Imposition of sanctions

This is the final stage of the disciplinary process and could include:

Suspension without pay, however this can only be done if it is provided for in the contract of employment. This sanction can be effective as a short, sharp shock, however, it may prove difficult to re-establish an effective working relationship.

Demotion to a lower position and salary, however this affects the employee's moral and motivation so may not be an effective solution

Dismissal is drastic and should only be used for the most serious offences. It is expensive, disruptive and may affect the morale of the team.

When considering serious disciplinary action, such as dismissal, you must ensure you follow the statutory disciplinary procedure. This is important as failure to do so would mean that any employment tribunal would automatically find the dismissal unfair.

Statutory disciplinary procedures are the minimum standard that should be followed and to comply with them you will have to do the following:

- You must write to T stating why disciplinary action is being taken and inviting him to a meeting to discuss the matter. T has a right to be accompanied at the meeting, so make sure he knows this.

- At the meeting, you must explain the problem and allow T to respond. After the meeting, you should explain your decision and inform T that he has the right to appeal.

- T may appeal against your decision and has a right to be accompanied to the appeal meeting. The person who accompanies T to this meeting should be a different or more senior manager than the one who accompanied him to the initial meeting.

To reduce the chances of facing a situation similar to the one you are experiencing with T, it is important that employees are aware that certain actions will lead to disciplinary action. You can ensure this is the case by making sure that rules and procedures relating to disciplinary are made clear and preferably are put in writing. They should be known and understood by all employees. Communication and training will help you to ensure that this is the case.

4 Sources of power

> **Text references.** These topics are covered in Chapter 1.
>
> **Top tips.** Don't just list everything you know about all the sources of power you can remember. Make sure you read the scenario and only describe in detail those sources of power displayed by KK. You will gain the most marks if you can use the information you are provided with to explain why she possesses these sources of power and include information on how each source of power can help her to successfully lead the change.
>
> **Easy marks.** There are some easy marks here if you have studied the section on power and are able to describe what the different power sources are.

Power is the ability to get things done. French and Raven classified power into six sources: coercive power; reward (or resource) power; legitimate (or position) power; expert power; referent (or personal) power; and negative power. The sources most relevant to KK, and how each could help her manage the changes in the Finance Department, are explained below.

Reward (or resource) power

This source of power is based on access or control over valued resources. KK is a senior manager in the Finance department and as such is likely to have access to, and a degree of control over, resources. This could be very helpful to her in managing the changes in the Finance department as she may be able to obtain resources such as additional budget or, more valuably, information.

Information is particularly important as failing to provide sufficient information and the lack of communication is a primary source of resistance to change from employees. Knowledge of the change and the reasons behind it will greatly increase the likelihood of a smooth transition to the new roles and responsibilities within the department.

Legitimate power (authority)

This source of power is associated with a particular position in the organisation, for example an individual may have the power to issue instructions because the authority to do so have been formally delegated to her, as is the case with KK.

KK has been formally asked to lead the changes. Her legitimate power will help her manage the changes as the other staff will be aware that she has been formally given the task and does, therefore, have the right to do certain things or make certain changes.

Expert power

Expert power is based on experience, qualifications or expertise. This source of power is dependent on others recognising that expertise.

KK's expert knowledge has been acknowledged and is held in high regard giving her significant expert power. This could help her to successfully manage the changes as her acknowledged expertise makes it more likely that people will accept what she says as fact and less likely to challenge her assumptions or processes.

Referent power

This power is based on force of personality or 'charisma' which can attract, influence or inspire other people.

KK is well liked and respected by her colleagues and is also known for showing interest in, and providing support to, all those who work for her.

KK's referent power could be very helpful to her in managing the change as the staff appear to have formed the option that KK is 'on their side' and will be much more likely to go along with her requests as a result.

5 Benefits of delegation

Text references. Delegation is covered in chapter 1.

Top tips. Start your answer with a brief explanation of delegation and develop this to explain the benefits of delegation. Strong answers will consider a wide range of benefits for both the Finance Manager and also his team.

Examiner's comment. This question was generally well answered. A few candidates lost marks by failing to explain delegation, and others spent unnecessary time discussing the process of delegation and the factors that can contribute to good/poor delegation. It is useful to note here that careful reading of the question is required so that the focus of the question is understood before commencing to write the answer.

Marking scheme

	Marks
Explanation of delegation	Up to 2
Benefits of delegation, for example:	
Motivational	Up to 2
Enhance decision making	Up to 2
Gain experience	1
Assessing performance	Up to 2
Training	1
Employee development	1
Development of specialist expertise	1
Make effective use of time	1
Focus on strategic aspects of job	1
Maximum marks awarded	<u>10</u>

Delegation involves assigning tasks and the associated authority to others. YT can only do this if his role allows him the authority to delegate. The outcome of his appraisal confirms he does have this authority.

YT would delegate by giving members of his team the authority to carry out certain elements of his job. The task would then be carried out by the team member, but YT himself would remain fully accountable, both for the task and for any decisions undertaken by his team on his behalf.

Both YT and his team could benefit from delegation in the following ways:

- **Motivation and development**: Delegating authority contributes to the job satisfaction and development of lower level employees. Increased job satisfaction means that the team are better motivated and also more likely to produce higher quality work.

- **Training, appraisal and succession planning**: Increased levels of responsibility supports training, appraisal and management succession planning as it gives staff experience and prepares them for promotion.

- **Shorter decision making chain**: Delegation brings decision making closer to the situation requiring decisions as it reduces the number of people the information must pass through. Better decisions may also be made as the decisions are made by those individuals with specific knowledge of the problems encountered.

- **More efficient use of resources**: YT is currently overloaded as shown by the exceptionally long hours he has been working. There are physical and mental limits to the workload of any individual and the hours they are able to work. If YT were to delegate some of his tasks to appropriate members of his team he will free up some time to focus on higher-level tasks, such as planning. This will ensure his time is more effectively used and should also lead to a higher standard of work.

- **Stronger team**: Delegation should not only provide YT with a more realistic workload but also will provide opportunities for knowledge and skills development to the staff and an overall improvement in the strength of the team as a whole.

6 Corporate governance issues

Text references. Corporate governance is covered in Chapter 2

Top tips. To score highly in this question, you will need to state the principles of corporate governance and relate this specifically to the case of X company by explaining exactly how their practices contravene best practice governance.

Easy marks. A few easy marks are available for describing the background to corporate governance, however, this should be an introduction to your answer only; do not fall into the trap of spending too long describing this in unnecessary detail.

Examiner's comment. This question was fairly well answered with most candidates able to gain a pass mark.

Some candidates spent rather too much time on elaborating the reasons for the development of the Combined Code of Corporate Governance. Others focused on the issues that did not arise in the scenario at the expense of time and effort that could have been spent on dealing with the specific issues raised in the scenario. Once again this points to the necessity of reading the question properly so as to correctly determine its focus.

Marking scheme

	Marks
Background explanation of governance	1
Balance of executive directors	1
Insufficient number of NEDs in X Company	1
Formal, rigorous transparent appointments	1
Appointments based on family membership in X Company	1
Diversity and external expertise	1
All directors from similar backgrounds	1
Quality and timely information to discharge director's duties	1
Important information not supplied	1
Maintaining a sound system of control	1
Major contamination suggests major weaknesses	1
Regular dialogue with shareholders	1
Breakdown in the normal level of communications	1
Maximum marks awarded	10

Corporate governance is the system by which organisations are directed and controlled. High profile corporate scandals and collapses over the last 25 years (such as Enron and Maxwell Communications Corporation) have demonstrated the need for guidance in this area.

X company currently faces a number of corporate governance issues. These include:

Appointment of directors

When directors are due to retire they are usually replaced by other family members. This is not in line with corporate governance principles which require new directors to be appointed via a clear and formal procedure. A nomination committee should make recommendations about all new board members.

Balance of executive and non-executive members

Of the nine members of X's board, only two are non-executive members. This is unlikely to be sufficient to prevent domination of the board by family members, who constitute the majority of the group. To remove this risk, the board should consist of a balance of executive and non-executive directors.

Diversity of the board

M's research of the directors highlighted that all of the directors were from similar backgrounds. By failing to recruit members with external experience and fresh ideas the diversity of the group is greatly reduced. This may limit the extent to which ideas and existing practices are challenged and could reduce the level of debate around strategic decisions.

Supply of information

M noticed at his first board meeting that the board papers for an important discussion had been omitted. This is not in line with the corporate governance requirement that the board should be promptly supplied with enough information to enable it to carry out its duties.

Internal control

The major contamination issue at one of the manufacturing plants indicates a failing of the board to properly manage the organisation's system of internal controls. Corporate governance guidelines state that a good system of internal controls should be maintained. The directors should review the effectiveness annually and report to shareholders that they have done so.

Communication with shareholders

Companies should be prepared to communicate with shareholders and should provide means for institutional shareholder intervention. This does not appear to be happening at X company as following a major institutional investor raising his concerns the executive chairman commented that "the shareholders should trust him to run the company as he sees fit".

7 Strong culture

> **Text references.** Culture is covered in Chapter 5 of your BPP Study Text.
>
> **Top tips.** To score well on this question you will have to provide wide-ranging positive and negative influences of organisational culture on performance.
>
> **Easy marks.** Some easy marks are available for briefly explaining what is meant by organisation culture.
>
> **Examiner's comment.** Some good answers, but many weak answers which tended to discuss general management issues impacting positively or negatively on organisational performance.
>
> Some candidates based their answers on structure rather than culture, or discussed the advantages and disadvantages of different types of culture, but did not relate to the scenario. Some candidates did not read the scenario carefully enough and thus failed to note that the answer required an explanation of the positive and negative influences of 'a strong culture'!

Marking scheme

	Marks
Up to 2 marks for explanation of concept of culture	
1 mark each to a maximum of 5 for each of	
Positive influences of culture	
Negative influences of culture	
Maximum marks awarded	10

Culture can be defined as ways of behaving and ways of understanding that are shared by a group of people. It is 'the way we do things around here'.

These deep rooted ways of doing things and routines that underpin an organisation mean that it has a significant influence over the organisation's strategy and structure and the relationship it has with its various stakeholders.

PCC Company's strong culture will have both positive and negative effects on organisational performance. Positive influences include:

Identity

A strong culture provides employees with a sense of identity and belonging. This can be motivational and impact positively on staff retention.

Communication

Culture can facilitate good communication and coordination.

Reduce differences

Differences between people, groups and members of staff within PCC Company will be reduced.

Regulation

A strong culture will regulate behaviours and norms. Dominant values and attitudes will be reinforced.

Image

A strong culture will reflect the philosophy of the founder or the dominant group. This will provide an image and identity to the company affecting the way it is perceived externally. This has the potential to differentiate PCC Company from its competitors and could be the basis for developing a competitive advantage.

Strategy

A strong culture will directly impact on the strategy of the organisation and its ability to react to change.

Negative influences of PCC Company's strong culture include:

Inflexibility

Strong cultures can be deeply ingrained and difficult to change.

Blinkered

It could create a blinkered view which may prevent PCC Company from learning new skills or taking on new challenges.

Inappropriate values

If the culture of PCC Company is based on inappropriate values it could cause the performance of the organisation to deteriorate. The effectiveness can also be hindered if PCC's strong culture does not have positive attributes in relation to stakeholders and change.

Conflict

Strong cultures have the potential to cause conflict when the organisation is in contact with another. This is of particular concern for PCC Company given that future developments may involve a merger with another company. If conflict does arise it will significantly reduce the likelihood of that merger being successful.

Environment

If PCC Company's strong culture is not aligned with the environment in which it operates it is unlikely to succeed.

8 CT

Text references. Culture is covered in Chapter 5 of the Study Text.

Top tips. This question examines candidates' ability to distinguish between the characteristics of culture and different stages within a company's lifecycle. First identify and explain the type of culture that KCC is likely to have had at start-up. Then consider what kind of culture it has now and how and why that may be different. Do not just list aspects of culture; make sure you relate your answer to KCC.

Easy marks. Identifying the start up culture (power culture) is easier than identifying the culture KCC has now.

Examiner's comments. This question was poorly answered, although some answers were good.. Many candidates simply repeated material from the scenario with no 'added value'. For example they did not make use of typologies of culture to help in distinguishing between the characteristics of culture. A number of those that did make reference to theory did not evidence a good grasp of the subject with incorrect application of typologies

Marking scheme

	Marks
Definition of culture	1
Culture when KCC established (max 5 marks	
Power culture	
Depicted by a web	
Power resides at centre	
CT keeps control of activities/makes decisions	
Few rules and procedures	
Control informal	
Other	5
Culture of KCC now (max 5 marks)	
Role culture	
Depicted as Greek Temple	
Impersonal – example from KCC	
Relies on rules and procedures for efficient organisation	
Hierarchy and authority	
Formal and rigid control	
Stifles creativity	5
Other	
Max	10

Organisational culture is **'the way we do things round here'**. The culture of an organisation, such as KCC's, may be differentiated by their structures, processes and management methods.

When CT first established her business its culture may be described as a **power or club culture**. A power culture is shaped by one individual. The culture of KCC would be based and shaped around CT. Much of the drive for growth would be through her own passion and enthusiasm. Much of her time would be spent on creating designs for cakes.

KCC was able to react quickly to change because it was adaptable, informal and decision-making was quick.

Within KCC, there was **little formalisation, and few rules and procedures**. As the organisation was relatively small, all the staff would know each other. CT was on first name terms with all her staff and CT had direct communication with all her employees.

As KCC grew it would have introduced more formal structures and control systems. The culture that emerged is likely to be a **role culture**. A role culture is a **bureaucratic culture, shaped by rationality, rules and procedures**. There is a presumption of logic and rationality.

The characteristics of the culture that KCC is likely to have now are those of a role culture and these contrast with the **power culture** of the company when it was first set up.

KCC now relies on **formalised rules and procedures** for work routines. This is seen by the employee who was overheard commenting that he felt he was just a robot on the production line, rather than a craft worker.

Decision making in a role culture, such as KCCs, will be **standardised and bureaucr**atic. Decisions also tend to be controlled at the centre. KCC has a senior management team, who are focused on achieving efficiencies, control and bottom-line performance.

KCC has managers who look after different functional areas of the business. **Communication** will tend to be **vertical** within these functions and creativity may be stifled. This can be seen by the fact that KCC has functional managers who seem to have little interest in the creative side of the business.

9 Role culture

Text references. Role culture is explained in Chapter 5 which also discusses organisational culture in general.

Top tips. In part (a), you are being directed towards a discussion of **role culture**. This organisation type is one defined by *Harrison* and later, *Handy* in his classification of four types of organisation culture. You need to define this first and then set out why it would no longer suit the company using the information found in the scenario.

In part(b) you can use Harrison and Handy's classification to select a suitable culture. This would be consistent with part(a). There are other possible cultural types such as those defined by *Denison, Miles and Snow* or *Deal and Kennedy*. These all look at **culture and strategy**. However Handy's model also considers the **employee**, which is a key aspect of the scenario. These other models don't do this to quite the same extent.

Easy marks. You should earn a couple of handy marks by defining role culture.

Examiner's comments. This question was generally well answered. Some answers were very good indeed.

Some candidates repeated bits of the scenario as part of their answer and for others to repeat points made in part (a) again in part (b), thus taking up examination time and yet gaining no additional marks.

Marking scheme

	Marks
(a)	
1 mark per valid, explained point (½ if not explained)	
to a maximum of 2 each for each of:	
Definition of role culture	
Advantage of role culture offset by disadvantages	
Too hierarchical and rigid	
Shift from monopoly position requires more flexibility	
Innovation stifled	6
(b)	
Task culture more appropriate	
Explain task culture: working across functional boundaries	
More flexible – focus on outputs	4
Culture of problem solving	
	10

(a)   <u>Role culture and why it may no longer be appropriate for the company</u>

Organisation culture may be defined as the complex body of shared beliefs, attitudes and values that shape behavioural norms in an organisation.

Examples of organisation culture include such elements as its **beliefs and values** ('the customer is always right', for example), and **symbols** such as corporate logos. Expected norms of **employee behaviour** (such as dress codes) and **rituals** (the staff summer party) are also manifestations of organisation culture. The concept of organisational culture is one that S Company needs to take into account, because it is running into difficulties in a changing market.

A **role culture** is a bureaucratic culture shaped by rationality, rules and procedures. It is typically stable, slow-changing formalised, and impersonal. Authority is based on position and function. Role cultures can be very efficient in stable environments where workers have the opportunity to gain expertise. This is one of *Harrison* and *Handy's* four possible **cultural** types for organisations.

S Company has experienced a **shift in its environment** away from a comfortable monopoly position to competition and is experiencing severe difficulties.

The stable, slow moving role culture is no longer suitable for a competitive environment where E needs to be flexible and innovative, quickly responsive to changes in the environment and competitor initiatives.

Workers have expertise but they are unwilling to collaborate and work outside their specialism or function. This hinders innovation and the ability to develop new services.

In summary, the role culture worked well or at least was more suited to S Company's situation as a monopoly provider. Once competition destabilised its environment, S Company found itself unable to cope with the need for organisational flexibility.

(b)   The type of culture to which the company now needs to move

Using *Harrison* and *Handy's* classification the 'best fit' type of culture would be a **task culture**. The task culture is one where management is directed at solving problems and completing projects. **The focus is very much on getting the job done.** The culture is team-based, horizontally-structured, flexible and values expertise.

Management in S Company clearly need to **direct their energies into solving any problems and getting projects completed.** This requires focusing on outputs ie products and on resolving staff problems especially 'work to rule' attitudes.

This would enable **new innovations** in services to be offered to customers **sooner** than at present.

Staff must learn to work in teams which cross functional boundaries and draw on specialisms as they are needed. They need to embrace a culture of problem solving and team working to get new products and services into the market place.

10   Task oriented management

Text references. These topics are covered in Chapter 1.

Top tips. You are specifically asked to make reference to theory, so you should apply these to the problems identified by TS consultants. Do not just re-phrase the problems, but consider them in conjunction with the theory in order to arrive at solutions. For example, management style is inappropriate (too task oriented) – how might this change?

Easy marks. There is a lot of information in this question, considering it is only for ten marks, so it is possible to find a way in to at least part of the answer, even if you do not get all the points.

Examiner's comment. Answers were generally good. Weak answers too much time explaining problems or repeating material directly from the scenario rather than discussing the recommendations. Also, no explicit use of theory or just a description of theory without application (e.g. describing the range of leadership styles without application).

Marks

1 mark per valid, explained point (½ if not explained)
to a maximum of 2 each for each of:
Explanation of reasons for motivation
Inappropriate management style
Need for participatory style
Empowerment and delayering
Feedback (appraisals)
Learning and development

<u>10</u>
<u>10</u>

Motivation theory

Staff in the Finance Department of YR Hospital enjoy competitive salaries and benefits, yet morale is low and they are performing poorly. Herzberg classifies salary and benefits as **hygiene factors,** rather than motivator factors. Hygiene factors are essentially **preventative**. They prevent or **minimise dissatisfaction** but do not give satisfaction, in the same way that sanitation minimises threats to health, but does not give 'good' health. They are called 'maintenance' factors because they have to be continually renewed to avoid dissatisfaction.

What the staff lack are **motivator factors.** Motivator factors **create job satisfaction** and are effective in motivating an individual to superior performance and effort. In this context, missing motivator factors include:

(a)   **Advancement and growth in the job**. Staff have not received any training.

(b)   **Responsibility and challenges.** Staff must keep within a narrow job description and have no chance take the initiative or make decisions on the department's activity.

(c)   **Recognition and achievement.** The focus on restricted tasks and close supervision stifles development and employees do not feel trusted. The main reason for this is that there is very little feedback on performance.

Herzberg suggested that if there is sufficient **challenge**, **scope** and **interest** in the job, there will be a lasting **increase in satisfaction** and the employee will work well; productivity will be above normal levels.

Task oriented management style

The lack of motivation is a function of management style. *Blake and Mouton* identified two basic dimensions of leadership: **concern for production** (or task performance) and **concern for people.** It is clear that in the Finance Department, management is task oriented, concentrating solely on achieving results and ignoring people's needs. In fact, if people's needs are ignored for too long, results often suffer.

Recommendations

(a)   A more **participative** management style is needed. A participative management style is defined by Likert as one where the leader has complete confidence in subordinates who are allowed to make decisions for themselves. Motivation is by reward for achieving goals set by participation, and there is a substantial amount of sharing of ideas, opinions and co-operation.

(b)   A more **consultative** management style, defined by Likert as one where leader has some confidence in subordinates, listens to them but controls decision making, motivates by reward and a level of involvement, and will use the ideas and suggestions of subordinates constructively

(c)   **Empowerment** of staff. This involves making staff responsible for achieving and in some cases setting work targets.

(d)   **Delayering.** This means cutting the number of levels (and managers) in the chain of command. This will overcome the 'them and us' culture that currently exists between management and staff, by pushing the responsibility further down.

(e)   **Feedback.** Currently staff do not receive feedback. An effective appraisal system would overcome this.

Learning and development. Training is needed, whether formal or in the form of mentoring. As staff take on more responsibility, they will need more knowledge and skills.

11   TR

Text references. Chapter 1.

Top tips. The question asks you to refer in your answer to theory about management or leadership styles. You must therefore decide which theory (or theories) you intend to use in your answer, and you should make it clear what or whose theory you are using. The question also asks you to explain the leadership styles that TR could adopt, so you need to include TR in your answer. Key phrases in the question are "his style of leadership is not effective in all instances" and "he has not been flexible in dealing with some of the issues that he has faced." This might suggest to you that your comments might also include a brief mention of the contingency view that the most appropriate leadership style varies with the circumstances.

Easy marks. Include a clear explanation of your selected theory of leadership/management style in your answer.

Examiner's comment. In general, this question was not very well answered, with some exceptions. Common errors involved insufficient knowledge of relevant theory, mixing up management and motivation theories and not applying theories to the scenario.

Marking scheme

	Marks
Introductory explanation of the nature of theories of leadership style	2
Examples of different leadership styles, identifying the originator of the theory.	6
The Ashridge Management College theory is used in this answer, but other theories of	
leadership style are fully acceptable.)	
Reference to TR	2
Mention of contingency theory or different styles for different circumstances	1
Maximum marks available	11
Maximum attainable	10

There are several theories about the leadership or management style that individuals might use. One of these theories was developed by the Ashridge Management College Research Unit, developing the views of Tannenbaum and Schmidt that leadership styles can vary along a continuum from autocratic to democratic.

Ashridge Management College theory

The theory put forward by the Ashridge Management College is that four leadership styles can be identified: tells, sells, consults and joins styles.

(a)   The 'tells' style is an autocratic style of leadership. If TR were to adopt this he would make all the decisions personally and tell subordinates what the decision is. The advantage of this style is that the leader is able to make decisions quickly and act forcefully. The disadvantage is that subordinates may resent being told what to do all the time, especially if they are not convinced that the leader's decisions are correct. TR thinks that he has not always been flexible in his approach to problems, and this may be the result of having a 'tells' style.

(b)   The 'sells' style of leadership recognises that subordinates should be persuaded to accept the decisions of the leader. If TR adopted this style, decisions would still be made by TR, but he would explain the reasons for his decisions to his subordinates and he would try to persuade them to accept that his decision is a good one. Since TR would make the decisions himself, an advantage of this style is the ability to make quick decisions. The disadvantage is that subordinates may understand the reason for the decision, but may disagree with it and may be dissatisfied with their inability to comment on it.

(c) The 'consults' style involves consulting subordinates before the leader makes a decision. If TR adopted this style, he would make the final decision, but would listen to the views and opinions of subordinates before making it. The advantage of this style is that the leader is able to consider a problem or decision from the perspectives of several people and so obtain a better understanding of the problem before making a decision. The potential disadvantage is that subordinates may resent the leader's decisions if they are eventually taken without seeming to take their advice or opinions into consideration.

(d) The 'joins' style is a democratic style of leadership. If TR adopted this style subordinates would be fully involved in the decision-making process and decisions would be reached jointly by the work group, and by consensus. The advantage of this style is that subordinates may be motivated to act on decisions that are taken. The disadvantages are that the subordinates may not have the skills or experience to offer a reliable opinion, and decisions reached by consensus are not necessarily the best decisions in every situation.

Contingency approach

TR thinks that his management style is not effective in all situations. This suggests that he should change his style, for example by adopting a consults style (because this may help him to be more flexible). Theorists such as Fiedler have argued that the most suitable and effective leadership style varies according to circumstances, and TR may wish to consider whether he is able to change his style according to the nature of the problem and the decision that has to be taken.

12 PW

Text references. This topic is covered in Chapter 2 of the text.

Top tips. It is best to start by explaining what is meant by social responsibility, then to discuss the benefits that socially responsible companies gain. Remember to show awareness of the arguments that might be made against social responsibility, particularly increased costs. If you were giving such a presentation in real life, you would need to anticipate the objections of your audience. However, make the point that these costs are short-term and are more than offset by the benefits...

Easy marks. The whole question is a good source of easy marks because it is flexible as to the points you can make.

Examiner's comment. This question was well answered.

Marking scheme

	Marks
Explanation of social responsibility, for example: (max 2 marks)	1
Takes account of more than shareholder interests	1
Stakeholder view – recognises many groups in society with interest in/interactions with the company	1
	1
Concerned with externalities	up to 2
Other	1
Key benefits for example:	1
Commercial	up to 2
Impact on corporate image	up to 2
Good public relations	up to 2
Attracts socially responsible customers	up to 2
Attracts socially responsible investors	up to 2
Improve staff morale and attracting/retaining staff	up to 2
Improves relations with government/regulatory bodies	up to 2
Other	up to 2
	10

PW has been asked to give a presentation on social responsibility to an annual conference. The audience will include cynics who view socially responsible business driven strategies as unrealistic, conflicting with profits and detracting from creating shareholder wealth. She should include the following points in her presentation:

The concept of social responsibility

Social responsibility is the duty the organisation has towards **the wider community or society**. A business that is exercising social responsibility acknowledges that its responsibility is wider than just meeting the needs of its shareholders. There are many groups in society with an interest in the organisation's activities. Businesses should provide goods and services which meet the needs of users and society as a whole. However, they should also acknowledge the costs that their activities impose upon society for which they do not themselves bear a direct cost (**externalities**). Businesses may then exercise social responsibility by minimising these external costs or through compensating society for their actions. Examples may include, amongst others, the activities of PW, such as recycling, community-based projects and reducing carbon footprints.

Key benefits that companies can gain from developing strategies which are socially responsible

PW should acknowledge that social responsibility from an organisation may have an adverse effect on profits and detract from creating shareholder value. Social responsibility may lead to a reduction in profits, at least in the short run through:

(a) **Additional costs** such as those of environmental monitoring,

(b) **Reduced revenues** as a result of refusing to supply certain customers,

(c) **Diversion of employee effort** away from profitable activities and

(d) **Diversion of funds** into social projects.

However, these costs may be outweighed by the benefits of developing strategies which are socially responsible:

(a) Socially conscious **customers and investors may be attracted** to buy the company's products and provide its capital and ethical investment funds may buy its shares.

(b) Socially responsible actions may have a positive impact on the **corporate image** of the company and improve its **public relations.**

(c) There may be an improvement in the **motivation and morale of management and staff** of a firm that behaves in a socially responsible way. It will also be easier to attract and retain staff. In addition, staff may be willing to accept lower remuneration.

(d) Businesses that do not conform to society's expectations and are not socially responsible may be **unsustainable in the long run**.

(e) Being socially responsible **improves relations with governments**, and may moderate moves to introduce strict legislation.

13 Megamart

Text reference. The topics mentioned in this answer are discussed in Chapter 2 of your BPP Study Text.

Top tips. The term 'management style' might put you in mind of models of management behaviour such as those developed by *Blake and Mouton*, *Rensis Likert* or *Tannenbaum and Schmidt*. This was not what the question is about. This question is actually about corporate governance, although it would have been clearer if the words 'management style' had been replaced by the single word 'conduct'.

That said, the scenario gives a pretty clear account of several very significant failures of corporate governance and it should be easy for you to write them up.

Easy marks. Rex Lord's transgressions are pretty blatant, so you should have no difficulty in securing one or two marks at least for each of the main issues we deal with in our answer.

Marking scheme

Marks

2 marks for each relevant issue identified and explained up to a maximum of
10 marks for corporate governance issues.
Issues should include:

	Marks
Chairman and Chief Executive roles combined	2
Remuneration packages	2
Monitoring and control	2
Role and independence of auditors	2
Communication	2
	(10)

Corporate governance relates to the conduct of an organisation's senior officers in running their organisation. In the case of MegaMart, Rex Lord is the dominant senior officer, and his style of running the company gives rise to a number of issues in terms of the way the company's purposes and priorities are decided.

Rex Lord has been using MegaMart plc as a vehicle to **pursue his own ends**, thus depriving the shareholders and other stakeholders of their legitimate expectations. In order to do this he has contravened several well-established **rules of corporate governance** that are incorporated in, for example, the London Stock Exchange Combined Code.

Leading management roles

There are **two leading management roles**: running the Board and running the company. There should be a clear division of responsibilities so that there is a balance of power and no single person has unfettered powers of decision-making. Rex Lord's clear **exploitation of his power** illustrates why this is a good rule.

Non-executive directors

There should be a **strong and independent** body of NEDs with a recognised senior member other than the Chairman. MegaMart does not have this.

Directors' remuneration

Remuneration levels should be sufficient to attract directors of sufficient calibre, but companies should not pay more than is necessary. Directors should not be involved in setting their own remuneration. A **remuneration committee**, staffed by independent NEDs, should determine specific remuneration packages.

Quite clearly, MegaMart has failed to conform with these requirements as far as Rex Lord's remuneration is concerned.

Communication with shareholders

Rex Lord has appears to have failed to abide by the rule that companies should be prepared to communicate directly with **institutional shareholders** and to use the AGM as a means of communication with **private investors**.

Auditors

There are two significant threats to the **independence of the auditors** that should be reviewed both by them and by MegaMart's audit committee (which should be made up of NEDs). The first is that having been in post for 20 years, there is a danger that the auditors have become **complacent and even acquiescent** in their relationship with Rex Lord. In any event, it is necessary that the partner in charge of the audit is changed after a maximum of five years.

The second threat is associated with the **provision of services other than audit**. This is called **management risk** and is the risk that the auditors effectively act in a management role, doing things that should be reserved to the directors and managers of the company.

Compliance with the Stock Exchange Combined Code

As a quoted company, MegaMart should include in its financial statements a narrative report of how it applied the **principles** of the Combined Code and a statement as to whether it complied with its **specific provisions**. We are not told whether or not this was done, but if it was, it must have made interesting reading.

14   SP Company

Text references. Corporate governance is covered in Chapter 2.

Top tips. Pick out the main flaws or issues in the company as you read through the question. Note these down using them to **sketch a plan** for answering the question. Your answer will be framed in terms of how these represent **corporate governance issues**. Make sure that you are familiar with the **UK Corporate Code,** or the relevant version in your country (for example the King Report in South Africa) as you will need to refer to its main features when answering the question.

Easy marks. As usual the easy marks are for definitions. You should be able to make at least a couple of clear points based on the flaws listed.

Corporate governance is the system by which organisations are directed and controlled. It addresses the need to ensure that directors use their power in the interest of the owners and shareholders, as **agents** appointed to run the business on their behalf.

There were three significant corporate governance reports during the 1990s. These were reports by **Cadbury, Greenbury** and **Hampel.** The reports were merged into a **Combined Code** in 1998 and listed companies are expected to comply with this code, now called the **UK Corporate Code**.

SP Company is listed and so the company will be expected to comply with the UK Corporate Code.

Poor corporate governance

The company shows signs of several poor **corporate governance** practices. These include the following:

Autocratic leadership. E is an autocratic leader. Many corporate governance failures have been as a result of a single board member dominating decision-making and other members merely agreeing to their actions.

Non-separation of the roles of Chairman and Managing Director. E holds both posts in the company. His dual roles, and the power that they hold, mean that it is difficult for others to challenge his decisions. The UK Corporate Code recommends that the two roles are kept separate to ensure good control and a balance of power.

Lack of board involvement. The UK Corporate Code states that all listed companies should be led by an **effective** board and also requires a board to meet regularly and have certain matters reserved for its decision. The board meets infrequently and irregularly. It is **ineffective** in its role as a board evidenced by its reluctance to challenge E's decisions. It is also unlikely to be involved in an overview of activities and risks which is crucial given the poor state of control systems and E's disregard for procedure.

Non-executive directors. The UK Corporate Code requires listed companies to include non- executive directors to ensure balance and so that no one group dominate. If SP Company does not have non-executive directors, then it must take steps to appoint some to ensure independent judgement on decisions.

Non-disclosure of directors' remuneration. The chairman has put pressure on the FD to cover up a remuneration package that he set for himself. The UK Corporate Code states that directors should not be involved in setting their own remuneration. The annual report should contain a statement about the remuneration policy for directors and details of each director's remuneration.

Lack of appropriate control systems and accountability in the company. The poor quality of accounting information in the company will be a major problem if the markets are trying to make a fair assessment of the company's value. The Code requires that a good system of control should be maintained and its effectiveness reviewed annually by the directors. The board should present a balanced and understandable assessment for the company's position and prospects in the annual report. An audit committee should be set up consisting of non-executive directors. This committee should review the audit and the independence of the auditors.

Other matters for concern are the **acceptance of bribes** and **insider dealing**. That E has (so far) got away with such practices reflects the lack of involvement and independence of the Board.

Finally, F is aware of some of the corporate governance issues and has voiced her concerns to the board. She may choose to **adopt an ethical stance** and '**whistle blow**' on E's activities. This may result in her losing her job, as the board have not shown any concern or inclination to confront E on his practices.

15 Code of Ethics

Text references. CIMA's Code of Ethics is covered in Chapter 2 of your Study Text

Top tips. Don't waste time diligently reproducing the full explanations of each of the fundamental principles and focus instead on just those you believe are being compromised. You might find it helpful to consider each individual in turn. An alternative structure would be to focus on each principle in turn stating the different ways you feel it is compromised by each of the people involved.

Easy marks. As a student member of CIMA you are already subject to CIMA's Code of Ethics and as such should be familiar with the five fundamental principles and so should be capable of picking up easy marks by described the principles that are being compromised by the individuals in the scenario.

CIMA's Code of Ethics lays out five fundamental principles: integrity; objectivity; professional competence and due care; confidentiality; and professional behaviour.

As both D and the Finance Director are CIMA members, they are both subject to the Code of Ethics and as such should abide by these fundamental principles.

If D accepts the bonus and the Finance Director is allowed to claim non-business related expenses then they would be compromising their ethical position as they would both would be taking part in actions that goes against some of those fundamental principles as follows:

<u>D</u>

By taking the bonus D is compromising the fundamental principles of integrity and objectivity.

Integrity would be compromised as the Code states that 'a professional accountant should be straightforward and honest in all professional and business relationships'. The bonus is effectively a bribe for D's silence and so, by accepting this, D is doing something that she knows to be wrong. Her honesty is compromised as she will no longer report an activity which she knows to be wrong.

Objectivity would be compromised as the Code states that 'a professional accountant should not allow bias, conflict of interest or undue influence of others to override professional or business judgements'. By accepting the bonus D is allowing the influence of the Finance Director to override her better judgement.

Professional behaviour would also be compromised as the accepting of a bribe is unethical behaviour which reflects poorly on the accountancy profession and could therefore be considered to discredit it in the eyes of the public or the media.

<u>Finance Director</u>

By claiming non-business related expenses the Finance Director is compromising the fundamental principles of integrity and professional behaviour.

Integrity would be compromised as the Code states that 'a professional accountant should be straightforward and honest in all professional and business relationships' and the Finance Director is not being honest with the authority he works for by claiming for expenses which he knows to be unrelated to his business. We know he is aware that his behaviour is wrong as he has offered the large personal bonus to D as a bribe for her silence. The submission of these non-business related expense claims is fraudulent behaviour and a serious violation of the principle of integrity.

Professional behaviour would also be compromised as by submitting fraudulent expense claims is not complying with the requirement to 'comply with relevant laws and regulations and should avoid any action that discredits the profession'. We are not told about the extent of the fraudulent claiming, but given his reaction and his offer to D we can surmise that it is substantial. Were his behaviour to be leaked to the media it is likely that behaviour such as this would show the accountancy profession in an unfavourable light.

The offering of bribes for silence is also unethical behaviour which again reflects poorly on the profession and cannot be regarded as 'professional behaviour' nor a sign of the Finance Director's 'integrity'.

16 Health and safety policy

Text references. Chapter 2 covers health and safety policy.

Top tips. You must emphasise that good health and safety is a **statutory** requirement and not just best practice. So a health and safety policy must comply with legislation. There are benefits too in an enhanced corporate image and good ethical practice. Remember that the company already has a health and safety policy so the question is not about putting one in place but about reminding management of their **responsibilities** in this area. Our suggested answer has only considered the viewpoint of the **employer** where senior management are representatives, though in fact senior management are also employees.

Easy marks. You can gain a few marks from listing employer responsibilities under the legislation.

Examiner's comments. This question was answered moderately well. Some candidates tended to give specific examples of health and safety rather than key areas that should be covered.

Marking scheme

	Marks
2 marks for mentioning and explaining (1 mark if not explained) to a maximum of 8 each of the following:	8
Employers' and employees' responsibility	
HSWA (1974)	
Corporate image	
Ethical practice	
Other valid, explained points	
½ mark for each employer's duty to a maximum of 2	2
Maximum	10

Key areas that H should cover in the health and safety seminar

H needs to cover the following areas in his seminar.

(a) Legal requirements

The **main legislation** dealing with health and safety in the UK dates back to the **Health and Safety at Work Act (HSWA)(1974)**. Secondary legislation is covered in several **regulations** covering topics such as manual handling, VDU, health and hygiene and consultation on health and safety matters.

Both employers and employees have responsibilities under the legislation. These require them to ensure that the systems, environment, equipment and conduct in the workplace are such as to minimise the risk to health and safety of employees and visitors alike.

Specifically, **employers** have the following responsibilities under the **HSWA**.

(i) To provide **safe systems** (work practices)
(ii) To provide a **safe and healthy work environment** (well-lit, warm, ventilated, hygienic and so on)
(iii) To maintain all **plant and equipment** to a necessary standard of safety
(iv) To **support safe working practices** with information, instruction, training and supervision
(v) To consult with **safety representatives** appointed by a recognised trade union
(vi) To appoint a **safety committee** to monitor safety policy, if asked to do so
(vii) To **communicate safety policy** and measures to all staff, clearly and in writing

The regulations impose additional duties on the employer, including to carry out risk assessments, to introduce controls to reduce risks, provide health and safety training, provide information to employees on health and safety and to employ competent health and safety advisors.

Where regulations cover specific areas such as VDU safety and manual handling, the employer must also make sure that appropriate **assessments** of the relevant operations are undertaken. Thus in the case of manual handling, the employer must ensure an assessment is made of all manual handling operations and take steps to reduce or eliminate the risks. Where VDU usage is concerned, the employer must arrange for adequate breaks, arrangement of the workstation and training and consultation to improve work practices.

(b) Corporate image and cost to the organisation

A business' **corporate image and reputation** as an employer may suffer if its health and safety record is poor. This would discourage potential employees and even customers. A **poor safety record** can lead to fines, lost productivity and the cost of hiring replacement workers.

(c) Ethical practice

Employees have a right to be protected from needless pain and suffering and employers have a **moral obligation** to ensure this right is upheld.

---

17 Health and safety

Text references. Health and safety is covered in Chapter 2.

Top tips. To score full marks in part a) you will need to not only identify hazards but relate these to the specific scenario of Z's department.

Easy marks. You should be able to pass part a) from general knowledge. Some easy marks can be achieved here be simply thinking about an office environment and brainstorming what accidents could occur and what could cause them.

Part b) can also be passed with little technical knowledge. Thinking about why health and safety is an important issue is likely to provide sufficient material to pass this part of the question.

Examiner's comment. Most candidates answered both parts of this question very well.

Marking scheme

		Marks
(a)	1 mark for background explanation of employer's responsibilities 1 mark per hazard identified to a maximum of 4	
		4
(b)	1 mark per benefit identified	6
		10

(a) There are a number of health and safety hazards that might be found in Z's department, including:

Trip hazards such as slippery or poorly maintained flooring (eg frayed carpet), trailing wires, obstacles in corridors or stairways, and standing on swivel chairs in order to reach high shelving. A filing cabinet could also topple and injure someone should it be overfilled.

Ambient issues that can cause **discomfort**, eyestrain or related problems. Examples include inappropriate control of temperature, insufficient lighting, poor ventilation, glare/reflections from screens, and insufficient space for the number of occupants.

Sanitary issues that may lead to related problems such as low levels of cleanliness, insufficient or unsuitable sanitary conveniences and washing facilities, and insufficient supply of drinking water.

Chemical hazards such as airborne particles of photocopier toner which could be damaging if regularly inhaled.

Physical hazards such as hot compartments of the photocopier, or back pain caused by inappropriately designed chairs.

(b)   There are a number of benefits to having a robust health and safety procedure. These include:

Compliance: a robust health and safety procedure assists employers and employees in meeting their legal obligations to take reasonable measures to promote safe and healthy working.

Protection of employees from needless pain and suffering.

Damage to the corporate image and reputation of the business may occur if it is found to have a poor health and safety record. This may alienate customers and potential employees

To **avoid or reduce the costs** associated with accidents, illness absence and impaired performance. A robust health and safety procedures should reduce:

- Time lost by injured employees

- Time lost by management and technical staff following accidents

- The cost of first aid materials and officers

- The cost of any damage to equipment or any cost associated with the subsequent modification of the equipment

- Costs associated with increased insurance premiums

- Reduced output from the injured employee on return to work

- The cost of possible reduced moral (eg absenteeism and increased labour turnover)

- The costs associated with recruiting and training replacements for injured workers

- The cost of compensation payments from employee claims for damages

18 Finance function

> **Text reference.** The finance function is covered in Chapter 3 of your Study Text.
>
> **Top tips.** This is a fairly straightforward test of knowledge, but you need to think why it benefits Minimart in particular to separate the two functions.
>
> **Easy marks.** Part (a) is a source of easy marks for reproducing textbook knowledge.

(a)   Although an organisation may operate a single finance function covering all its financial activities, within this function a **distinction** can be made between financial control activities and treasury activities.

Financial control activities involve the **allocation and effective use of resources**. This comprises:

(i)   Advising on investment appraisal
(ii)   Analysing performance (management accounting)
(iii)   Reporting results (financial accounting)

The **treasury function** is involved in **obtaining suitable types of finance**. This includes:

(i)   Advising on sources of finance and dividend policy
(ii)   Financial risk management (hedging)
(iii)   Liaising with financial stakeholders (banks / key shareholders)

Examples of interaction between the two functions are:

(i)   **Financial control** reports on and identifies currency risk whilst **the treasury function** decides on hedging strategy.

(ii)   **The treasury function** assesses the cost of capital and **financial control** then applies it to proposed investments.

The financial control function is concerned with **determining whether** the **various activities** of the organisation are meeting their **financial objectives.** This function will therefore be interested in a **wide variety** of **stakeholder relationships,** for example, with customers, suppliers and employees. By contrast, the treasury function is mainly concerned with the relationship of the company to the **providers of**

finance. In a geographically dispersed company such as MiniMart Co, it is likely that financial control functions will exist at a variety of local levels, while the **treasury department** will be centralised at the head office.

(b)   The **balanced scorecard** approach can be used to appraise the finance function in the following areas:

(i)   **Customer satisfaction.** This focuses on the strength of relationships between the finance function and other stakeholders and whether the finance function is viewed as delivering the right mixture and quality of transaction processing, risk management and decision support.

(ii)   **Enhancement of internal processes.** These focus on the processes that the finance function must carry out efficiently and effectively in order to report accurately and give customer satisfaction.

(iii)   **Financial.** Success here could be measured by the frequency of forecasts and the average preparation times for key elements of the business planning process.

(iv)   **Learning and growth.** These measures concentrate on the organisation's ability to adapt to change and also the development of finance staff's skills and competencies. Possible measures include turnover of finance staff and what percentage of staff have a recognised financial qualification.

19   Mentoring

Text reference. Mentoring is covered in Chapter 2 of your Study Text.

Top tips. This is a fairly straightforward question. Notice that you are asked for the benefits to the new member of staff, rather than to the organisation, although these overlap to some extent, for example improved performance.

Easy marks. The benefits of mentoring can be listed easily from memory from the Study Text.

Examiner's comment. Performance was mixed, with some good answers. Weak answers tended to discuss what happens as part of induction and general training and hence did not evidence appreciation of the concept of mentoring.

Marking scheme

	Marks
General points/explanation of mentoring	1
Process of mentoring:	
Valid points – 1 mark per valid, explained point (½ if not explained) to a maximum of 4	4
Benefits of mentoring:	
Valid points – 1 mark per valid, explained point (½ if not explained) to a maximum of 5	5
Maximum	10

What is mentoring?

Mentoring is a form of on-the-job development, focused more on personal and career development than on specific skill training. It is a long-term relationship.

A mentor is a guide, ideally both more experienced and more powerful in the organisation, whose concern is the trainee's long-term personal development. (S)he may occupy a role as the trainee's teacher/coach, counsellor, role model, organisational champion, encourager, constructive critic and so on, as appropriate to the situation over time.

Process of mentoring

The process of mentoring involves:

(a)   Helping the trainee to **greater self-awareness**.

(b)   Helping the trainee to formulate and clarify his or her work and non-work **needs and ambitions**.

(c)   Helping the trainee to identify **opportunities for development** at work.

(d)   Encouraging the trainee to **take responsibility** for his or her development, while offering support where required, and

(e)   Collaborating with the trainee to **plan his or her own development**.

The role of the mentor may be summarised as follows.

Manage the relationship
Encourage the mentee
Nurture the mentee
Teach or coach the mentee
Offer mutual respect
Respond to the mentee's needs

Benefits of mentoring

Mentoring is a long-term relationship designed to support learning and career development. It has the following benefits for JB as the person being mentored:

(a)   Improved motivation and performance, and faster career progression

(b)   Access to a role model who can be trusted

(c)   Advice on dealing with administrative, technical and people problems.

(d)   Information on 'the way things are done around here' (corporate culture and management style)

(e)   Coaching in specific skills

(f)   Guidance in tackling projects (ie helping JB to help herself)

(g)   Encouragement: if she can do it, so can you

(h)   A sympathetic ear, where a line manager or colleague might be more difficult to confide in

Mentoring focuses on **facilitating and reinforcing actual changes** in a person's work style and habits. It is beneficial both to the new employee and to the organisation.

20 LS Company

Text references. Conflict is covered in Chapter 3 of your BPP Study Text.

Top tips. Pay attention to the requirements: you are asked to 'compare and contrast' the 'sources' and 'types' of conflict. Resist the temptation to write all you know about conflict. It is a good idea to plan out the structure of your answer. Ours is one possible structure, where you identify the two types and within each type, the source or sources. This is the recommended approach, as it follows the text. Note that you are not asked for a conclusion, but we include one for illustrative purposes.

Easy marks. Distinguishing the two basic types of conflict (vertical and horizontal) will earn easy marks. There are plenty of clues in the question about the sources of the conflict.

Examiner's comment. There were some good answers, showing appreciation of the different types and sources of conflict. Weaker answers explained *how* to manage conflict rather than comparing and contrasting the sources. Other weaker answers repeated information directly from the scenario and did not develop to discuss the different sources of conflict.

Marking scheme

	Marks
Explanation of types of conflict: 1 mark per valid, explained point (½ if not explained) to a maximum of 2	2
Sources of horizontal conflict – 1 mark per valid, explained point (½ if not explained) to a maximum of 5	5
Sources of vertical conflict – 1 mark per valid, explained point (½ if not explained) to a maximum of 2	2
Other valid points – maximum 1	$\frac{1}{10}$

Introduction

Conflict is the clash of opposing **'forces'**, including the personalities, interests, opinions or beliefs of individuals and groups. Conflict can be of different types (within an individual, within and between teams) and have its source in a number of different factors (power and resources, goals and priorities and personality.

Types of conflict

It is useful to distinguish between two basic types of conflict:

(a)   **Horizontal conflict**, between individuals and groups at the same broad level in the organisation. This is often based on competition for limited influence and resources, and

(b)   **Vertical conflict**, between different levels in the organisation hierarchy. This is often based on conflict of interest and power imbalance.

LS Company is showing symptoms of both types of conflict.

Sources of horizontal conflict

LS Company is suffering the effects of **horizontal conflict**. The conflicts are arising between the Marketing and Sales Department and the Finance Department, groups and individuals that do not have a hierarchical relationship and are of more or less equal status in the company.

The various disputes have occurred for several reasons.

Differences in goals. The primary goals of the various departments involved, rather than supporting the overall objective of a successful business, are effectively incompatible. For example, the Finance Department is concerned about profitability, which is why they put pressure on the Marketing and Sales department to increase the price. The goal of the Marketing and Sales department is to increase market share, and ultimately revenue and profits. In the short term, at least, these goals conflict.

Differences in personality types. People working in different functions tend to have rather different personal priorities, interests, attitudes and values. For example, the Sales and Marketing Department perceives the Finance Department as short-sighted and too focused on cost at the expense of the wider sales environment. This perception may reflect the fact that finance staff are seen, rightly or wrongly, as too conservative and narrowly focused. In contrast, the Finance Department sees Sales and Marketing as complacent, and believes they have not worked hard enough to develop an appropriate strategy. This perception may come from the fact that sales staff are believed to be lacking in conscientiousness and attention to detail.

Both these perceptions may be wrong in some cases, but probably not here.

Task interdependence. it is necessary for all the departments to cooperate closely if the company's fortunes are to improve. Any lack of co-operation from any department, perhaps rooted in one of the other causes of conflict mentioned here, is likely to produce significant frustration and further conflict as a result.

Work pressure. LS Company is facing difficult business conditions, which is likely to produce stress effects all responsible members of staff, both because of awareness of the need for improved performance and as a result of pressure from above. Conflict is a possible symptom of this stress.

Sources of vertical conflict

A potential conflict is developing between senior management and the Production Department, and also between senior management and the trade union. This is a **vertical conflict**, because senior management is above the Production Department in the hierarchy, and holds the balance of power.

The source of the potential conflict is the **proposal to cut jobs** in response to the downturn in sales. If the trade union takes industrial action, there is potential for considerable disruption, loss of production and consequent loss of customer goodwill. This will almost certainly have a knock-on effect on staff in other departments, where morale is already low.

Conclusion and priorities

The horizontal conflict, that is the conflict between Marketing/Sales and Finance, needs to be resolved first. If the criticism of each department is justified, then a better pricing strategy and a more aggressive marketing strategy needs to be implemented. If successful, there will be no need to cut jobs in the Production Department, so the vertical conflict will not arise.

21 ZEZ Company

Text references. Conflict is covered in Chapter 3. Negotiation is covered in Chapter 4.

Top tips. A good way to approach Part (a) is to use Thomas's conflict handling model. Give a brief explanation of the model before applying it to the scenario. In Part (b), you will need to relate your knowledge of the stages of negotiation to the specifics of the question, explaining a range of tactics for effective negotiation. You don't need to draw the diagram – this is for information only.

Easy marks. These are a available for an outline of the Thomas model and for knowing the four stages of negotiation.

Examiner's comment. Candidates familiar with Thomas's typology were able to answer part (a) of this question very well. A significant number of candidates appeared to have no knowledge of conflict handling strategies and therefore scored very few marks for this question. Part (b) was generally well answered. Several candidates could have improved their performance by elaborating on the respective phases of negotiation.

Marking scheme

	Marks
Explanation of conflict handling framework	3
1 mark per valid, explained point (½ if not explained)	
to a maximum of 2 each for each of:	
Avoidance	
Accommodation	
Compromise	
Competition	
Collaboration	<u>10</u>
	13
1 mark per valid, explained point (½ if not explained) to a maximum of 2 each for each of:	
Explanation of negotiation	
Listening and understanding the other's objectives	
Persuasion, determine what willing to settle on, preparation	
Opening phase	
Bargaining phase	
Closing phase	
	<u>12</u>
	<u>25</u>

The Senior Management team of ZEZ Company has a range of possible responses to his problem of potential conflict with the staff. *Thomas* (1976) suggests that individuals' conflict-handling styles can be mapped on two dimensions, according to the **intentions** of the parties involved. He labelled the two dimensions *assertiveness* (trying to satisfy one's own concerns) and *co-operativeness* (trying to satisfy the other party's concerns).

He describes five strategies for resolving conflict but feels however that **compromising** was the optimal solution.

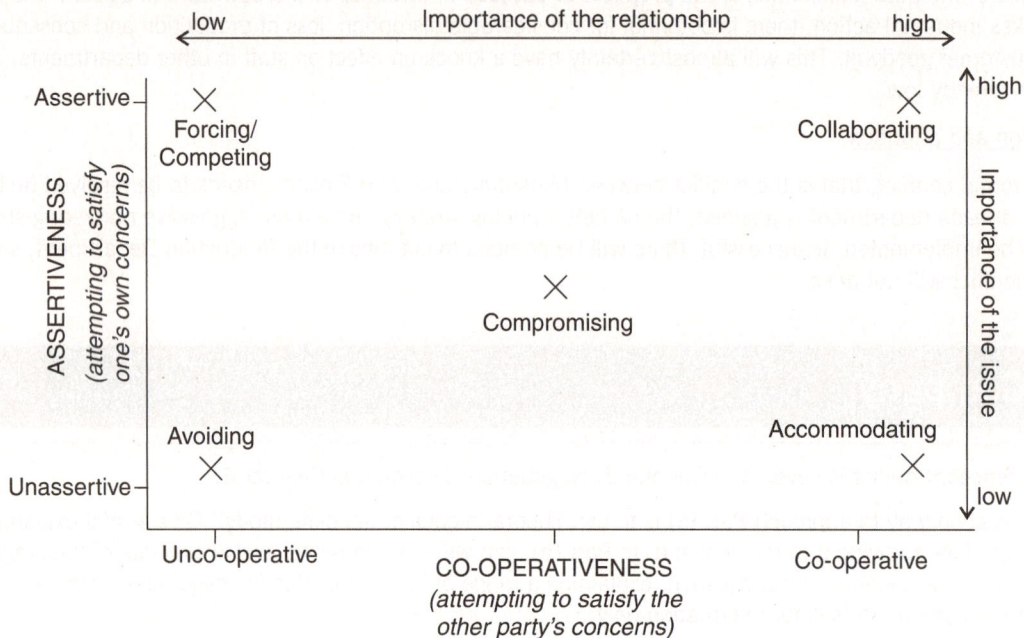

(a) Conflict handling

Avoidance. Some essentially trivial problems blow over without particular management effort. This type of problem can be ignored. If ZEZ Company feels that this is the case here, it can effectively deny that a problem exists and withdraw from considering it further. However, the redundancies and proposed changes to the contractual terms, together with the threat of industrial action mean that it is unlikely that denial and withdrawal would be a satisfactory response. If the conflict is not resolved in some way, the future of the company is in jeopardy.

Accommodation. A more active policy would be to suppress the problem by smoothing over any overt disputes, if possible, in order to preserve working relationships. This approach is unlikely to produce the changes evidently required at ZEZ company, so the Senior Management team may have to combine it with a certain amount of coercion, imposing necessary changes unilaterally. Unless costs are reduced, ZEZ may not survive, and so there is little room for negotiation.

Compromise. A more positive approach for the management of ZEZ to take would involve a willingness to make compromises *via* a process of bargaining, negotiation and conciliation with the trade unions. It is likely that there is some room for manoeuvre in such matters as the criteria for redundancy, the number of redundancies, the redundancy package and changes to terms and conditions.

Collaboration. The compromise approach may, perhaps, be extended into a more sophisticated process of integration and collaboration, in which a continuing dialogue can establish both common ground and general agreement as to what is necessary for the achievement of the overall task. This is a positive approach to managing conflict, but it does not always work. Specifically in the case of ZEZ Company, harsh choices need to be made. Collaboration with the unions can only work if the unions accept the there will need to be changes to contractual terms and redundancies.

Competition. The most assertive conflict handling strategy – to be applied where there relationship matters least – is competition or forcing. This is where the parties do not co-operate, but seek to maximise their own interests, and one party wins and the other loses. This approach would not be appropriate in ZEZ Company, because it would be damaging to working relationships in the long term.

(b) Negotiation

Negotiation is, a process whereby two parties come together to confer with a view to concluding a jointly acceptable agreement. It is a method of conflict resolution, closest to the 'compromise' approach in

Thomas's model discussed in part (a). It involves argument and persuasion and a certain amount of undermining of the opposition.

In this case the Senior Management of ZEZ Co will need to negotiate an agreement with the trade unions who are representing employees. This process is usually known as 'collective bargaining'.

In broad terms, in order to be effective, Senior Management should approach these negotiations with an understanding of the elements involved with the process. The process involves two main elements:

(i) **Purposeful persuasion**: whereby each party attempts to persuade the other to accept its case by marshalling arguments, backed by factual information and analysis. That is, to be successful, Senior Management will need to persuade the unions to its viewpoint.

(ii) **Constructive compromise**: whereby both parties accept the need to move closer toward each other's position, identifying the parameters of common ground within and between their positions, where there is room for concessions to be made, while still meeting the needs of both parties.

Initially, the trade union will not want to agree to job losses, but it might recognise that they are inevitable and concentrate instead on persuading management to provide generous severance pay above the legal minimum and to consider redeployment opportunities. Senior Management, might anticipate this and work out a compromise solution.

Effective negotiation should go through a number of stages:

(i) Preparation

A framework for preparation for the negotiations that ZEZ might use to ensure that the negotiations themselves are effective might be:

- Set objectives for the negotiation. Decide what ZEZ wants from the negotiations.

- Gather information on the issues over which negotiations are going to be concluded. For example, the market rate for similar outsourcing services.

- Identify potential areas of conflict.

- Identify potential areas of movement.

- Formulate a negotiating strategy.

(ii) Conducting the negotiation

Some of the considerations of ZEZ for conducting negotiations might be:

- Identifying the common ground.
- Considering new proposals or counter proposals.
- Making concessions.
- Having a skilled negotiating team.
- Using effective communication skills.
- Ensuring good leadership, so that meetings can be well facilitated.

(iii) Closing the negotiation

At the conclusion of negotiations, both parties must be satisfied that all issues have been discussed, and they must understand exactly what has been agreed. ZEZ should ensure that once there is agreement, the points are written up as a draft agreement. It can then be printed, formally signed and communicated to those affected by its provisions.

22 FPC Company

Text references. Communication is covered in Chapter 4 and appraisal in Chapter 2.

Top tips. Part (a) of the question is about communication skills (or the lack of them). Training sessions in communication skills should be directed at helping individuals to understand the nature of communication and why attempts at communication are often unsuccessful and messages unclear or ignored. Although the question is mainly about the problems of poor communication, it is worth thinking as well about the purpose of training, and making a brief introductory comment about what the training sessions should aim to achieve.

There are specific problems within FPC Company, and you should mention these in your answer, indicating the training that might be required to enable staff to understand the nature of these problems and the effect they are having.

Part (b) is concerned with performance appraisal and how this might improve the performance of staff. It is important to remember that staff appraisals often have three different purposes: to assess performance and reward good performance; to provide a historical review of performance and whether the individual has met planning targets; and to discuss an individual's weaknesses in a constructive way and plan for future improvement through training and development initiatives. Appraisals are not carried out for the sole purpose of motivating individuals. You should also take note of the fact that none of the staff have had an appraisal in recent years. This should encourage you to comment in your answer that appraisals will have only limited effect if they are carried out occasionally and forgotten during the time in between.

Easy marks. For part (a), think about problems with communication, and suggest ways in which training might help individuals to recognise the problems and be conscious of the need to deal with them. Training can also include practising or the learning of techniques to improve communication. For part (b), you should explain the purposes of staff appraisal and make sure that you explain how each of these could help to improve staff performance. Don't forget that individuals are possibly motivated by concern for their future training and development, and also by financial rewards for achieving a target.

Examiner's comment. Answers were mixed. In Part (a), too many candidates lost focus after reading the scenario and tended to discuss the problems of conflict between the departments rather than tackling the question to do with the improvement of communication skills for members of the Finance Department. In answering Part (b), a surprising number of candidates failed to make good use of their knowledge of performance appraisal when applying it to the scenario for this particular question. Some candidates simply described the stages involved in staff appraisal rather than developing the answer to explain how it could help improve staff performance.

Marking scheme

		Marks
(a)		
	Purpose of training sessions in communication	2
	Discussion of the elements of a communications model and its elements	2
	Need for the sender to understand purpose of communications	1
	Need for sender to understand level of knowledge and interests of recipients	2
	Problems with use of technical language and jargon	2
	Problems with the form of messages and channels of communication: e-mails and spreadsheets	2
	Value of combining non-financial with financial performance indicators	1
	Value of feedback and monitoring use of information	2
	Communications planning	2
	Other valid points may be included in answers, such as a discussion of 'noise'	
	Maximum for part (a)	15
(b)		
	Defining performance standards and giving direction to individuals. Reference to FPC Company	2
	Monitoring performance of individuals against targets	2
	Appraisal schemes and incentive/reward schemes	2
	Identifying good performance and weaknesses in performance. Identifying ways to improve	2
	Development of the individual: using appraisal schemes to plan training and development measures	2
	Motivation of individuals	2
	Other valid points may be included in answers	
	Maximum for part (b)	10
Maximum		25

(a) <u>The purpose of training in communications</u>

Training should have a purpose. In FPC Company, PR has recognised a problem of poor communication by finance staff that is ongoing, with no effort to resolve it. The overall aim of the training sessions should therefore be to create awareness among finance staff that there is a problem with communication, for which they are responsible. They also need to understand the consequences of poor communication, which is that the information provided is not understood and acted on in the way that it should be. Having recognised the problem of poor communication, staff should then be trained to learn methods that can be used to improve their communication skills. It will then be the responsibility of PR to ensure that these skills are then applied in practice, by introducing change into the way that financial (and non-financial) information is communicated by the finance team.

<u>Communication problems and a communications model</u>

Training should initially focus on the problems that exist in FPC Company. As a way of structuring the problems, it will be useful to discuss a simple communication model. Communication occurs between the creator of a message and its recipient or consumer of information. The information is provided through messages, which are delivered in a language used by the creator that the consumer must interpret and 'decode'. The information is delivered through chosen media. A basic communications model therefore consists of creator and consumers, the message, the language of the message and the medium for transmitting the message. Training should encourage finance staff to understand that problems in communication can occur with any of these, making the communication process ineffective.

Training sessions should go on to cover the nature of communication problems in more detail, how they arise in FPC and what can be done to deal with the problem.

<u>The creator and the message</u>

A training session might focus on the creators of information and the content of the messages they send.

Finance staff should be trained to think about the purpose of the information they send out and what they should be trying to achieve with the information. This includes recognising that the purpose of much communication is to prompt a reaction by its recipients. To do this, the recipients need to be aware of the information and understand what it means.

Staff should be taught about the need to recognise the level of understanding of the recipients of information. In the case of financial information, it is particularly important to recognise that non-financial staff do not have a strong understanding of the technicalities of finance and accounting and are unlikely to understand or use the jargon that finance staff commonly use. Awareness needs to be established that in FPC messages are often too complicated and there is excessive use of financial jargon. Training should include methods of presenting relatively simple messages in language that the recipients can understand.

<u>The recipients of messages and the medium</u>

Another training session might focus on how recipients get the messages and how they use them. This might also include training on the choice of medium or channel for sending the information.

Communications should mean something to the recipient and should prompt the recipient into action where appropriate. This means that the messages should 'grab their attention' and sustain their interest. Messages should therefore highlight information that matters to the recipients, and should be seen and understood by them. Finance staff need to understand that recipients of information respond to messages about non-financial as well as financial matters, and may be disinclined to study financial indicators alone.

Training should also help staff to recognise the importance of using suitable communications channels for messages. We are told that there is excessive use of e-mails, in which it is difficult to identify relevant information. It might help to make finance staff aware of the number of e-mails that managers in FPC have to deal with each day, and how they respond to the many e-mails they receive.

Staff should also be encouraged to think about the form in which the message is delivered. We are told that financial spreadsheets are used, in which it is difficult to identify the significant information. Training should address the issue of whether non-financial staff are familiar with spreadsheets, and whether other methods of presenting information – for example in graphical form, or by highlighting significant information in another way, might be appropriate.

Feedback

A training session should try to get finance staff to understand the value of feedback, and the need to monitor how recipients have responded to the messages sent out. Information has value only if it is used for decision-making, and finance staff need to be aware of how the information they provide is used by managers within the company. If the information is not being used in the ways that are intended, measures need to be taken to make the messages more effective.

To bring the training to an end, PR should lead a session on what needs to be done to improve the quality and effectiveness of financial (and supporting non-financial) information within the company. He might do this by announcing that he wants to establish a communications plan in which all the issues – the purpose of information sent out by the finance department, its content, form, timing, avoiding the use of technical language or jargon, and monitoring how it is understood and used – are all considered. Training in best practice needs to be converted into actual best practice.

(b)   Staff appraisal

Staff appraisal schemes usually have several purposes.

In FPC, staff do not have clear targets or objectives. When there are annual appraisals for members of staff, the process can be used to establish performance standards and targets that are expected from individuals. Informing individuals about what is expected of them might encourage them to work in conformity with standards or towards the stated goals.

Having established targets or standards for individuals, annual appraisals can be used to monitor actual performance by comparing it with the target. Individuals can be made aware of how well or how badly they have performed. Giving praise for good performance may motivate individuals to maintain their standards in the future.

Appraisal schemes are often linked to reward schemes, and annual bonuses for achieving or exceeding targets. Pay is considered a strong motivator, and the offer of rewards can help individuals to focus on achieving the targets they have been set. A criticism of reward schemes is that individuals may focus on achieving targets to the exclusion of all other considerations, and incentive schemes must be carefully structured if they are to have the desired effect on overall performance.

Another use of appraisal schemes is to encourage the personal development of individual employees. Appraisal interviews can be used by a boss to discuss with each team member individually what they have achieved in the year, and what they have done well or badly. This constructive discussion can then be used to consider ways of improving performance and helping the individual to develop in the future. The outcome of an appraisal interview may be an agreement to send the individual for training in particular subjects in order to develop their knowledge and skills. There may also be agreement on how the individuals can be encouraged to improve by doing more varied work in the future or taking on more responsibility.

Appraisal interviews that are used to agree measures for training and development for the individual can motivate the individual. It should create awareness that the organisation is concerned about the individual and wants to encourage the individual to develop and improve. It also helps the individual to recognise more clearly the ways in which he or she should be trying to improve.

To have any value, appraisal interviews should happen regularly, typically once a year. If they are held only infrequently, as in FPC Company, they will be ignored as nothing more than an occasional wasteful administrative exercise by the HR department. Line managers need to take ownership of the appraisal process for the process to be effective. It may also be argued that although formal appraisal interviews should occur annually, there should be continual monitoring and mentoring of individuals throughout the year, to improve and sustain their personal development.

23 RM Company

> **Text references.** Chapter 2 contains material on teams and Chapter 3 considers conflict and includes information of managing disputes and negotiation.
>
> **Top tips.** This question is a real test of your ability to produce an answer that is more than just a general analysis. You must be able to make points that apply to the specific circumstances of RM Company. Note the word 'nature' in the requirement for part (a). The question is actually using the word with a specific meaning. He is asking you to put conflict that is taking place into some sort of classification of type or category. As you will see in our answer we classify the problems at RM Company as **horizontal conflict**.
>
> **Easy marks.** There are few easy marks in this requirement. You would glean a mark or two for pointing out the different attitudes of the departments, but this would not count as a full analysis since both **goal incompatibility** and **cognitive and emotional orientation** are involved.

(a)   The nature and sources of conflict at RM Company

RM Company is suffering the effects of **horizontal conflict**: that is, the conflicts are arising between groups and individuals that do not have a hierarchical relationship and are of more or less equal status in the company.

The various disputes have occurred for several reasons.

Incompatibility of goals. The primary goals of the various departments involved, rather than supporting the overall objective of successful NPD, are themselves effectively incompatible. For example, the apparent slowness of the R&D department may reflect a goal of high technical excellence, while the anxiety of the sales department and the frustration of the marketers may, in turn, reflect goals of continuing growth and good customer relations.

Incompatibility of personalities in different business functions. People working in different functions tend to have rather different personal priorities, interests, attitudes and values. For example, the perception of the finance department as unhelpful controllers of resources may say more about the attitudes prevailing in the other departments than the actual nature of the finance department's motivation.

Task interdependence. It is necessary for all the departments to cooperate closely if successful NPD is to take place, since information, in particular, must flow effectively back and forth between them. Any lack of co-operation from any department, perhaps rooted in one of the other causes of conflict mentioned here, is likely to produce significant frustration and further conflict as a result. This may be behind some of the production department's complaints about lack of co-operation from the R&D people.

Work pressure. RM Company is facing difficult business conditions, which is likely to produce stress effects all responsible members of staff, both because of awareness of the need for improved performance and as a result of pressure from above. Conflict is a possible symptom of this stress.

(b)   Leading and managing the NPD team

> **Easy marks.** As with any question on teams, when thinking about this requirement, your mind should instantly make an agile leap to the work of *Tuckman* and that of *Belbin*. In fact, the Examiner's marking scheme indicates that discussing these two topics could almost take you to a pass mark. Naturally, you would not overlook the fact that the leader is part of the team and a consideration of management style would provide the remaining marks required.

The task of developing a new team might be considered under three headings: the individuals needed, the functioning of the group, and the leadership of the team.

The individuals

F must ensure that the members of the new project, between them, possess the skills, experience and aptitudes necessary to develop successfully his new range of luxury foods. Past disputes mean that perhaps the most important personal quality the team members will require a **commitment to working productively together**. They must retain their orientation towards the role of their own departments, but they must supplement that with a willingness to understand the needs and priorities of their colleagues.

The emphasis must be on a judicious **balance of departmental concerns** in order to **support the overall goal**.

Belbin suggests that the effective functioning of a team depends, at least in part, on the ability of the members to play a range of important team roles, so F should select his team using a mix of roles. These roles are co-ordinator, shaper, implementer, monitor-evaluator, resource investigator, team worker, specialist and completer/finisher.

The group

New teams develop and mature over time, finding ways to operate and relate. The leader can build the team by controlling and accelerating this process. The development process was described by *Tuckman* as taking place in four stages.

(i)   **Forming** is the process of bringing the group together and beginning to work out its aims, structure and processes. The 'getting to know each other' process should be encouraged here since team members come from different functions and may not even know each other. The team members are likely to be wary of one another and social relationships will be unformed.

(ii)   **Storming** is a period of open conflict between members about objectives, methods and relationships during which priorities and roles emerge. It should lead to a robust basis for co-operation in the future.

(iii)   **Norming** is a period of settling down with the development of group norms about work requirements and methods and social expectations. The leader may need to encourage 'overarching' norms and goals in order to overcome inter-functional differences.

(iv)   **Performing** productive work follows as the final phase, when the team is ready to collaborate on efficient task performance.

Leadership

Leadership style will be important. The project team will include experienced professionals with their own competences and expectations. An autocratic style is unlikely to be the most productive when working with such people. The **maturity** of the team, in *Hersey and Blanchard's* terms, needs to be considered. Maturity of a team is not defined as age but as:

(i)   A desire for achievement

(ii)   The willingness and ability to accept responsibility

(iii)   Education, experience or skills relevant to the particular task

The leader must map his style (for example delegating) to the maturity of the team. In this team, the **maturity** of the team is high, therefore a low degree of directive behaviour on the part of the leader will be appropriate.

Participation in decision-making and a high degree of **delegation** will be important. In addition, it will help maximise the potential synergy of cross-functional working by drawing on the various stakeholders and areas of expertise.

The complexity of the task and the need for a wide range of co-ordinated inputs will make **communication** very important. Providing for this will be a major leadership role. F must, in the first place, ensure that he communicates effectively with his team himself. He must provide clear objectives and decisions, brief future activity and plans clearly and give feedback on progress. He must also ensure that the team members communicate effectively with each other. No doubt much important communication will be **verbal, face-to-face and informal**, but there should also be **meetings** held at suitable intervals to ensure that important matters are not overlooked and there is general understanding of work and progress.

24 Sales targets

Text references. Teamworking is covered in Chapter 2.

Top tips. This question brings teambuilding and teamworking theory into a realistic commercial setting and demonstrates how teams can either work very well or not at all. A key theme that seems to stand out from the question wording is the lack of control that the team members now have over their working environment – from a happy and participative group there is now a disjointed series of insular teams that seem to have forgotten all about overall organisational objectives in the pursuit of non-participative sales targets. The problems with the new structure are evident and wide-ranging. It is important in part (b) to provide **practical** advice not waffley theory. In part (a), the examiner suggested up to six marks for the benefits of sales teams and seven marks for the problems of sales teams. In part (b), there were **up to two marks each** available for each strategy listed.

The examiner's comments on this question show the importance of understanding and applying the CIMA active verbs. Students failed to **discuss** or **explain** in their answers.

Easy marks. For part (b), as there are twelve marks on offer so make sure that you come up with at least six suggestions.

Examiner's comments. In part (a), most candidates were able to pick out the pros and cons of teamworking. However these were not always applied to the scenario given. In part (b), candidates needed to write more about than just the balance of roles identified by *Belbin* when discussing teams. In both parts, common errors included missing out key points or not 'discussing' or 'explaining' as required.

Marking scheme

		Marks
(a)	1 mark for introduction/overview stating that explaining schemes are a motivational technique	
	1 mark per benefit to a maximum of 6	
	2 marks per valid, explained problem to a maximum of 6	
	Maximum for part (a)	13
(b)	Maximum for part (b)	12
		25

(a) <u>Benefits and problems of introducing sales teams and the sales target system</u>

The introduction of the sales target system in the A Insurance Company would have had the achievement of organisational sales growth targets as its main aim. It is not stated how the targets were set, but unless the teams were allowed to set their own targets, and measure their own progress, it is likely that the targets could be resented when they are not achieved.

Incentive schemes such as the one described are a common **motivational** technique. Given that 'the Centre' had been achieving such good results in the past, it was probably never anticipated that the restructuring that has taken place could have such a negative impact on working relationships, morale and productivity.

<u>Benefits</u>

Organising work groups into teams is a common form of work organisation, and a powerful motivator for performance. Teams combine the skills of different individuals, and fear of 'letting the side down' can be a powerful motivator. Effective teams could bring the following benefits to 'the Centre'.

(i) Loyalty and hard work is encouraged
(ii) Skills and information are shared
(iii) New ideas can be tested
(iv) Individuals are encouraged to participate
(v) Goodwill, trust and respect can be built up
(vi) Targets may be regularly exceeded

Problems

These benefits do seem to have occurred in Team X, the most successful team. The success becomes self-generating. Unfortunately, teamworking of this kind is rarely an unqualified success and Teams Y and Z are struggling in different ways. Some obvious problems can be identified.

(i)   **Conflict** and personality problems can arise, as has happened in Team Y. Informal networks come to the fore, which may work against overall organisational objectives.

(ii) The **rigid nature** of the new team-based structure has meant that Team Z has abandoned the rest of 'the Centre'.

(iii) Differences of opinion are always likely to occur.

(iv) Group consensus (groupthink) can stifle thought and close the team off from the rest of the organisation. This appears to have happened to Team Z.

When teams rather than individuals are rewarded, it is easy for unmotivated or otherwise undeserving individuals to get by with little effort. There is no direct evidence from the scenario that this is the case with some members of Team X, but if it were then it would add more fuel to the resentments and difficulties faced by the other teams. As the reward is in the form of cash, it is very easy for unsuccessful teams to feel resentful and become increasingly alienated. When this happens, inter-group conflict is likely to arise.

(b)   ### Strategies that could be used to minimise problems

Assuming that B cannot disband the team structure, here are some ideas for B to consider on how to manage the current situation, minimise its problems and improve morale in 'the Centre'.

Participation in target setting

This would have the effect of gaining the 'buy-in' of team members to the targets, and encourage them to see the targets as achievable.

Split teams by product

It may be desirable, if the product portfolio allows it, to give each team its own product (one team for vehicle, one for home and one for contents insurance) and, rather then having them compete directly, reward them on percentage improvement each month or quarter. Because the products may all be bought by one customer, it would encourage cross-team co-operation to reward all teams when overall sales are increased.

Different incentives

It may be time to remove the cash incentive, and replace it with a reward that is a little less emotive and less likely to cause resentment. It may be worthwhile to replace it with a 'team of the month' trophy or similar prize. A 'suggestion box' system, independent of team membership, should be set up to reward individual ideas.

Mix up the teams

This is going to be needed to shake up some of the cliques and insularity that have been formed and which are proving to be a barrier to proper co-operation. B may need to refer to *Belbin's* roles to ensure that teams have a good mix of people. The current leader of Team Y needs to be replaced.

Regular meetings of all team members

These will encourage cooperation between the teams, reinforce organisational objectives and provide a mechanism for conflicts and disagreements to be aired and resolved. Informal networks can be given an outlet, and valuable insights gained by management as to future staffing of the teams. Social events involving all teams should be encouraged.

Counselling and discipline

The leader of Team Y is not performing in his role and this is affecting his team members adversely. This needs to be sorted out by way of counselling or some sort of disciplinary procedure as it is affecting his team.

Team leader briefings

These should be held regularly with B, so that team leaders can keep their members up to date, and be made to feel that they are part of the decision making process. This should reduce any potential for animosity between them as they should be reminded that they are all working for the same organisation.

25 T4M

Text references. Outsourcing is covered in Chapter 3 in the context of the finance function and again in Chapter 11 in the context of strategy. Negotiation is covered in Chapter 4

Top tips. You should make sure you cover benefits and drawbacks of outsourcing as well as explaining what outsourcing is. In part (b), you should give examples of the types of negotiation the finance director will be involved in if the outsourcing strategy goes ahead. Do not just say what negotiation is – apply it to the scenario.

Easy marks. Some aspects of part (b) on negotiation should be a straightforward memory test.

Examiner's comment. Weaker answers used Mendelow's matrix to discuss stakeholder power and interest but didn't then use this to develop an answer linked to negotiation. Others provided practical examples of what F could negotiate on, which is fine but they did not go on to discuss how to approach negotiations so that they are effective.

Marking scheme

		Marks
(a)	Benefits, for example:	
	Reduces labour costs	up to 2
	Reduces fixed costs	up to 3
	More accurate prediction of cost	up to 3
	Best practice/expertise	1
	Finance function can focus on strategic role	1
	Other	1
	Drawbacks, for example:	1
	Cost of managing contract	1
	Expertise needed to manage contract	1
	Loss of managerial control	1
	Erosion of internal knowledge	1
	Risk re confidentiality of customer information	1
	Cost of potential legal action for non compliance with Service Level	up to 3
	Agreement	up to 3
	Unsatisfactory customer service	up to 3
	Other aspects, language, union problems, cultural differences	up to 3
	acceptable	1
	To a maximum of 12 (flexibility)	
		12

(b)	Explanation of negotiation	up to 2
	Negotiations on contract with G20	up to 3
	Negotiations with employees and union re redundancies	up to 3
	Understand objectives	1
	Focus on primary objective	1
	Listen to both sides	1
	Anticipate reactions	1
	Be aware of cultural differences	1
	Be prepared to settle for what is fair	1
	Avoid win-lose or lose-lose	1
	Use of persuasion	1
	Test understanding	1
	Planning preparation stage	up to 3
	Opening phase	up to 3
	Bargaining phase	up to 3
	Closing phase	up to 3
	Other	
	To a maximum of 13 (flexibility)	
		13
		25

(a) Outsourcing involves the organisation sub-contracting business activities to external providers. Often these providers are located in the same country as the organisation but international providers, as in this case, can also be used. Where a part of an organisation's business activities is relocated to another country, it is termed **offshoring**.

There are a number of benefits T4M could gain from outsourcing to G20:

(i) Costs

    (1) T4M may be able to substantially reduce the costs of customer service on bill queries and payroll. G20 will be able to provide these services at a **lower cost** than T4M is currently paying. This may be a result of lower input costs, such as labour and IT infrastructure.

    (2) T4M will save on **recruiting and training** of staff.

    (3) T4M may be able to enter into a fixed price contract for the outsourced services. This will give them **increased certainty** for decision making and planning.

(ii) Specialism

G20 may be a specialist provider of the services required. It may therefore bring **specialist skills** and best practice. This may have efficiency benefits for T4M, as well as providing a better level of service for its customers and employees.

(iii) Strategic Focus

The use of G20 as an external provider of services will allow the finance team to **concentrate on tactical and strategic decision-making** rather than being concerned with activities at the operational level.

There are also, however, a number of drawbacks with T4M's proposal:

(iv) Loss of control

Outsourcing may result in a **loss of control** over the activities outsourced. This is because the staff carrying out the activities are no longer direct employees.

(v) Loss of skills

Once the activities have been outsourced then the **skills will be lost** from T4M and it will mean that financial transactions will be difficult to bring back in-house.

(vi)   <u>Transition to Outsourcing</u>

    (1)   In order to save costs 300 staff will be made redundant, and this may lead to **conflict** with employees and their representatives.

    (2)   The transition to outsourcing may lead to a **loss of morale** amongst those remaining in the organisation.

(vii)   <u>Confidentiality</u>

    (1)   Another drawback associated with using external providers concerns **confidentiality** of information given to them. There may be a loss of confidential information that may be used either for commercial use or fraud.

    (2)   In order to prevent the leak of confidential information, **security measures** would need to be put in place and this would take both time and money.

(viii)   <u>Disagreements</u>

    T4M and G20 may find themselves in **dispute** after the transition to outsourcing. This may produce a break in activities, together with additional costs.

(ix)   <u>Costs</u>

    Although a reduction in costs was cited as one of the benefits of outsourcing, there may be some financial drawbacks:

    (1)   T4M could end up having to pay increased costs for **additional services required after the service level has been agreed**.

    (2)   After the initial contract period, T4M may be faced with substantial increases in costs.

    (3)   There will be costs associated with managing the outsourced contract, along with developing the **expertise needed to manage the contract**.

    (4)   Finally, the outsourcing activities will need to be **monitored** to ensure compliance with predetermined standards, and this will have associated costs.

(b)   **Negotiation is**, a process whereby two parties come together to confer with a view to concluding a jointly acceptable agreement.

In this case F, the Finance Director, will need to negotiate in agreement with several partners in a **number of potential scenarios** if the decision to outsource goes ahead. These might include:

- Negotiating the **contract between T4M and G20**.

- Negotiating with **employees and trade unions** regarding possible redundancies resulting from the outsourcing decision.

In broad terms, in order to be effective, F should approach these negotiations with an understanding of the elements involved with the process. The process involves two main elements:

(i)   **Purposeful persuasion**: whereby each party attempts to persuade the other to accept its case by marshalling arguments, backed by factual information and analysis. That is, to be successful, F will need to persuade the other parties to his viewpoint.

(ii)   **Constructive compromise**: whereby both parties accept the need to move closer toward each other's position, identifying the parameters of common ground within and between their positions, where there is room for concessions to be made, while still meeting the needs of both parties. Here F will need to be willing to compromise on his position.

It is likely that constructive compromise will be needed in both the negotiations cited above. T4M will wish to minimise its costs and maximise the level of service it receives from G20. Whereas G20 will wish to maximise its income and minimise the resources it needs to devote to the contract. F should be prepared to compromise in a constructive manner.

Similarly, in the trade union negotiations, the trade union will not want to agree to job losses, but it might recognise that they are inevitable and concentrate instead on persuading management to provide generous severance pay above the legal minimum and to consider redeployment opportunities. F, on behalf of T4M, might anticipate this and work out a compromise solution.

Effective negotiation should go through a number of stages:

(i)　Preparation

A framework for preparation for the negotiations that F might use to ensure that the negotiations themselves are effective might be:

- Set objectives for the negotiation. Decide what F wants from the negotiations.

- Gather information on the issues over which negotiations are going to be concluded. For example, the market rate for similar outsourcing services.

- Identify potential areas of conflict.

- Identify potential areas of movement.

- Formulate a negotiating strategy.

(ii)　Conducting the negotiation

Some of the considerations of F for conducting negotiations might be:

- Identifying the common ground.

- Considering new proposals or counter proposals.

- Making concessions.

- Having a skilled negotiating team.

- Using effective communication skills.

- Ensuring good leadership, so that meetings can be well facilitated.

(iii)　Closing the negotiation

At the conclusion of negotiations, both parties must be satisfied that all issues have been discussed, and they must understand exactly what has been agreed. F should ensure that once there is agreement, the points are written up as a draft agreement. It can then be printed, formally signed and communicated to those affected by its provisions.

26　TFX Company

Text references. Shared servicing is covered in chapter 3.

Top tips. To score highly in part (a) you will need to provide a strong discussion of the advantages and disadvantages to moving to a shared service model which is specifically tailored to the organisation in question.

Tuckman's framework provides a good structure for you answer to part (b), referencing back to theory rather than relying on broad, generic points above building teams will help ensure you earn enough marks to pass this part question.

Easy marks. Some marks will be available in part (a) for simply describing what is meant by a shared service model.

Examiner's comment. Part (a) overall had some strong answers but a number of weaker ones due to incorrect interpretation of SSC model. Weaker answers tended to confuse the Shared Service Centre Model with outsourcing. Generally candidates were better able to articulate the benefits rather than the disadvantages of the SSC model.

Part (b) was a mixed performance. High scoring scripts used theoretical principles associated with team development. Weak answers made few practical suggestions, and some approached the question from a project management point of view of setting up the SSC, rather than relating their answers to developing and building teams.

Marking scheme

		Marks
(a)	Up to 2 marks for explanation of SSC model	
	Up to 2 marks for rationale for SCC model	
	Up to 1 mark per benefit of SSC	
	Up to 1 mark per disadvantage of SSC	
	Maximum marks awarded	13
(b)	Up to 2 marks for overview of need to be proactive in building new teams	
	Up to 1 mark for explanation of Tuckman's view of team development	
	1 mark per valid, explained point (½ if not explained)	
	to a maximum of 3 each for each of:	
	Forming	
	Storming	
	Norming	
	Performing	
	Up to 8 marks for other approaches to team building	
	Maximum marks awarded	12
	Maximum marks awarded for question	25

(a)   Each of the business units of TFX company currently has its own finance department. A recommendation has now been made that the finance function is transformed to become a shared service centre (SSC). This would involve consolidating all of the existing finance functions into a single central function which would serve the entire organisation.

There are a number of benefits that TFX would enjoy should they go ahead with this proposal:

Cost reduction

Consolidation into an SSC would reduce inefficiencies by removing the duplication of work that is currently carried out in each of the individual finance units. This would greatly reduce both overheads and headcount and therefore unit transaction costs would also be reduced. There would also be a reduction in premises and associated costs given that the function would now be based in a single location. These reductions in cost would allow TFX to benefit from economies of scale.

Improved quality

Consolidating the finance functions into a single SSC would facilitate knowledge sharing which should lead to an improvement in quality of the service provided.

Standardisation of approach

The establishment of an SSC would allow standard approaches to be adopted across the organisation. This would allow TFX to develop more consistent management of business data and ensure best practice is followed throughout the organisation.

However, there are a number of disadvantages to moving towards an SSC that TFX should be aware of:

Loss of working relationships

Whilst the individual finance departments are embedded within the business units they will have established good working relationships with the rest of that business unit and a degree of trust will have been built up. By removing the finance functions from the business units and moving towards an SSC it is likely that these strong relationships and levels of trust would be lost.

Reduced local knowledge

Finance functions that are embedded into the business unit that they serve are more likely to have increased levels of knowledge and understanding of the day to day running of that business unit. This allows the finance function to better understand the needs of the business unit and make a more valuable contribution to its strategic decisions. By moving the finance functions of TFX out to a shared service model this local knowledge would be lost. This may reduce the value of the service that can be provided.

Cultural issues

TFX is a multinational company which operates in a number of different countries globally. It may not be very practical for a diverse company of this nature to move to an SSC. For example, there is the possibility that culture differences, time differences and language barriers may be encountered which may make a centralised service difficult to operate in practice.

(b)   If the move to a shared service centre goes ahead, TFX will need to develop and build the new finance team. This team is likely to be made up of groups of staff from across the organisation who are not used to working together and may have very different established ways of working.

The management at TFX that is responsible for this team will need to be proactive in helping it to develop into an effective and efficient team. An understanding of Tuckman's stages of group development would be helpful as, for a team to be effective, it is important that it is allowed to pass through each of the developmental stages. Only once each of the stages have been passed through will the new team be able to focus on achieving its purpose as the finance function of the SSC.

The stages identified by Tuckman are as follows.

Forming

This is the beginning period where the group is only just coming together. Each member of the team will wish to impress his or her personality on the group. The individuals will be trying to find out about each other and about the aims and norms of the team. It is unlikely at this stage that any member of the team will wish to introduce new ideas. Initial roles and responsibilities as well as codes of conduct and acceptable behaviours will be worked out at this stage.

Strorming

The storming stage of team development normally involves more or less open conflict between team members. There may be changes agreed in the original objectives, procedures and norms established for the group as the various members of the group suggest their different views on how best to work together in order to achieve the targets of the SSC. The effectiveness of the team will fail during this stage, however, if the team is developing successfully this may be a fruitful stage. This is because more realistic targets will be set and trust between the group members will be increased.

Norming

This is the period of setting down where the team will start to reach agreements and conflicts will be resolved. Compromise and negotiations will take place between the individuals to allow procedures and standards of behaviours to be established. Individual requirements and output expectations will also be agreed. Norms and procedures may evolve which enable methodical working to be introduced and maintained.

Performing

The final stage of team development occurs when the team sets to work to execute its task. The objectives of the group will no longer be hindered by the difficulties of growth and development of the team. The team's energies will all be task focused with the aim of achieving the objectives of the SSC rather than conflict focuses. As such, the team will now be at its most effective.

If the new team is to successfully pass through the stages identified above and become an effective team the company will have needed to consider a number of factors prior to putting the team together. For example, it will be necessary to ensure that appropriately skilled individuals are selected for the team and that the team as a whole is balanced. Belbin's nine team roles will be helpful here in ensuring there is an appropriate balance of the various roles within the team.

27 Project network

> **Text references.** Chapter 8.
>
> **Top tips.** We have shown both the activity-on-node style diagram and the activity-on-line style diagram but you only need to draw one of these. Choose the style with which you are most comfortable.
>
> **Easy marks.** If you draw the diagram correctly, you already have the answers to parts (a) and (b).

(a) Either of the following diagrams.

Activity-on-node style

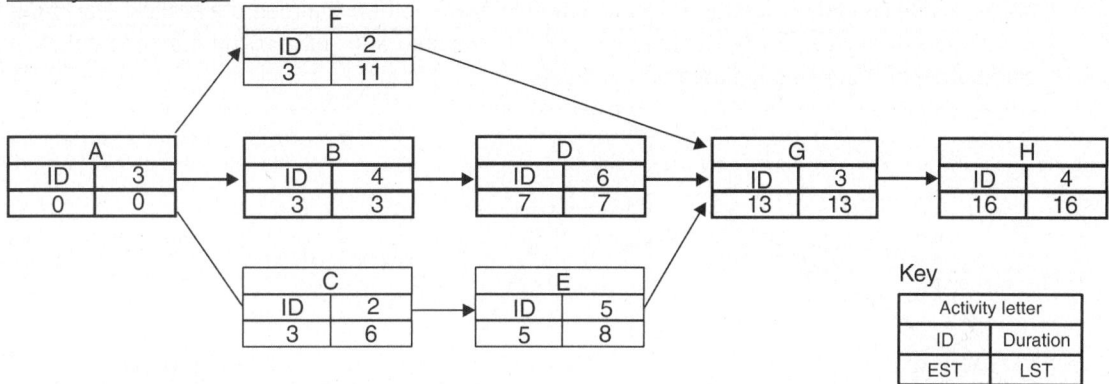

Activity-on-line style

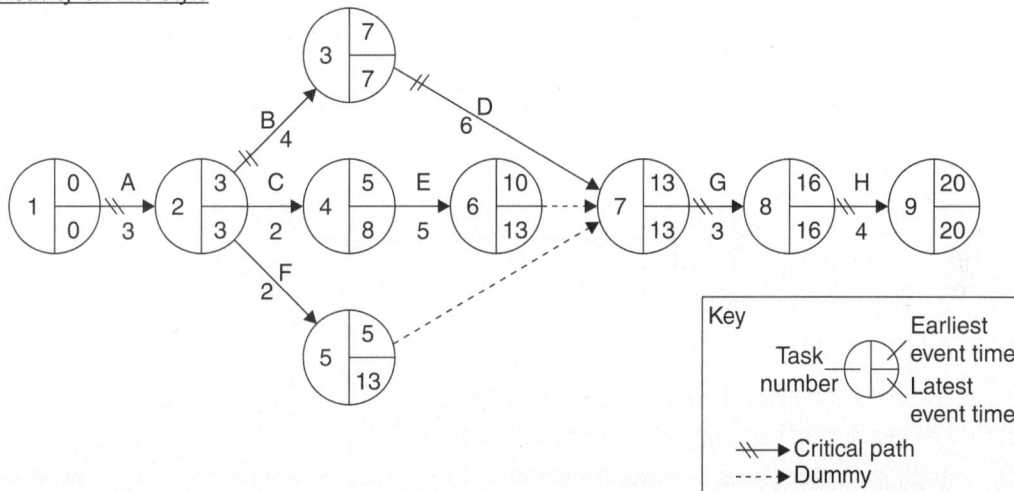

(b) Activities on the critical path are A, B, D, G, H.

(c) 20 days.

(d) Task C overrunning by two days would not change the elapsed duration.

(e) Task B overrunning by one day would increase the elapsed duration to 21 days.

28 F Bakery

Text references. Network analysis is covered in Chapter 8 of your Study Text.

Top tips. Part (a) of this question is a reasonably straightforward network diagram. You should present it clearly (use a whole page) and correctly labelled so that the critical path can be identified easily.

Easy marks. If you draw the diagram correctly you will be able to identify the critical path.

Examiner's comment. There was a marked difference between candidates who had prepared well for this question and those who had missed the necessary preparation. A large proportion of well prepared candidates gained full marks for their answer while the less well prepared scored only a handful of marks or even zero marks. Some candidates omitted to calculate float/slack, others claimed the earliest start time for recruitment was week 34 rather than week 24 as required and some made minor mistakes in their completion of the network diagram.

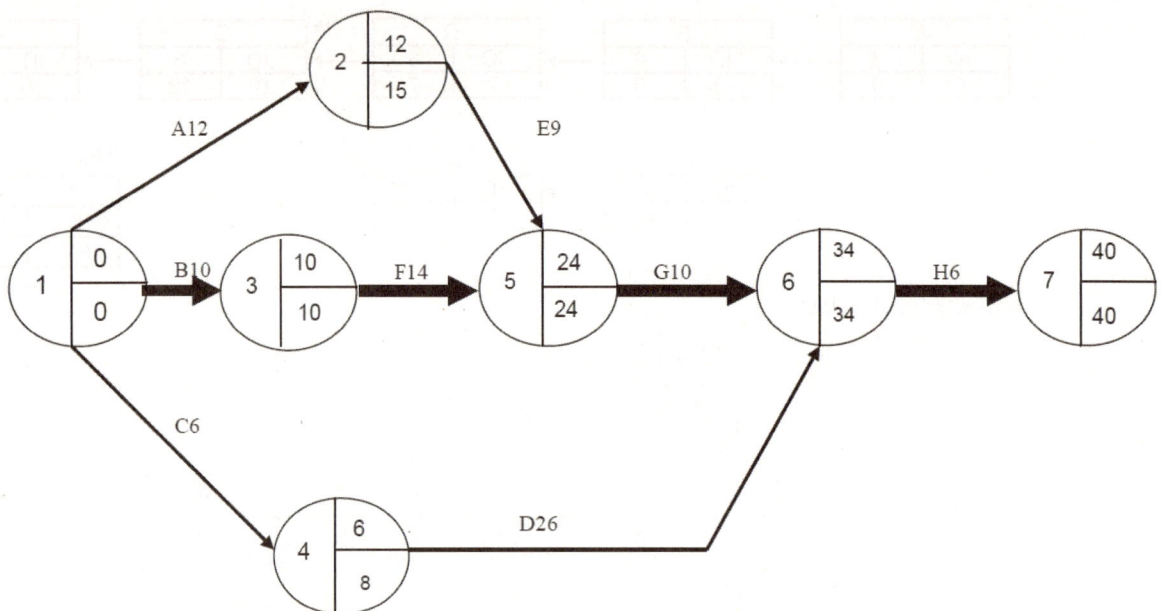

(a)   Activities on the critical path are B, F, G, H.

   The overall duration of the project is 40 weeks.

(b)   The recruitment campaign can start in week 24.

(c)   Activities A and E have 3 weeks' float time.

   Activities C and D have 2 weeks' float time.

29 V

Text references. These topics come under the heading of project implementation, and are covered in Chapter 8.

Top tips. Part (a) of this question is a reasonably straightforward network diagram. You should present it clearly (use a whole page) and correctly labelled so that the critical path can be identified easily. In Part (b), you need to explain the difference between 'scenario planning' and 'buffering', and also to apply this knowledge to the scenario and discuss the usefulness of these techniques to V in planning the start up of her new business.

Easy marks. These are available for text book explanations in Part (b)

Examiner's comment. In part (a), most candidates were able to produce a network diagram that enabled them to identify the critical path. However, some simply did not know how to construct a network diagram In part (b), the better candidates were able to apply the explanations to the scenario. Quite a few candidates were unable to differentiate between the concepts of contingency/scenario planning and buffering.

Marking scheme

		Marks
(a)	Network diagram	3
	Identification of critical path	1
		4
(b)	Explanation of contingency/scenario plans (up to 2)	
	Explanation of buffering (up to 2)	
	Explanation of the applicability of these to V (up to 2)	
	Identification of 1 week between critical path and business opening time	1
		6
Max		10

(a)

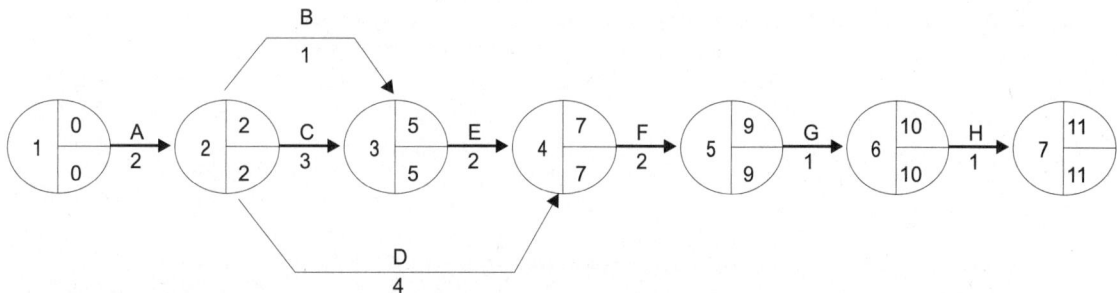

Critical Path = ACEFGH
Duration of project to set up V's business = 11 weeks

(b) **Critical Path analysis (CPA) aims to ensure the progress of a project on time**. The critical path of this project is 11 weeks and V wishes to open a business in 12 weeks. She is concerned that there is a degree of uncertainty in the timescales of some of the activities needed to establish the business, and these may delay the opening of the business. If there is a delay in any of the activities along the critical path, this would lead to a corresponding delay in the completion of the project as a whole.

To help V plan for these uncertainties she could use **contingency / scenario plans**. V would examine the various activities involved in setting up her business and have alternative courses of action ready in place if there were occurrences that may delay a critical activity and hence the completion of the project on time. For example, if finding a rental office took longer than two weeks then she may decide to reduce the time spent on training staff by a corresponding amount. Alternatively she may choose to design tests on web design systems and test the web design systems herself, and recruit staff and train the staff at a later date.

Buffering is an alternative method of planning for uncertainty. Buffers are periods of time added to a project schedule to protect the promised due date from slippage. A buffer can be added to risky activities. These activities can be either critical tasks or non-critical tasks where they feed into critical tasks so that the critical task can begin on time. For example, V could add additional time to activity A (finding a rental office) or B (procuring equipment). This approach, however, may cause the build up of slack in her plan and may lead to complacency.

30 Netcrit

Text references. Chapter 8.

Top tips. Do not waste time drawing more than one diagram.

Further question practice. If you struggled with this question try Critical path analysis and Blake.

(a)   12 days are needed for the critical path A-E-G.

Activity-on-node style

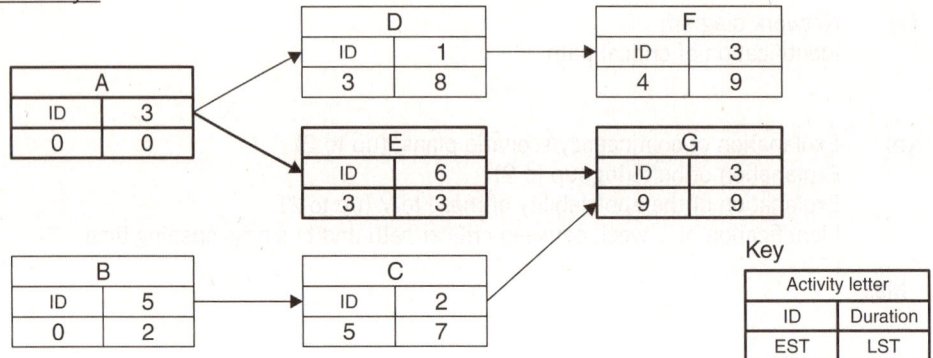

Activity-on-line style

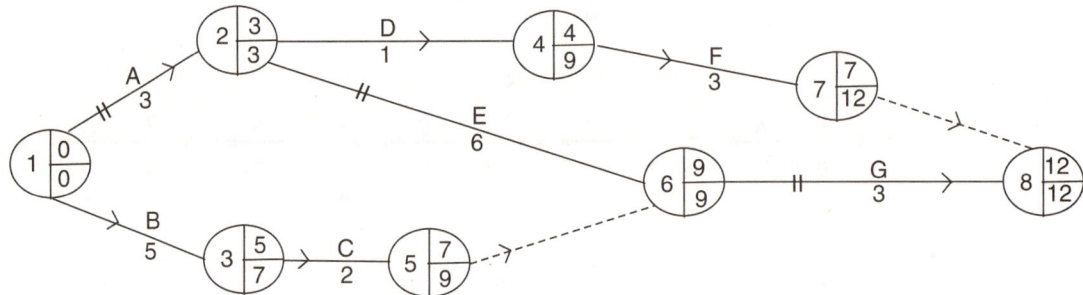

Duration of critical path is 12 days

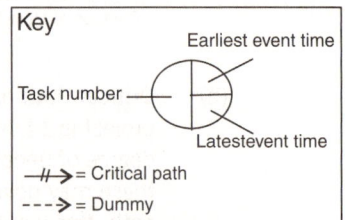

(b)   The dependencies given mean that the activities can be thought of as forming three main strands as shown in the Gantt chart below. Two of these strands can be manipulated to reduce the staff requirement on day 6 to the five people needed for activity E.

(i)   Activity B is started on day 1 and is therefore complete by the end of day 5

(ii)   Activity C, which depends on activity B, is not started until day 8. This allows it to be completed by the end of day 9 so that activity G is not delayed.

(iii) Activity D can be undertaken on any day from day 4 to day 9 inclusive. We show it happening on day 4.

       The disadvantage of this manipulation is to produce a requirement for thirteen staff on day 9.

1	2	3	4	5	6	7	8	9	10	11	12

A   E   G

| 6 | | | | | 5 | | | | 3 | | |

B   C

| 3 | | | | | | 2 | | | | | |

D   F

| 4 | | | | | | | | 3 | | | |

Total

| 9 | 9 | 9 | 12 | 8 | 5 | 5 | 7 | 7 | 6 | 6 | 6 |

The minimum number of staff is therefore **five** workers.

31 Risk

Text references. Chapter 6 covers project management and Chapter 7 covers risk management.

Top tips. This question brings together two topics – risk and project management. In your answer, try to make it clear that you understand how the two can be related. The linkage is specifically referred to in the question, but draw it out to demonstrate your understanding.

This was set as a predecessor syllabus exam question. The examiners then only awarded up to two marks for explaining risk. So the bulk of the marks were given for identifying the stages in risk management and strategies for managing risk. It is easy to forget the mark allocations in the 'heat of the battle'. Look back at the advice on **key skills** in the front pages on how to approach questions. This is **not an application question**, but **requires two key skills**. You need to **show your knowledge of the topic** and that **you understand** and **can apply the verbs in the question**.

Easy marks. A definition of both 'project' and 'risk' is a good starting point. An example of a typical project can also provide a framework upon which to hang your answer.

Examiner's comments. Answers should start with an explanation of what project risk is. They should then continue with a discussion of how risk can be managed and strategies for dealing with risk in projects. Weaker candidates failed to answer the specific question which asked for the ways in which risk can be managed in a project.

Marking scheme

	Marks
Definition of project	1
Explanation of risk	2
Risk avoidance strategies	2½
– ½ mark for need to take an overview	
– ½ mark for each strategy	
Stages of risk management	2½
– ½ mark for each stage	
Overall risk of project	1
Other valid points	1
– ½ mark per point to a maximum of 1	
Maximum	10

Organisational management involves making decisions about what needs to be done to further the strategy of the organisation. In general, the work which organisations undertake involves either day-to-day operations, or specific projects.

<u>Projects</u>

A **project** is defined as 'an undertaking that has a beginning and an end and is carried out to meet established goals within cost, schedule and quality objectives'. This may include developing a new product, changing the organisational structure, or implementing a new business process.

Projects need to be carefully structured, as they often cut across organisational boundaries. A new product development project team, for example, might involve staff drawn from the production department, sales and marketing and finance. This can prove challenging to large and traditionally operated organisations, and constitute a risk that the project will not be successful.

<u>Risk</u>

Risk exists in the possibility that unplanned, undesirable events may occur. It is possible to differentiate risk from **uncertainty**: in this strict sense, risk implies that it is possible to assign a specific numerical **probability** to the event in question; uncertainty implies that this cannot be done. In normal business contexts, including project management, risk analysis is about specifying and assessing **potential threats** to expected operations or progress.

<u>Managing project risk</u>

In the context of project management, identification of risks involves taking an overview of the project at the start, in order to establish what could go wrong, and the consequences. The project manager needs to consider whether the project involves an unacceptable amount of risk.

Dealing with project risk involves four possible strategies.

(a)	**Avoidance**	Factors giving rise to the risk are removed
(b)	**Reduction/mitigation**	Ways to mitigate the risk are found
(c)	**Transference**	Risk is passed on, such as via insurance
(d)	**Absorption**	Risk is accepted, and coped with if it occurs

Risk management may be viewed as a five stage process.

STAGE ①   Identify the risks

STAGE ②   Assess risk impacts and their likelihood (low, medium, high)

STAGE ③   Plan and record responses to these risks. A contingency plan may be needed for risks that are regarded as high impact and high likelihood.

STAGE ④   Carry out risk reduction activities

STAGE ⑤   Review the risk management approach

The chief risk facing any project is, perhaps, the overall risk that the project itself is inappropriate for the organisation – for example, the new product being developed fails to find a ready market. Risk management here might include undertaking rigorous market research to estimate the likelihood that the new product under consideration will be adopted quickly by customers.

32 Project initiation stage

Initiating a project is usually the first stage in the project planning process. Initiation includes mission, goals and objectives and creating the **Project Initiation Document (PID)**. The PID sets out fundamental progress and success criteria. It establishes a benchmark against which progress is measured. The first productive stage of the project is planned during this process. So the PID defines the **terms of reference** for the project. It contains the statements of the project manager, team, stakeholders and sponsors about:

(a)   **Overview of the project** including key dates
(b)   The **scope of the project** so what it should and shouldn't cover
(c)   The **objectives for the team** during and on completion of the project
(d)   **Project team organisation**, **roles** and **responsibilities**

P needs to apply these four features to the project for rebuilding the school. An explanation of the main features in the PID follows.

Overview of the project and objectives for the team

This should set out the **objectives** of the project, which are its quantified goals. What does the project want to achieve? Clearly the intention is to have the school rebuilt and equipped in twelve months. Remember that objectives should be SMART. So the objectives need to state the time taken, the cost of the project and the quality of the output. Any constraints must be identified and factored into the planning process. Funding is clearly a major constraint so the project should include an estimate of the funding needed.

The project scope

This is all of the things that have to be achieved if the project is to succeed. So it is all of the work that has to be done. This is an essential stage of the project. As volunteers with charitable motives largely run the project, there is a danger of the project expanding to have too many aims. The scope also determines anything **not included** in the project. This also helps avoid the number of aims increasing too much.

There are a few approaches that can be used to work out what needs to be done for the project to succeed.

(a)   **Gap analysis**. This looks at the gap between what is currently available and what is desired. This obviously includes funding but may also apply to personnel and expertise.

(b)   **Reverse engineering** identifies the features of an existing product or system by taking it apart.

(c)   **Functional decomposition** starts with the desired result and works out what must be done to achieve it. It starts with a broad approach and hones in on tasks and elements that must be achieved.

Project team

A project team made up of volunteers will need to have clear roles and responsibilities to ensure **accountability** and **responsibility** are maintained. Meetings and reporting deadlines should also be agreed upon.

33   Matrix structure

Text references. Chapter 8 on project implementation covers this area.

Top tips. You should start by explaining what a matrix structure is, and why it is different from a functional structure and a pure project structure. The point of doing this is not to reproduce textbook knowledge of theory but to apply that theory to the particular case of M. You need to explain why M needs to balance the needs for many project managers with the need for the stability of the traditional functions.

If you are uncertain how to start your answer refer back to the advice on 'Approach to questions' in the front pages.

Easy marks. Easy marks were available for explaining what a matrix structure is. Also there are a lot of clues in the question about why such a structure would be appropriate.

Examiner's comment. Candidates did not perform well on this question. Many candidates were unable to identify the characteristics in terms of developing to say why a matrix structure is appropriate.

Marking scheme

	Marks
Explanation of matrix structure and how it differs from functional structure and pure project structure	3
Why it is appropriate for M	1
Need for many project managers	1
Flexibility/adaptability	1
Need for functions: expertise	1
Other valid points – 1 mark per valid, explained point (½ if not explained) to a maximum of 3	3
	10

Matrix structures versus other structures

The Management Consultant's review has recommended that M adopts a **matrix structure.** This is where team members in different functions report both to their departmental manager (for on-going work in that function) and to a project manager (for work pertaining to the project). It requires the use of cross functional project teams to work on specialist projects. In practical terms this will involve each project team member reporting to both a project manager and to a functional head.

A matrix structure can be contrasted with a **functional structure,** where the project is 'housed' within a particular function (eg a marketing research project within the marketing department), alongside the on-going work of the function. This takes advantage of the shared resources and pooled expertise of the function. It also provides continuity when individuals leave the project, and when the project ends.

A matrix structure is also different from a **pure project structure,** where the whole organisation is structured permanently for project work and project management is built into the line management structure.

Why a matrix structure is best for M

There are a number of reasons why a matrix structure is better for M than a functional structure or a pure project structure.

Better than a functional structure

(a)   **Number of project managers.** The firm has many projects underway at any one time, and so will need a lot of project managers. A functional structure would find it difficult to provide enough project managers to deal with the number of projects.

(b)   **Flexibility.** The projects vary in duration and complexity. Flexibility is therefore needed to cope with the unpredictable. A functional structure could be too rigid to provide this flexibility.

(c)   **Adaptability.** Staff working on a variety of different projects develop the ability to adapt to change, which is important in the competitive world of computer information systems.

<u>Better than a pure project structure</u>

M operates in a complex industry where **functions** such as sales, marketing (and market research), customer relations, budgeting and finance are just as important as the specialist skill required for particular projects. M needs the other side of the matrix to be functional so that it **can pool and harness the expertise** of its employees.

If employees work continuously on projects, there is a danger that the **organisation could fragment** and lose sight of its core values.

<u>Conclusion</u>

A matrix structure is particularly appropriate for M because it combines the best of generalist and specialist skills, and combines stability with flexibility.

34   WBS and Gantt charts

> **Text references.** Both project management techniques are covered in Chapter 8. Chapter 6 also gives general background on project management.
>
> **Top tips.** This question is a good example of the level of complexity you can expect in this exam. It assumes you know *what* work breakdown structure and Gantt charts are, and asks you *how* they assist in the project management process. Our answer is much longer than you would be able to produce in the exam.
>
> **Easy marks.** Planning and control are the main benefits of the WBS approach. You should also have had no problem in coming up with budgeting: this is a management accounting exam, after all.

<u>Work Breakdown Structure (WBS)</u>

This is the analysis of the work involved in a project into a structure of **phases, activities and tasks. Dependencies** determine the order in which tasks must be carried out, while **interactions** between tasks affect them without imposing order. The essence of WBS is analysing the work needed to complete a project into manageable components. WBS works backwards from the required outputs to plan what processes and components are then needed. **Responsibilities** are then assigned to these processes or tasks.

There are **four main areas of project management** that benefit from the use of WBS.

(a)   **Budgeting.** WBS gives a clear statement of the **work** that is involved in a project. This is valuable in itself, since it prevents any misapprehension of the extent and complexity of the project. It is also the first step towards preparing a **budgeted cost**, since it is unlikely that the same levels of cost or cost techniques can be applied to all types of activity.

(b)   **Planning.** Even the simplest project may display complex **interactions** and **dependencies** between activities. Clear understanding of dependencies is obviously fundamental to any project planning.

An example of an interaction arises in a building project, where –damp proofing is taking place. If any kind of waterproofing barrier is applied to the walls, it is obviously vital that its integrity is not compromised by driving nails or screws through it; this will have a significant effect on the way that subsequent work is done.

Quality is another important aspect of planning, in that there may well be quality-related choices to be made about methods and materials. These too will have implications for time and cost. There is generally a **trade-off between time, quality and budget** (known as the 'iron triangle').

(c)   **Control.** WBS can be useful in deciding the structure and application of controls. While a project manager takes **overall responsibility**, it will be useful to divide up the **operational responsibility** for individual activities and tasks to other people as far as possible.

This division can be complicated when it becomes necessary to have input from the same person on more than one occasion. Taking a building project again, this might arise when an electrician returns to the house to fit switch and socket accessories after plastering has been done. The responsibility for such dangling tasks must not be overlooked.

The other important aspect of control facilitated by having a WBS is that small but important factors and activities are less likely to be overlooked during the implementation phase.

(d)   **Risk**. An awareness of the relative riskiness of different phases and activities is an important aspect of project management; it will usually be appropriate for the project manager to **direct extra attention and resources to the areas of highest risk** in order to give the best chance of success and take appropriate action if things start to go wrong. WBS allows particularly risky elements to be identified and managed separately from less risky but connected items. In a house renovation there is always a risk of tradesmen misinterpreting instructions, so, for example, if a wall is to be demolished, it might be a good idea to be on hand to ensure that the correct wall is dealt with.

Gantt charts

The **Gantt chart** is a horizontal bar chart used to plan the time scale for a project and estimate the resources required. Once again the project is broken down into tasks, which are listed on the chart in order of commencement. Tasks are listed on the horizontal axis and weeks taken on the vertical axis. A Gantt chart can draw on information from the Work Breakdown Structure.

This is an **easy visual tool** for those involved in a project to understand their responsibilities, resources required for the project and to monitor progress. Such monitoring can be on a daily or weekly basis. One advantage of a Gantt chart is that it can illustrate both the **planned duration of an activity and the actual duration**, so any variances can be easily identified. It can also be used to show the **workload of individual members of the team,** which can be useful in identifying problems and assessing staff contribution to the project for staff appraisal purposes.

A Gantt chart **does not show the interrelationship between the various activities** in the project as clearly as a network diagram, so often a combination of Gantt charts and network analysis will be used for project planning and resource allocation.

35   Graphical planning techniques

Text reference. The topics mentioned in this answer are discussed in Chapter 8 of your BPP Study Text.

Top tips. This is a fairly demanding question for 10 marks. Part (a) requires a clear description of WBS and Gantt charts. Part (b) then requires an explanation of how both these techniques contribute to project communication. If the communication aspects of these techniques are unfamiliar to you, it will not be easy to construct an answer in the time available. The key to an answer to part b) is to think about the need for communication in project management (or in any aspect of management): communication helps with planning, co-ordination of activities and control. You should try to demonstrate in your answer how WBS and Gantt charts may do this.

Easy marks. The only easy marks in part (a) come from knowing what WBS and Gantt charts are. In part (b) you need to recognise the importance of 'communication' in the question, and you must refer to communication in your answer.

Examiner's comment. This question was generally well answered. The most common error was to repeat in part (b) what had already been covered in part (a).

Marking scheme

		Marks
(a)	Description of WBS	2
	Description of Gantt charts	2
	Maximum for part (a)	<u>4</u>
(b)	One mark for each valid point, which may include:	
	Both techniques are valuable in providing information for planning, coordination of activities and control	1
	WBS used in planning to communicate the nature of the project tasks	1
	WBS also used to communicate deliverables and responsibilities	1

WBS used in control to inform individuals of progress (time, resources, costs) for which they are responsible	1
Gantt charts presenting project activities in graphical form, possibly more effective than written form	1
Gantt charts useful in planning for showing the planned timings for starting and completing activities and the project as a whole	1
Gantt charts useful for presenting resource requirements for each day/week of the project	1
Other points may be valid and justify one mark	
Maximum for part (b)	6
Maximum	10

(a)   <u>WBS and Gantt charts</u>

WBS is a technique for the planning and control of projects, in which the work required to complete the project is **divided into manageable units or components, also known as work packages**. For each work package, there is a defined outcome (or 'deliverables') and defined responsibilities. All the work packages are then organised into a sequence of processes to be undertaken.

A **Gantt chart** is **a diagrammatic presentation of the work packages in a project, in the form of bar charts**. Each work package is shown as a bar and the length of the bar indicates its expected completion time. The chart as a whole represents a time line, showing when each work package can or should begin, and when it can or should end. It therefore shows the planned starting and finishing times for the project as a whole. Work packages that can be done at the same time are shown in parallel in the chart. The Gantt chart also indicates the resources required for each work package, so that the chart also shows the total resources required for the project at any given time.

(b)   <u>Use in the project communication process</u>

WBS and Gantt charts are used in the project communication process.

(i)   The division of a project into work packages using WBS is used in the **planning process.** Individuals are informed what their tasks and responsibilities are, so that everyone in the project team understands his or her role and what is expected of them. WBS can also be used to provide information for control purposes, whereby individuals are informed of the costs and the resources they are consuming (for which they are responsible) and for monitoring the timely completion of each work package in the project.

(ii)   Gantt charts provide a visual presentation of work packages, and the **planned starting and finishing times and planned resource** requirements for each project. It can also show the **delays** that can be allowed in activities without affecting the completion time for the project. A visual presentation can be more effective in communicating plans and responsibilities than written communication. Gantt charts can also be used to monitor progress in the project, on a daily, weekly or monthly basis (depending on the nature of the project). The chart can be used to record actual progress, compared with the plan. This can help with both co-ordination of activities and management control of the project – for which clear communication is required.

36 Project stakeholders

Text references. The roles and management of project stakeholders is covered in chapter 7

Top tips. Although some marks will be available for identifying the general responsibilities of the various stakeholders, to ensure success in this question you will need to discuss the more specific responsibilities of each of these stakeholders in the given scenario.

Examiner's comment. This question was generally well done. Some candidates discussed the power and interest of different stakeholder groups and did not go on to discuss the roles – an explicit requirement of the question.

Marking scheme

1 mark per valid, explained point (½ if not explained)
to a maximum of 2 each for each of:
Explanation of project stakeholders
Explanation of the ERP system stakeholders and explanation of their role – up to 2 marks
available for each stakeholder identified
Maximum marks awarded

<u>10</u>

Project stakeholders are the individuals and organisations who are involved in or may be affected by project activities. It is important that X Company identifies the key stakeholders, their expectations, and their level of interest and power so that they can be appropriately managed. Powerful stakeholders may have the ability to block the project and prevent it going ahead so careful management is required to reduce the level of disruption to the project.

In the case of the enterprise resource planning (ERP) project, the main stakeholders are:

Project sponsor

The project sponsor provides and is accountable for the resources invested into the project and is responsible for the achievement of the project's business objectives. The project sponsor will oversee the project and take responsibility for the project budget. The sponsor will provide authority and guidance and will liaise between the project manager and the Board of X Company.

Project owner

The project owner is the person for whom the project is being carried out, ie the client. In this case the project owner is the finance director of X Company. The owner of a project is primarily interested in the deliverables achieved and that the project meets his needs. His role will be ensuring that the ERP resolves the problem of insufficient information.

Users

These are the individuals or groups that will utilise the end product. In X Company, the users are the functional managers who will use the ERP system. It is important that the needs of these people are clearly identified and documented prior to commencing work on building the system. However, it is possible that each functional manager will have different needs and so any possible conflict that arises will have to be managed and resolved.

As the ERP will allow real-time connections to outside stakeholders including suppliers and customers, they will also be end users of the system. It is therefore important that the system is user friendly and that their buy-in is achieved. Without this the overall benefits of the project will be reduced.

Software supplier

A software supplier will need to be selected to deliver the ERP. The aim of the supplier will be to maximise the price they charge in order to get the best deal for their software company.

Project team

The team are the individuals who actually carry out the work of delivering the project within the constraints of quality, time and cost. The project objectives and the work required to deliver those objectives must be made clear to the team. The team contributes a range of skills to the project to facilitate its completion and as such it is important that the team is committed to the project's overall success.

X Company Board of directors

The Board is responsible for allocating resources and ensuring this is in line with the expectations of shareholders. The Board will need assurance that the ERP system will improve the efficiency and effectiveness of X Company and that the project with worth committing resources to. The Board will require regular project status updates and reports so that it remains well informed with regards to the delivery of business objectives.

37 Project control processes

Text references. Chapters 6 and 7 cover this area.

Top tips If your mind has gone completely blank, you may be able to generate some marks using a common sense approach. Put yourself in the role of the project manager and think about how you make sure you kept it under control. You would probably come up with things like comparing actual progress and costs to the budgets and plans, researching deviations from the plan and taking action as quickly as possible to prevent it getting out of control. All of these are valid points and would earn valuable marks.

Easy marks If you have studied the project management sections of the Study Text, you should be able to earn a number of easy marks by simply repeating what you have learnt. If not, the common sense approach described above should mean you are still able to earn enough marks to pass the question.

The project manager is dedicated to the running of the project so long as it is in existence and takes ultimate responsibility for ensuring the desired result is achieved on time and within budget.

In order to do this, the project manager will need to take a number of actions during the life of the project to ensure that project is effectively monitored and controlled in order that the above outcome will be achieved.

Monitoring

The monitoring role of the project manager begins directly after the planning stage and will involve collecting actual data relating to the costs, progress and schedule of the project and comparing these to the corresponding figures laid down in the initial plans and budgets. This will make the project manager aware of any problems, such as overspends or delays, at the earliest possible opportunity.

Controlling

The project manager should investigate the causes of any departures from the plan and ensure that the necessary control or corrective action is taken to get the project back on track.

Consultation

The project manager should ensure possible courses of corrective action are discussed with other members of the project team and their views taken into account. This inclusion in the problem solving and decision making processes will give the team members a sense of ownership and they will be more committed to ensuring the successful completion of that project.

Communication

Whatever corrective action is decided about must be communicated and taken as soon as possible. All relevant stakeholders in the project must be aware of the action that has been taken and the impact this will have.

Revised plans

Following the corrective action, a number of calculations such as revised budgets, forecasts and project schedules may need to be carried out depending on the findings that led to the corrective action being taken. By doing this, it will help to ensure that any future deviations from the plan are avoided wherever possible.

The most important thing a project manager can do to ensure a project remains on track and is well controlled towards a successful outcome is to ensure the monitoring of the progress of the project is carried out **regularly**. To be effective, the project manager will need to implement systems which regularly gather data on the actual progress and performance of the project, and carrying out the corrective action as discussed above as soon as possible.

Reporting

The project manager should define a regular project reporting period (monthly or weekly for instance) depending on the nature and complexity of the project. The more complex the project the more frequent the updates required is likely to be.

Lessons learned

The project manager must ensure anything learned from the updates, reports and corrective action is fed back into the project cycle to prevent similar problems occurring further down the line or with future similar projects the organisation carries out.

38 Risk management in projects

> **Text references.** Managing project risk is coved in Chapter 7.
>
> **Top tips.** Read the question requirement carefully. Note that part a) asks you to 'describe the steps', so your answer should be presented as a series of logical steps rather than just a general discussion about risk management.
>
> Make sure that the examples you give in part b) are specifically related back to the given scenario.
>
> **Examiner's comment.** This question was generally well answered. Some candidates produced long rambling answers about how project managers might best manage risks rather than the more concise and focused answer required by the question.

Marking scheme

		Marks
(a)	Introduction	1
	Identification	1
	Assessment (likelihood and impact)	Up to 2
	Prioritisation	1
	Management	1
	Reporting (on effectiveness)	1
	Monitoring (of evolving risks)	1
		Max 6
(b)	Each strategy discussed (1 identification, 1 example)	Up to 2
		Max 4
		10

(a) All projects contain an element of risk, for example the risk of developing an inappropriate system. Risk management involves identifying such risks and implementing policies to minimise their impact and likelihood of occurring.

It involves the following steps:

Risk identification: All possible risks that the project may face are identified and documented. The project manager then reviews this list to identify which risks could affect performance.

Risk assessment: This is the process of assessing the likelihood and impact of each risk on the organisation. Plotting the likelihood and consequences of risks on a matrix allows unquantifiable risks to be considered alongside those to which a numerical value can be given. This helps the project manager to ensure resources are directed towards the most significant risks.

Risk management: A strategy for each risk will then be determined by the project manager. There are four basic strategies: risk reduction, risk avoidance, risk transference and risk absorption. At this stage each risk will also be allocated an 'owner' who will be responsible for monitoring and managing the risk.

Risk monitoring: This involves both monitoring the identified risks to ensure they are being appropriately managed by the risk strategy and ensuring no new risks have arisen as the project develops.

(b) A project manager might address a project risk by implementing one of the following strategies:

- **Risk avoidance**: Removing the factors which give rise to the risk by aborting or changing specific project goals, or choosing not to undertake the project all together.

- **Risk reduction/mitigation**: Implementing a strategy or process such as internal controls to reduce the likelihood of the risk occurring and/or to minimise the impact of the risk should it occur.

> **Alternative solutions**
>
> Other strategies that are equally valid and would have scored marks are:
>
> - **Risk transference**: The risk is passed on to or shared with another party, such as an insurer.
>
> - **Risk absorption**: The risk is accepted and no action is taken. This is done in the hope or expectation that either the risk will not occur, or its impact can be dealt with, or both. This frees up resources allowing the project manager to focus on more specific risks.

39 Project planning and roles

Text references. Chapter 6.

Top tips. This is a very practical question, so avoid talking about the many interesting but rather theoretical aspects of project management, such as the project life cycle and project stakeholders. Stick very much to what the project manager has to do. So you are required to **identify** and **explain** in part (a) and **contrast** and **compare** in part (b). You must be clear what the examiner means in the verbs used in these questions. Look back at the advice on key skills in the front pages and refer to 'What the examiner means' if you have forgotten what the verbs mean.

Notice that we make an assumption in response to the ambiguous wording of the requirement. Should you find that you are not quite sure what is required, choose the simplest option and state the assumption you have made.

Easy marks. You have been given some clear indications of the matters the project manager has to deal with for part (a). Make sure you include these topics and the work related to them in your answer, if only as examples of work to be done.

Examiner's comments. Some candidates lost their way , going into too much detail on specific planning phases rather than giving an overview of the whole planning process

(a)   Activities in the planning phase

(Note. We have assumed that the requirement for 'setting up a customer service contact team' means bringing the existing team to a state of operational readiness in the new premises rather than setting up a new team from scratch, with all that that implies in the way of recruitment, selection, training and development.)

Clarifying objectives

Very little planning can be done for any activity without a fairly clear idea of the **objectives** that are to be achieved. In this case, the overall objectives are indicated quite well and we might say that the aim is to prepare for and execute the move of S Company headquarters staff to their new premises. This overall aim will be supported by several **subsidiary or enabling objectives**.

(i)   Ensure that all necessary and appropriate building services and facilities are in place and functioning properly.

(ii)   Design, install, test and commission an upgraded office IT support system.

(iii)   Close down the existing headquarters building.

(iv)   Move portable equipment to the new building and install it.

(v)   Brief and execute the transfer of existing staff to the new building.

(vi)   Deal with any HRM problems arising from the move.

The subsidiary objectives listed above give a fair idea of the **scope** of the project; that is to say, the overall amount and type of work that has to be done to complete it. Establishing the project's scope in detail is the first step towards the **work breakdown structure** necessary for detailed project planning.

Stating roles and responsibilities

It is clear that the project has, effectively, already been authorised by the board of S Company and will be undertaken. Nevertheless, there will still be a need for a clear statement of roles and responsibilities in a **project authorisation document** (or project charter), so that all concerned know what is to be done and who is responsible for which parts. This will be particularly important in relation to the IT system, since its development must involve specialists who are likely to have their own ideas and priorities. If **external contractors** are involved, clear objectives and standards must be set for them from the outset.

Detailed planning

Once the objectives are in place and the scope of the work is agreed, detailed planning can commence. This will require the establishment of a **project team**, which should include an appropriate level of project dedicated staff and representatives from the various headquarters departments. For a project of this size, D will probably be able to manage with an assistant, so long as he or she can call upon departmental representatives for advice when required.

The detailed planning of the work to be done to enable the move to take place will revolve around three main areas of work: the IT system, the new building and the details of the move. **Network analysis** and **Gantt charts** will be useful for establishing time and resource requirements and constraints. The use of these methods also provides for detailed progress control by the project manager and the establishment of major review gates at which progress can be checked by P.

Budgeting

Other important aspects of planning are **risk** and **cost**. Costs must be estimated and a **budget** created so that expense can be monitored. Risk assessment leads to **risk management actions**, such as avoidance, minimisation and insurance.

(b)   The role of project sponsor and project manager

> **Top tips**. This is a rather easier question than part (a), dealing as it does with a much more specific and limited aspect of project management activity. Try to provide something more than two lists of bullet points by giving overall accounts of the two roles and, in particular, the ways in which their general natures differ.
>
> **Easy marks**. Some of the project manager's tasks, such as monitoring progress and leading the project team, are fairly obvious.
>
> **Examiner's comments**. Unsurprisingly, candidates tended to do quite well with this question.

P as project sponsor

The project sponsor is the person whose **overall authority** requires and permits the project to be undertaken. P will initiate the project, appoint the project manager and provide the resources used in the project.

P will exercise **general supervision** over the progress of the project without becoming involved in the detail of project management. This will involve giving **approval to plans, budgets and specifications**; receiving and approving **progress reports** and bids for changes; and ensuring that a clear focus is maintained on the project's **objectives and priorities**.

A further possible role for the project sponsor is that of '**project champion**', promoting and defending the project and providing moral support to the project manager D, particularly when delays occur and problems arise.

D as project manager

D, as project manager is responsible to the project sponsor for the **success of the project**. This means delivering the required results in accordance with planned requirements for **cost, time and quality**. To do this D must **manage and lead the project team** and may have a hand in its selection. He or she must also be responsible for the proper **planning** of the project; the **management of the resources** allocated to it; overall **progress management** and control; and reporting on progress to the project sponsor, P.

D will also have to **manage the expectations** of the various project stakeholders. These include P, the various headquarters groups that are involved in the move and any external contractors or consultants involved in the project. This is likely to involve extensive communication, negotiation and dispute resolution, especially when there are delays or changes of plan become necessary.

40 P Company

> **Text references.** Chapter 6.
>
> **Top tips.** Part (a) addressed the fundamental attributes of project work and, as such, was a straightforward question. However you need to **tailor** your answer to the circumstances found in P Company to gain good marks.. We have deliberately kept our answer concise, to demonstrate this. Part (b) asks for the **responsibilities** of the project manager. We have taken responsibilities to be obligations to others as this follows the general theme of the scenario: that the project manager has obligations to other departments, management and the project team, and have answered in this way. Again you need to tailor your answer to the database project.
>
> **Easy marks.** Easy marks are available in part (a) for identifying the characteristics of project work that distinguish it from 'business as usual' and only a modest amount of additional effort is needed to relate these characteristics to the website development project undertaken at P Company. In part (b), there are marks available for general aspects of the role of the project manager.
>
> **Examiner's comment.** This question drew a range of answers, good and bad. There was a tendency for some candidates to lose focus and to stray into a discussion of project management skills and the detail of project management tools rather than sticking with the requirement of explaining the role and responsibilities of the project manager of the website development.

(a) <u>Characteristics of the website development project</u>

In general the work which organisations undertake may be classified as either '**business as usual**' or **projects**. Whether an activity is classified as a project is important, as projects require management using specialised project management techniques.

A project has a number of attributes that distinguish it from 'business as usual'.

(i) **Projects have a defined beginning and end** – unlike operations which tend to be on-going. So, for example, the database project has a defined duration of six months to meet its deadline, which is business critical. This often allows them to be perceived in terms of a 'life cycle' of defined stages, from project definition and planning through implementation and control to closure and review.

(ii) **Projects have resources allocated specifically to them**, although often on a shared basis. Thus, P has manpower from other departments At the close of the development project, staff will return to their departments. The project is likely to have a budget, although details of this are not given, and time appears to be the main constraint.

(iii) **Projects are often unique or 'one-off'**: intended to be done only once, in contrast to operations which involve recurring tasks. Thus the development of the new customer database is distinguished from on-going customer service operations.

(iv) **Projects follow a specific plan towards a clear intended end-result** (in this case, implementation of the customer information database), in contrast to operations for which goals and deadlines may be more general. There will be a specific schedule and resource plan for the system development project.

(v) **Projects often cut across organisational and functional lines**, while operations usually follow the organisation or functional structure. Here, for example, P is able to draw on expertise of staff from the Customer Service, Finance and IT Departments, and from other parts of the organisation.

(vi) **Projects have stakeholders,** who are all those with an interest in the progress of the project and its final outcome. These could include:

– The project sponsor, that is the individual or group providing the funds

– The project steering committee or board, to whom the project manager reports

– The project customer, or end user

– The project owner

(b) The role and responsibilities of G in her role as project manager

As project manager, G is the person who takes ultimate responsibility for ensuring the project is completed on time and within budget. G will also have responsibilities to management, other business areas and the project team. It is her responsibility to deliver the completed website to the satisfaction of its users. She is new to this position, and was selected on the basis of his technical skills rather than his wider management skills.

(i) The project manager must **establish an organisation structure** for planning, communicating and control of the project. G should already have developed a framework for the procedures and structures needed to manage the project (for example, deciding to have weekly team meetings, performance reviews and so on).

(ii) **Detailed planning. The project manager is responsible for the project plan and will oversee the planning process, such as the preparation of the** work breakdown structure, network analysis for scheduling or Gantt charts for scheduling and resource planning. The project manager must also take responsibility for the project budget.

(iii) **Team building and co-ordination.** The project team members have been drawn from different departments, and a responsibility of G is to organise these individuals as a team, allocating tasks and delegating responsibilities to individuals within the team. An effective team will co-ordinate the efforts of the team members towards the common goal (completing the project on time, on budget and to specification), and the project manager must ensure that these efforts are properly co-ordinated. The project manager must also ensure that co-operation is obtained also from external parties, such as suppliers and external service providers. This is probably one of the areas where G feels particularly weak.

(iv) **Building an effective team, and being a team leader.** G has a responsibility to ensure that the team is high-performing. Her role may therefore involve trying to motivate team members, to create a positive attitude and team identity and to provide support to individuals if they have any difficulties or problems in their home life that affects their work. G also has a supervisory or monitoring role, to ensure that the team members are performing in a satisfactory way.

(v) **Monitoring and control.** The project manager should estimate the causes for each departure from the project plan, and take corrective measures. This involves monitoring costs, progress towards completion and achieving the specifications for the planned web site.

(vi) **Problem resolution.** Even with the best planning, unforeseen problems may arise and G will be required to deal with them and find workable solutions.

(vii) G must **ensure resources are used efficiently** and strike a balance between cost, time and results. Essentially, G is responsible for completion of the project on time, to the end users' satisfaction and on budget.

(viii) **Responsibilities to management.** G has responsibilities as project manager to senior management, represented perhaps by the project steering committee. G must also **keep management informed** with timely and accurate communications. The project sponsor and steering committee will want to be informed.

(ix) **Maintain a customer orientation.** G must maintain an awareness of the requirements of the project's 'customers' and understand that the project has been undertaken for their benefit. G therefore has a responsibility to meet customer requirements in the best way possible.

Conclusion

G is certainly correct in recognising that project management calls for management skills rather than technical IT skills. It is surprising that she thinks she does not have these skills because senior management appointed her (presumably) in the belief that she would perform the role well. A useful way forward may be to appoint a member of the project steering committee to act as a mentor, and provide advice and support to help her carry out the project management role successfully.

41 Project Management Software

Text references. Project management software is covered in Chapter 8 and Mendelow's matrix in Chapter 7.

Top tips. Project management software is a fairly specialised area of the syllabus but this scenario does not give enough detail to allow you to become totally bogged down in technicalities. By expressing the main principles and features of project management software, and relating these to the circumstances of M University in part (a), you will produce a good answer.

In part (b), analyse the scenario carefully to find all of the interested stakeholders. As a rule of thumb, look for at least five to be sure of satisfying the ten mark allocation. A good starting point is to consider the stakeholders in terms of *Mendelow's* matrix of power and interest. Make sure you refer to the factors in the matrix when commenting on each stakeholder. This shows how important it is to **tailor** your analysis to the particular scenario. The examiner suggests between two and three marks for each general heading in her marking guide.

Easy marks. You should be able to identify five stakeholders fairly easily.

Examiner's comments. In part (a), candidates need to explain where project management software can help in a project. A detailed discussion of how the software will help the finance team is also required. In part (b), answers need to explain who the stakeholders are in the context of the project. Then, candidates should explain why the finance director needs to consider the interests of the different stakeholders. Common errors included not explaining how the software could help in managing a project. Some candidates confused project management software with project management. In part (b) candidates needed to explain why the director should consider particular stakeholders.

Marking scheme

		Marks
(a)	Identifying inputs to system – 1 mark per input to a maximum of 4 Main features and functions of software – Types of tool (Gantt charts network diagram, 'what if' analysis: 3 marks) Functions – 2 marks per valid, explained point (1 mark if not explained) to a maximum of 8 Maximum for Part (a)	15
(b)	2 marks per stakeholder identified and explained (1 mark if not explained) to a maximum of 10) Maximum for Part (b) Maximum	10 25

(a) <u>How project management software may help make the project successful</u>

Software might be used for a number of purposes in helping the project manager with his job. Most packages involve a process of identifying the main steps in the project, and breaking these steps down into specific tasks. **Typically, a system requires the following inputs:**

(i) **The length of time required for each activity** – how much time does the project have?

(ii) **The logical relationships between each activity** (as an obvious example, building the student village cannot begin until the land has been acquired and architectural drawings have been produced)

(iii) **The resources available** – how much is likely to be invested by local businesses?

(iv) **When the resources will be available**

We can look at the role of software under the main general headings which are used when outlining the task of the project manager.

Planning

Network diagrams (showing the critical path, perhaps from the initial approach to the authority with the planning proposal for purchasing the land) and **Gantt charts** (showing resource use) can be produced automatically. Packages also allow some flexibility with variables such as start and finish dates, likely level of investment from local business, cost of the land, or available resources. This will allow **contingency plans** to be made following **'what if' analysis**.

The **complexity** of the M University project means that planning will also be complex and difficult to carry out accurately and quickly. The project software will help here with the scheduling of different activities.

Estimating

As the project progresses, actual data can be used to provide more accurate estimates of the likely duration or costs (for example) associated with the project. Estimates can be changed many times and new schedules produced almost instantly. This ability will enable the finance director to satisfy the project sponsors' need for reassurance that project costs are under control.

Monitoring

Actual data can be entered to monitor progress constantly, and automatically update the plan. **Budgeting** and **control** features of project software can help comparisons to be made between actual and budget costs during the project.

Reporting

Software packages allow both **standard** and **tailored progress reports** to be produced and circulated to interested parties at any time. This helps with keeping the stakeholders in the project informed, and with the co-ordination of activities.

The sponsors will require that monitoring and control of the project are undertaken in a competent fashion. They will also require regular, detailed progress reports: the features above will therefore assist the finance director to keep their needs satisfied.

(b)   Why the finance director should consider stakeholder interests

Stakeholders are the individuals and organisations who are involved in, or may be affected by, project activities. The various stakeholders will differ in their attitudes and priorities concerning this building project. The following stakeholders can be identified from the scenario. All of their interests need to be considered as early in the project as possible.

Stakeholder mapping could be used to classify these stakeholders, so **Mendelow's matrix** of power and interest could help identify which stakeholders have power and the extent of their involvement in the project.

Regional authority

The **interests** of this stakeholder are clear, because it currently owns the land that the University wishes to acquire. It has considerable power of veto over this project. The authority needs to consider its own policies concerning development, as well as the interests of local residents (the electorate) who will be affected by the planned proposal. M University must make sure that its planning application is sound and addresses any concerns that the regional authority may have about the proposed development.

Residents

They are said to be unhappy about the proposal. The project manager needs to meet with their representatives to understand their concerns, as they will have a significant **influence** on the decision of the regional authority whether or not to sell the land to the university. Alternative plans that address the main queries of the residents may be able to be drafted.

Local business investors

These stakeholders are going to require an adequate return on their investment, and the project manager must be sure exactly what their expectations are, as part of the collaborative agreement. For example, if there are cost overruns there will need to be an agreement as to who will finance them.

Staff

Most members of staff are very unhappy about the extra travelling time that will be required. They may need to be compensated for this in the form of an additional allowance, which will add to the costs associated with the project. Some ways around this problem (free shuttle bus from the main campus, extra allowance for travel costs/time) may need to be made. Their interest is high but their influence is limited.

Students

The students will be **interested** in high quality accommodation, teaching rooms and other facilities. Their interests will need to be incorporated into the architect's plans. The prospect of high quality accommodation and other facilities could prompt some students to choose M University over another.

Corporate clients

As with students, these are the 'customers' of the project and so will expect the business and conference facilities to be top quality, or they will prefer to book conferences with other organisations.

42 Project management

> **Text references.** Project planning is covered in Chapter 7 of your Study Text. Project tools and techniques are covered in Chapter 8.
>
> **Top tips.** In part (a), as always, make sure you relate your knowledge of project planning to the scenario. The main focus is what will happen in the absence of project planning rather than the process of project planning.
>
> **Easy marks.** Textbook knowledge of project management tools and techniques will get you some easy marks, although to score well you will need to apply them to planning the hotel project.
>
> **Examiner's comment.** This question was generally well answered.There was a tendency, in part (b) for some candidates to confuse 'tools and techniques' with 'methodologies' and so lose marks by concentrating on the latter at the expense of the former.

(a)   Potential problems faced by the hotel project without good project planning

Projects are often seen as having a **lifecycle** and this idea helps when managing the project. Thus a project is broken down into manageable parts, which can be monitored as the project progresses.

Project **planning** takes place during the stage when the project is being **defined** and involves setting **objectives** and the time and resources needed to achieve these. If objectives aren't set clearly then they are open to changing specification by the client with likely knock-on effects on the project. It is possible that E will try to do this given her hands-on approach to managing the project.

The aim of planning at the **definition stage** should be to avoid the chaos of unplanned activity, provide a basis for accepting the project and identify problems in advance.

The hotel project could well end up with these problems if there is no planning. So activities would not be planned in sequence failing to take account of available manpower and funding, and unrealistic timetables end up in place. Resources are not planned for so budget overruns occur and delays may arise where resources aren't available.

Plans are refined further during the **design stage** of the project where they are fleshed out to include details of timings, costs, quality and risk and contingencies. At this stage **project management techniques** are used to plot out the **timetable** for the project. Resource plans are used to specify the types of resources needed and communication plans can be used to co-ordinate stakeholders in the project. If the hotel does not have a detailed timetable, it will be impossible to monitor progress. The project will not have contingency plans in place in case of slippage or unforeseen events.

Feasibility studies can be used to assess whether a project can achieve its objectives in a cost-effective manner. Technical feasibility can be used to assess whether the project can be completed with the available technology or whether further development is needed. This also includes technical expertise in other areas such as marketing and finance. Social feasibility applies to the effect a project has on people inside and outside the organisation. So will the project mean significantly increased workloads for employees or redundancies for instance? Financial feasibility includes a cost-benefit analysis and this may need the project team to look at intangible benefits.

The hotel clearly has an effect on its local environment and local planning must be adhered to. Local residents should be consulted on the plans and the disturbance caused by building works.

In the early stages, the **roles and responsibilities** of project members are defined. Clearly if these are not agreed upon, members of the project team will find it difficult to work together as they will be confused about their roles.

Also **control systems** are set in place. Without an adequate control system, there is a good likelihood of lack of cost control and resultant overspend.

(b)   Contribution of project management, tools and techniques to planning the project

P can use a variety of project management tools and techniques to help at the detailed planning stage of the project. Some of the most common are **Work Breakdown Structure, Gantt charts** and **Network analysis**.

Work Breakdown Structure (WBS)

This is the analysis of the work involved in a project into a structure of phases, activities and tasks. **Dependencies** determine the order in which tasks must be carried out, while **interactions** between tasks affect them without imposing order. The essence of WBS is analysing the work needed to complete a project into manageable components. WBS works backwards from the required outputs to plan what processes and components are then needed. **Responsibilities** are then assigned to these processes or tasks.

The hotel project could be broken down into manageable tasks by working back from the output, which is a hotel to the tasks and resources needed to achieve this. P can then develop a task list to assist in planning, control and monitoring the various stages of the project. These tasks can be analysed between dependencies and interactions. Individuals can then be given responsibility for certain tasks.

Gantt charts

The **Gantt chart** is a horizontal bar chart used to plan the time scale for a project and estimate the resources required. Once again the project is broken down into tasks, which are listed on the chart in order of commencement. Tasks are listed on the horizontal axis and weeks taken on the vertical axis. This is an easy visual tool for those involved in the hotel project to understand their responsibilities, resources required for the project and to monitor progress.

Network analysis

Network analysis is used to plan the sequence of the tasks making up the project scope and to determine the **critical path**. The project is broken down into tasks, which are arranged in a logical sequence. Each task then has an estimated duration. The analysis also reveals which tasks are **dependent** on others and that are known as **dependencies**. Dependencies are very important in project planning so that resources can be channeled into tasks on which others rely.

The project would be plotted on a **network diagram** showing all of the activities, their sequence, and **earliest event** and **latest event times** for each activity. The minimum possible duration of the project is found by plotting the **critical path**, which consists of critical activities. The critical path shows the elements which if delayed will delay the completion of the entire project. The analysis can also reveal where there is **slack** time, which is spare time.

The hotel project will find network analysis is a useful tool to work out what sequence activities must follow. So when the project is viewed overall, management can see what **activities are critical** and make these a priority. Where there is slack this can be used to cover unforeseen circumstances.

PERT

A variation on network analysis, which includes uncertainty, is known as the **Project evaluation and review technique** or **PERT**. Each activity has optimistic, most likely and pessimistic estimates of time calculated and these are used to calculate an expected time based on the mean value of these estimates. The technique also allows a standard deviation to be calculated for each activity.

43 COL

Marking scheme

		Marks
(a)	Award up to 3 marks for: Each element of the project plan identified Each element of the project plan discussed Each element of the project plan applied to the scenario To a maximum of 15 (flexibility)	
		15
(b)	For each skill identified 1 For each skill discussed in relation to D, up to 2 To a maximum of 10	10
		$\overline{25}$

(a) Outline Project Plan

Project Name: Upgrade of COL on-line course delivery system project

Project Manager: The project manager is Project Manager D. D is responsible for all of the key stages of the project management process. He is responsible for leading the project team.

Project Team: The project team consists of SYS designers, COL IT staff and users from COL.

Purpose/ Business Need: To update the online course delivery to meet the objectives set out by the Board of Directors and senior managers of COL.

Deliverables: The project must be delivered within 12 months at a cost of no more than $3 million.

Communication and Reporting: The project manager D will communicate with and report to Mrs Y, the senior IT manager at COL. This section of the plan would include how plans will be communicated to members of the team, the nature and timing of meetings and reports, as well as details of how other stakeholders will be kept informed of project progress.

Technical Plan: This section of the plan would include the technical features of the project, such as system specifications, systems diagrams, and so on.

Project schedule: This may include Gants charts or network diagrams and will describe the main phases of the project and key milestones. A work breakdown structure will need to be provided to the project team to identify all of the tasks and those responsible for them.

Resources: The resources required for successful implementation of the project would be listed here. Resources should be identified for all key activities and a resource histogram may be used to show resource requirements.

Budgets: A detailed budget and cash flow forecast would be required. There is no overrun allowed in the project from the original budget of $3 million. Any overrun will be borne by SYS.

Risk: Risks should be identified, assessed and where possible quantified. One of the main enhancements to the updated system required by COL is the security of candidates' details.

Change management: Requests for change to this plan may be initiated by either SYS or COL, represented by Mrs Y and D respectively. All change requests will be reviewed and approved or rejected by the project board.

Post-implementation audit: The final project will be reviewed post-implementation to evaluate success and as an aid to future projects.

(b)   The main skills required of project manager D to lead the project team and create customer confidence are described below.

Leadership and team building

A participatory style of leadership is appropriate for much of this project. However, an autocratic decisive style may be required on occasions.

D will be required to delegate tasks appropriately. This may be a particularly delicate task as some of the project team are not SYS employees. D must empower the project team members and not take on too much personally.

D will need to build team spirit through the co-operation of the various members of the project team.

Organisational

D should ensure that all project documentation is clear and distributed to all who require it. He should ensure that appropriate project management tools are used to analyse and monitor project progress.

Communication and negotiation

D must be a skilled communicator. He will need to communicate formally with COL (per the project plan). However, he will also need to communicate informally with all stakeholders involved. This will involve listening to project team members as well as other stakeholders.

D will need to persuade reluctant team members or stakeholders to support the project. He may need to negotiate on staffing and other resources, quality and disputes.

Personal qualities

There are a range of personal qualities that D should demonstrate. These include:

(a)   **Flexibility**, as circumstances may develop which require a change in the plan.

(b)   **Creativity**, if one method of completing a task proves impractical then a new approach may be required.

(c)   **Technical skills**, although D is the project manager, in order to gain customer confidence he should appear to be technically competent.

Change control and management

Changes in any project are inevitable. Changes to this project could arise from a variety of sources and have the potential to disrupt the progress of the project. D must be able to minimise the effects of these on the quality, time and cost of the project.

44 Sporting facility

Text references. Project management software is covered in Chapter 8 and Mendelow's matrix in Chapter 7.

Top tips. Project management software is a fairly specialised area of the syllabus but this scenario does not give enough detail to allow you to become totally bogged down in technicalities. By expressing the main principles and features of project management software, and relating these to the circumstances of the proposed new sporting facility you will produce a good answer to part (a).

In part (b), analyse the scenario carefully to find all of the interested stakeholders. As a rule of thumb, look for at least four to be sure of satisfying the mark allocation. A good starting point is to consider the stakeholders in terms of *Mendelow's* matrix of power and interest. This will suggest strategies for managing the stakeholders. Make sure you refer to the factors in the matrix when commenting on each stakeholder. This shows how important it is to **tailor** your analysis to the particular scenario. Note that you will not be required to produce the diagram of *Mendelow's* matrix in the exam; this is for illustrative purposes only.

Easy marks. In part (a) there are marks available for general points about project management software, straight from your Study Text. You should be able to identify the stakeholders fairly easily in part (b).

Examiner's comment. A few answers to Part (a) were good, but many were weak. Many candidates did not do well on this part of the question because they described general aspects of project management tools and techniques, rather than explaining how project management software could help during the life of the project. Some candidates scored highly in Part (b). Weaker answers identified stakeholders, but did not develop their answers to recommend appropriate strategies to manage the different stakeholder expectations.

Marking scheme

		Marks
(a)	Identifying inputs to system – 1 mark per input to a maximum of 3 Main features and functions of software – Types of tool (Gantt charts network diagram, 'what if' analysis: 2 marks) Functions – 2 marks per valid, explained point (1 mark if not explained) to a maximum of 7 Maximum for Part (a)	12
(b)	2 marks per stakeholder identified and explained (1 mark if not explained) and 1 mark per managing strategy explained to a maximum of 12) Other valid points on managing stakeholder expectations (1 mark per point to a maximum of 1) Maximum for Part (b) Maximum	<u>13</u> <u>25</u>

(a) <u>How project management software may help make the project successful</u>

Software might be used for a number of purposes in helping the project manager (the Finance Director) with his job. Most packages involve a process of identifying the main steps in the project, and breaking these steps down into specific tasks. **Typically, a system requires the following inputs:**

(i) **The length of time required for each activity** – how much time does the project have?

(ii) **The logical relationships between each activity** (as an obvious example, building the sporting facility cannot begin until the specialist building contractors have been consulted and architectural drawings have been produced)

(iii) **The resources available** – how much is likely to be invested by local businesses?

(iv) **When the resources will be available**

We can look at the role of software under the main general headings which are used when outlining the task of the project manager.

Planning

Network diagrams (showing the critical path, perhaps from the discussions with building contractors) and **Gantt charts** (showing resource use) can be produced automatically. Packages also allow some flexibility with variables such as start and finish dates, likely level of investment from local business, cost of the land, or available resources. This will allow **contingency plans** to be made following **'what if' analysis**.

The **complexity** of the sporting facility project means that planning will also be complex and difficult to carry out accurately and quickly. The project software will help here with the scheduling of different activities.

Estimating

As the project progresses, actual data can be used to provide more accurate estimates of the likely duration or costs (for example) associated with the project. Estimates can be changed many times and new schedules produced almost instantly. This ability will enable the finance director to satisfy the project sponsors' need for reassurance that project costs are under control.

Monitoring

Actual data can be entered to monitor progress constantly, and automatically update the plan. **Budgeting** and **control** features of project software can help comparisons to be made between actual and budget costs during the project.

Reporting

Software packages allow both **standard** and **tailored progress reports** to be produced and circulated to interested parties at any time. This helps with keeping the stakeholders in the project informed, and with the co-ordination of activities.

The sponsors will require that monitoring and control of the project are undertaken in a competent fashion. They will also require regular, detailed progress reports: the features above will therefore assist the finance director to keep their needs satisfied.

(b) Why the Finance Director should consider stakeholder interests

Stakeholders are the individuals and organisations who are involved in, or may be affected by, project activities. The various stakeholders will differ in their attitudes and priorities concerning this building project. The following stakeholders can be identified from the scenario. All of their interests need to be considered as early in the project as possible.

Stakeholder mapping could be used to classify these stakeholders, so **Mendelow's matrix** of power and interest could help identify which stakeholders have power and the extent of their involvement in the project.

Level of interest

	Low	High
Low	A	B
High	C	D

Power

Regional authority (V)

The regional authority is the **instigator of the project and one of the main investors**, the others being the three local businesses.

V is concerned about the financing – the Board of V have made it clear that overspending is not allowed – but the stake is not purely financial. This is a high profile project, and the reputation of the regional authority with local residents will be severely affected if anything was to go wrong.

V is therefore a **key player** (segment D of the matrix). The Finance Director/Project Manager's strategy **must** be acceptable to V, and V will probably participate in decision making. The key word for this strategy is **participation.**

Three large business investors

These stakeholders are going to require an adequate return on their investment, and the project manager must be sure exactly what their expectations are, as part of the collaborative agreement. For example, if there are cost overruns there will need to be an agreement as to who will finance them. There may be conflict with each other the V, the regional authority, which has been told not to overspend.

The business investors are unlikely to be involved in decision making and therefore belong in segment C of *Mendelow's* matrix: **low interest, high power.** Such stakeholders must be **kept satisfied,** because although often passive they may move to segment D, for example by threatening to withdraw their investment. The key word for this strategy is **intervention.**

Residents

They are said to be unhappy about the proposal, because the sporting facility would be located in their area. These stakeholders may be placed in segment B of the matrix: **high interest, low power.** However, as wealthy local residents, they are not without influence, particularly if the local newspaper takes up their cause . They may be able to win the influence of more powerful stakeholders, such as the business investors.

The project manager would be advised to **keep these stakeholders informed,** taking account of their views where possible. The key words for this strategy are **education/communication.**

Relocated staff

The staff from the smaller sports centres are very unhappy about being relocated to the new site. The site is not central and may involve extra travelling time.

The relocated staff belong in segment B of the matrix: **high interest, low power.** However, unhappy staff will not help the project be successful, particularly if they leave and get jobs elsewhere, so their views need to be considered. Some ways around this problem (free shuttle bus from the town centre, extra allowance for travel costs/time) may need to be made. The key words for this strategy are **education/communication**

Local people and school children

The people the sporting facility is designed for **do not fit** neatly into *Mendelow's* matrix. At the moment they could be said to have low interest and low power and to require minimal effort (key word: **direction**), but their interest should grow if the project is publicised. Ultimately the **local people will determine the success** of the project, which will not be viable in the long term if they do not use it.

Managing stakeholder disputes

Should conflicts arise between stakeholders, this may be resolved by:

(i)   **Negotiation.** The parties discuss the issue with a view to finding mutually acceptable solutions.

(ii)   **Mediation.** A third party facilitates the negotiation process.

(iii)   **Partnering.** Communication links are created between project participants in order to direct them towards a common goal.

(iv)   **Arbitration.** A third party may be asked to intervene to impose a solution.

45 Project initiation

Text references. Project initiation is covered in chapters 6, 7 and 8.

Top tips. Don't forget to relate the contents of a project initiation document directly to the hotel refurbishment.

Easy marks. If you know the basics you can gain a number of easy marks in part a) by defining what a project initiation document is and explaining what it would include.

The problems threatening the success of the project are described in the scenario - a number of easy marks can be earned by simply picking them out. However, in order to pass this part question it will be necessary to go on to clearly explain the way in which these threats can be minimised.

Examiner's comment. Most candidates were able to answer part (a) of the question though a few candidates struggled with the question. A number of candidates struggled to identify the key components of a project initiation document because of lack of preparation.

Part (b) of the question was generally well answered. A significant number of candidates lost marks because, although they accurately identified the problems threatening the success of the hotel refurbishment, they omitted to explain the ways in which B, the project manager, could have reacted in order to minimise the threats identified.

Marking scheme

		Marks
(a)	Purpose	Up to 2 marks
	Content (1 mark for description and 1 mark for application to the hotel project):	Up to 2 each
	Purpose statement	
	Scope statement	
	Deliverables	
	Cost and time estimates	
	Project constraints	
	Stakeholders	
	Project organisation structure	
	Other	
	Maximum	<u>10</u>
(b)	Up to 2 marks for each of the following:	Up to 2 each
	Unrealistic deadlines	
	Resource estimates unrealistic	
	No detailed project plan	
	Moving targets	
	Lack of control measures	
	Lack of milestones	
	Insufficient budget information	
	Reliance on project management software	
	Maximum	<u>15</u>
	Maximum marks awarded	<u>25</u>

(a)   A project initiation document defines the terms of reference for the project and provides the project manager with the authority to apply resources to project activities. It is approved by the project board and will define the roles and responsibilities of the various stakeholders involved in the project and provide the basis against which the project's progress can be assessed.

The project initiation document for the hotel refurbishment should have included the following:

Purpose of project

This should detail why the refurbishment of the hotel is necessary.

Overview of project

This will provide a summary of what is to be done as part of the project. This will include key dates for which elements of the project will be completed.

Scope of the project

This relates to what the project is to cover and, importantly, what will not be covered by the project. This helps to prevent 'scope creep' which occurs when the number of activities covered by the project gets increasingly larger as the project progresses. This causes delays and significantly increases the cost of delivering the project. This appears to be happening in this scenario as B has been informed that the hotel wishes to add additional specifications to the project.

Objectives

There should be a detailed description of both the objectives of the completed project and also the objectives for the team over the duration of the project. The tangible outcomes of the project will need to be clearly documented. In this case, it would detail the exact requirements of the refurbishment of the hotel.

Project team

The document should detail who will be involved in the project team and their specific roles and responsibilities should be clearly laid out. Authorisation and signoff controls should also be documented to ensure suitable controls are in place for any changes to the project. Key communications that will be made in relation to the project (eg meetings or reports) will also be detailed here.

Stakeholders

The project's key stakeholders and their interest in the project should be documented. This helps the project team to manage those stakeholders, particularly if any stakeholder group should attempt to prevent the project from going ahead.

Constraints

The budget of the project and the anticipated timescale will be clearly documented. The hotel refurbishment project is already showing signs of being behind schedule. S company is funding this project and so details of anticipated expenditure at the outset are necessary for the company to understand how much it is committing to and can monitor expenditure to ensure actual spending remains in line with these constraints.

Any other constraints (eg resources) should also be clearly laid out in this document. The scenario states that some of the core staff has had to be released from the hotel refurbishment project. This has had a negative impact on performance.

(b)   The hotel refurbishment project has experienced a number of problems. These include:

Unrealistic deadline

The project timescale was agreed at 30 weeks which is considered to be a 'very fast completion for this sort of project'. The project is now running two weeks behind schedule. Given that the hotel will host a very high profile event at the end of the 30 weeks, there is not for such delays and this time must be caught up.

The timescale needs to be urgently reviewed; key (critical) activities and dates need to be identified and controls must be put in place to prevent any further slippage.

Vague requirements

There is no detailed project plan in which the specific objectives and requirements of the project were documented. The key project objectives now need to be defined and a detailed work breakdown structure needs to be developed to identify key activities, deadlines and targets to allocate responsibility for achieving these to specific individuals.

Reliance on project management software

When questioned about tools and techniques to be used on the project, B seemed unsure and stated that he would 'rely on project management software'. While this will help to support the management of the project and can help to monitor actual time and costs against the budgets, it will not be able to match tasks to individuals, nor understand how they work. As the project manager, B needs an understanding of who is involved in the project, what they do, and how their departure would impact on the plan. Use of project management software is no guarantee of success.

Lack of control

It is noted that the project team is concerned about the lack of control over the project. This is linked to the reliance on software described above. A monitoring process needs to be established so that B can understand how the project is progressing and how this links back to the plan. Comparing performance to the plans will allow him to quickly identify where the project is going off track and take remedial action.

For the hotel refurbishment this is particularly urgent given the tight deadline, the lack of contingency and the fact that the project is two weeks behind. Monitoring may need to be done on a daily basis to get this project back on track.

Lack of milestones

There appears to be no project milestones defined for this project. Milestones are key targets or events within the project that need to be met, eg a milestone for this project might be 'all external paintwork complete'. Specific milestones and their outputs should be identified so that progress can be monitored and potential delays flagged immediately.

Poor resource allocation

In addition to the hotel refurbishment project, S company has a significant amount of other project work. Due to this volume a number of core staff were taken off the hotel project leaving it under resourced. Staff allocations should have been better considered at the outset and a realistic amount allocated given the number of other projects running. The removal of resource from the hotel project will obviously have a direct impact on the cost and timescale of the project.

S company needs to have a procedure in place for top level allocation of resources between projects. Where the resources are not available, additional projects should not be taken on.

Budgetary control

Costs incurred by a project should be compared to the cost plan produced at the initiation stage. The delay within the project has led to a delay of the first stage payment from the hotel. This will no doubt be putting pressure on costs as less cash will be available for the project. Getting the project back on track to avoid any further payment delays is therefore a key issue for B. A cashflow forecast should be prepared to ensure S company is aware of cash requirements and can take any steps required to maintain cash availability.

Scope creep

The scope of the project should be clearly defined in the project initiation document. Any changes made at a later date will incur additional costs and will increase the timescale for delivery of the project. The hotel is suggesting additional activities are added to the project yet are unlikely to be willing to accept a later completion date in order to host the wedding event. B must ensure that only essential changes are agreed to and such changes are fully authorised by the project sponsor.

46 Entertainment attraction project

Text references. The project lifecycle is covered in chapter 7

Top tips. In order to pass part (a), it is vital that you relate your answer to the scenario and use the project lifecycle as a framework to identify the steps that could have been taken in the Entertainment Attraction Project. A general description of the concept of the project lifecycle is unlikely to earn sufficient marks.

Note that there are actually two requirements to part (b). First the concept of continuous process needs to be explained, and then it needs to be applied to Z Company by describing the practices the company could put in place to achieve continuous improvement.

Examiner's comment. Overall for part (a) some candidates achieved high marks. The main two weaknesses included either not applying the answer to the project lifecycle, or not making reference to the scenario and specific problems being experienced.

Overall part (b) was a low scoring answer. Many candidates repeated points from part (a). Very few developed their answers in terms of the practices associated with continuous project improvement. Many answers simply referred to project completion.

Marking scheme

		Marks
(a)	Explanation of project lifecycle	Up to 2
	For each stage in the lifecycle, how problems can be avoided	
	Identification of need	Up to 4
	Development of a solution	Up to 3
	Implementation	Up to 4
	Completion	Up to 3
	Maximum marks awarded	15
(b)	Explanation of continuous improvement	1
	Explanation of the importance of continuous improvement	Up to 3
	Explanation of the activities – for each activity; eg	Up to 2 each
	Setting the culture	
	Education and training	
	Policies and procedures	
	Benchmarking	
	Feedback	
	Maximum marks awarded	10
	Total marks for question	25

(a) Projects, particularly larger projects such as the entertainment attraction (EA) project undertaken by Z Company, are considered to have a lifecycle. The project lifecycle is considered to have four main phases: Identification of need; development of a solution; implementation and completion.

Steps could have been taken at each of these four stages to avoid the problems the EA project has experienced.

Step 1: Identification of need

The first stage of a project involves identifying the need for that project. The steps that could have been taken by Z Company at this first stage are as follows.

Feasibility study

Z Company should have carried out an initial feasibility study to determine if the project has merit. This will consider the benefits of going ahead with the project and what, if any, alternative solutions exist.

Following on from this, Z Company should then have sent out an invitation to tender to a number of external contractors asking them to submit proposals. These proposals would detail how the work could be carried out along with estimates of costs and the timeframe in which it could be achieved. The tender process would provide Z Company with a number of potential solutions for carrying out the work. Z Company would then review these tenders by carrying out feasibility studies on each of them in order to help Z Company choose the most appropriate contractor.

A SWOT analysis would be a useful tool at this stage as it would provide Z Company with an understanding of the various strengths, weaknesses, opportunities and threats of each proposed project. This would allow Z Company to determine which would provide the best fit for the organisation and its needs. Had Z Company carried out this process it may have highlighted the overly ambitious target visitor numbers. This would have allowed contingency plans to be put in place early and perhaps prevented the ultimate failure of the entertainment attraction.

Project specification

Z Company should have produced a detailed project specification document that clearly defined exactly what it wanted the project to achieve and how this would be done, along with details of the resources that would be used to achieve this. This is vital for reference throughout the project to allow the progress of the project and its eventual success to be monitored.

Step 2: Development of a solution

This stage involves agreement on what is to be done. It will involve showing how the needs are to be met, computing costs and benefits and obtaining sponsor agreement.

Steps that could have been taken at this stage include:

Budget

Z Company should have produced a budget that realistically assess the finance required, the timescale and the resources that are available for meeting the objectives of the EA project. This budget would provide an outline for the project manager and project team.

Organisation plan

An organisation plan should then have been developed to document the structure of the project team and define the responsibilities of individuals. The responsibilities of any sub-contracted staff to be used would also be documented here. This would have helped to avoid issues relating to management structure and lack of understanding such as those encountered by Z Company.

Work breakdown structure

A work breakdown structure (WBS) would also have been useful for Z Company to calculate the cost of the project. A WBS breaks down the work required to complete the project into manageable components, or work packages, which have defined outcomes and responsibilities. The individuals responsible for each of the work packages would provide estimates of cost and time required by that particular work package. Involvement of individuals directly involved in this work may have improved the accuracy of the cost estimates which were shown to be poor in the EA project.

Step 3: Implementation

The next stage of the project lifecycle involves actually implementing the proposed solution. A number of steps could have been taken by Z Company at this stage.

Staff selection

Appropriate staff should have been selected to work on this project. Factors such as staffing levels, motivation and team management should also have been considered and an appropriate style of leadership should have been adopted by the project manager.

Communication

Plans relating to communication and the distribution of information would have helped Z Company to avoid some of the conflict that arose between the various stakeholders. It is important that Z Company take their stakeholders into consideration and determine the levels of interest and power possessed by each. This information should be used to manage the various relationships to help the project run smoothly. Stakeholder mapping would help Z Company understand which stakeholders are the most influential, and therefore where their efforts should be focused.

Monitoring

Z Company should have monitored performance on an ongoing basis to ensure it is in line with the plans and is on track for delivering the objective of the project. If necessary, changes to the plan should be made to take account of any new information or changes in circumstances. Any such changes should have been communicated.

Performance reporting

Actual costs and other resources used should have regularly compared to the budget and plans. This could have prevented the financial management issues encountered by Z Company as any discrepancies between the planned and actual figures would have been quickly identified and appropriate corrective action taken.

Project meetings

Regular project meetings should be held for the duration of the project. Z Company did schedule meetings but later cancelled them. Had they committed to a regular schedule of meetings both the project team and the project sponsor would have been better informed of project progress and performance.

Stage 4: Completion

At the end of the project, Z Company should evaluate the project and establish lessons learned that can be applied to future projects and improve the project management process. As part of this, Z Company will need to establish the reasons for the large overspend so that suitable procedures can be established to prevent similar overspends in the future. The reasons behind the timeframe slippage should also be investigated.

Post completion audit

As post completion audit would be highly beneficial to Z Company to help these issues be fully understood and ensure that lessons learned are fully embedded into the project management process.

(b) Continuous improvement is a long-term approach to improving the project management process via small incremental changes.

Continuous improvement is important for improving efficiency and quality of projects for a number of reasons:

- Internal evaluation meetings of the project team members provide the opportunity to discuss the successes and failures of the project to establish ways in which future projects can enjoy the same successes while avoiding making the same mistakes

- Evaluating the project from a business perspective to determine whether or not the benefits are being successfully delivered will allow Z Company to determine what has worked. Lessons learned can again be fed back to the process where elements have been found to be unsuccessful

- Continuous improvement encourages innovation and breakthroughs can be made to prevent future restriction of project results.

Z Company will need to take the following action to set up continuous project improvement:

Commitment from senior management

Obtaining this commitment is crucial if a continuous improvement culture is to be established.

Structure

An appropriate organisational structure will need to be put in place. A matrix structure is particularly well suited to a project focused organisation/team as it will facilitate knowledge sharing.

Reward systems

A performance linked reward system that recognises those who contribute to the improvement of the process will help to reinforce the continuous improvement culture.

Recruitment, education and training

Z Company will need to recruit staff with strong project management methodology knowledge and skills. Training and education will need to be provided to develop these skills in existing staff.

Defined processes

Processes, procedures and methodology should be clearly defined and documented. Z Company should develop standard management processes as well as supporting guidance and templates.

Benchmarking

Comparing its own project processes to industry best practice would assist Z Company in improving its own processes and bringing them up to best practice standard.

Feedback

To ensure a defined repeatable process for solving the problems exists, Z Company will need to ensure it obtains sufficient feedback from future projects. For example a Plan-Do-Measure-Act cycle could be established.

---

47   J Company

> **Text references.** Project slippage is covered in Chapter 9 of your Study Text. Project teams are covered in Chapter 8 and teams in general are covered in Chapter 2.
>
> **Top tips.** Part (a) is reasonably straightforward and you should be able to generate a number of marks by suggesting possible action that the company could take. However, notice that you are asked to **analyse** the strategies that are available so make sure that, as well as listing your suggestions, you relate this back to the specific scenario to determine how appropriate you think each of your suggestions is likely to be.
>
> **Easy marks.** In part (b) you can gain some easy marks by using the information given in the scenario – the feedback from the project team relating to lack of visibility and lack of communication of plans and priorities should indicate to you that these are areas that CW should address when managing future project teams.

(a)   There are a number of options available to J Company to address the issue of time, cost and quality in the website project. These include:

Do nothing

After considering all options, it may be decided that the best option is simply to let things continue as they are. This, however, is unlikely to be the case here as the impact of the rising costs and time needed to improve the functionality are significant enough for the Board of J Company to call an emergency meeting to discuss solutions to the slippage.

Add resources

It may be possible that additional resources, such as extra staff, could be provided to the project in order to help get the project back on track. However, although this would address the time slippage it is likely to increase the cost of the project even further. There is often a trade off between the three project objectives of cost-time-quality and whether adding resources is considered viable will depend on which of these objectives are more important. It will of course also depend on sufficient and appropriately qualified staff being available.

Work smarter

It may be possible to change working methods and improve productivity if those being used at present are inefficient. To explore this possibility CW would need to carry out an analysis of the current working methods to develop an understanding as to whether or not there is potential for improvement.

Replan

If the assumptions the original plan was based on have been proved invalid then a more realistic plan should be devised. It could be possible that this is the case here, as unforeseen problems have arisen relating the to the functionality of the site. If J Company chose to replan, however, they will have to accept the additional time and cost that will be involved in completing the project to these new requirements.

Reschedule

Sometimes it is possible, rather than completely re-planning, to save some time by changing the phasing of certain deliverables. This may or may not be possible for this project. CW would have to look into this to establish whether or not rescheduling could save time.

Introduce incentives

If one problem contributing to the slippage is found to relate to team performance then incentives such as bonus payments could be linked to work deadlines and quality. However, incentives are unlikely to be the correct solution in this case. It appears that it would be much more effective for the project manager to involve the team more in the decisions relating to the project and communicate with them much more effectively so that they are clear about deadlines, schedules, priorities and their own role and contribution. Ways this might be done are considered in part (b) below.

Change the specification

If the original objectives of the project are unrealistic given the time and money available it may be necessary to negotiate a change in the specification. As the problems relate to the functionality of the site, and that the reason for undertaking the project in the first place related to improving customer service by making the website more user-friendly, it is unlikely that this would be the best solution. However, if there is no leeway at all with regards to the time and budget available, and no methods of improving the existing processes exist, then this might become something that J Company might want to explore.

Conclusion

In order to determine the best strategy that J Company could use to address the project slippage CW and the Board will have to ensure that they have obtained a sufficient understanding of the causes of the slippage, what they consider to be essential outcomes to for them to view the project as a success and what is tolerable in respect of changes to time, budget and quality constraints.

They will also have to gain a full understanding as to what other resources are available to them in order to complete the project.

Only once they have the answer to all these questions can the assess the possible solutions and make a decision as to the appropriate action to take to address this problem.

(b) The factors that CW should consider to ensure the project teams he manages in the future are effective might be considered under three headings: the individuals needed, the functioning of the group, and the leadership of the team.

The individuals

CW must ensure that the members of the project, between them, possess the skills, experience and aptitudes necessary to successfully complete the project.

Belbin suggests that the effective functioning of a team depends, at least in part, on the ability of the members to play a range of important team roles. These roles are co-ordinator, shaper, implementer, monitor-evaluator, resource investigator, team worker, specialist and completer/finisher. CW must ensure his team covers these roles.

The group

New teams develop and mature over time, finding ways to operate and relate. As the leader, CW can build the team by controlling and accelerating this process. The development process was described by *Tuckman* as taking place in four stages.

(i) **Forming** is the process of bringing the group together and beginning to work out its aims, structure and processes. The 'getting to know each other' process should be encouraged here since team members come from different functions and may not even know each other. The team members are likely to be initially wary of one another.

(ii) **Storming** is a period of open conflict between members about objectives, methods and relationships during which priorities and roles emerge. It should lead to a robust basis for co-operation in the future.

(iii) **Norming** is a period of settling down with the development of group norms about work requirements and methods and social expectations. The leader may need to encourage 'overarching' norms and goals in order to overcome inter-functional differences.

(iv) **Performing** productive work follows as the final phase, when the team is ready to collaborate on efficient task performance.

<u>Leadership</u>

Leadership of the team will be fundamental in determining how well the team performs. This will be particularly important for CW to as the feedback from the current project team would indicate that there have been a number of problems in this area. CW himself may need training in effective project management.

A key criticism of CW throughout the current project was his **lack of visibility**. This must be addressed with any future teams so that the team know that he is contactable and available and also so that they can see what exactly he is doing in relation to the project.

Roles should be clearly defined and CW is responsible for ensuring that all members of his team have a clear understanding of their role and the way in which they are expected to contribute to the project.

Communication is also vital when leading a team and is, again, an area on which CW has been criticised. CW must ensure that he communicates effectively with his team himself. He must provide clear objectives and decisions, brief future activity and plans clearly and give feedback on progress. He must also ensure that the team members communicate effectively with each other. No doubt much important communication will be **verbal**, **face-to-face and informal**, but there should also be **meetings** held at suitable intervals to ensure that important matters are not overlooked and there is general understanding of work and progress.

Participation in decision-making and problems will also be important as this will provide the members of the team with a sense of ownership over the project and will help them to understand how they can contribute to its ultimate success.

The project team will include experienced professionals with their own competences and expectations and so a leadership style appropriate to this kind of team will have to be developed by CW.

48 SBU

Text references. This is covered in Chapter 11, which deals with levels of strategy.

Top tips. Start with an explanation of what is meant by a strategic business unit. You should then go on to explain the different levels of strategy within an organisation and the links between strategies of an SBU with corporate and functional strategies

Easy marks. The definition of an SBU will get you around three easy marks.

Examiner's comments. Answers were generally very poor. Many candidates had no understanding of what an SBU is.

Marking scheme

Explanation of strategic business unit (up to 3), to include, for example:
Division in organisation with degree of autonomy
Responsible for developing and marketing own products and services

3

Links to other levels of strategy, for example:
Reference to hierarchy
Strategic decisions are independent
Corporate level will inform decisions on investment for SBU
Influences products/services developed
Influences competitive position
Issues of centralisation versus decentralisation
Functional level strategies translate business level into action
Need to support SBU rather than conflict to deliver objectives
Other

(1 mark each, max 7)

$$\frac{7}{10}$$

Strategic business unit

A strategic business unit (SBU) may be defined as 'a division within a large organisation that has a significant degree of autonomy, typically being responsible for developing and marketing its own products and services.' *(CIMA Official Terminology)*.

There is a hierarchy of strategies within an organisation. These strategies may be divided into three distinct levels:

(a)   **Corporate strategy** is the most general level of strategy in an organisation. Corporate strategy is ' concerned with what types of business the company as a whole should be in and is therefore concerned with divisions of scope' (Johnson and Scholes).

(b)   **Business strategy** defines how an organisation approaches a particular market or the activity of a particular business unit.

(c)   **Functional strategy** (also called operational strategy) involves decisions of strategic importance but which are made or determined at operational levels.

The strategies of a strategic business unit are thus in **the middle of this hierarchy.** SBU strategies should be consistent with the strategies both above and below it in the hierarchy.

Corporate strategy

It is important that SBU strategies fit with the overall direction of the company, its purpose and scope as set out in its corporate strategy.

(a)   **Purpose.** A strategy developed at the SBU level should aim to meet the objectives of the strategies set at the higher corporate level.

(b)   **Scope.** The SBU's strategy should align with the direction of the corporate as a whole. For example, decisions such as which products / services should be developed, how the SBU might gain competitive advantage, and how the SBU may segment its market.

A strategic business unit must **obey** corporate strategic priorities, for example to work to ensure that the overall performances of the group matches promises made to shareholders. It must also work to maximise synergies and avoid action that may undermine corporate strategy, such as inter-divisional competition for clients or actions that undermine brands.

Functional strategies

Functional strategies are **also called operational strategies**. These decisions include product pricing, investment in plant, personnel policy, and so on. It is important that these strategies link to the strategic business unit strategies and through those strategies, in turn, to the corporate strategy, as the successful implementation of these is necessary for the fulfilment of both corporate and business objectives.

An SBU strategy must determine the functional strategies to ensure that finance, IT, marketing, production and other functions are pursuing courses of action that contribute to the realisation of business goals, rather than 'empire building' or 'doing his own thing'. In addition, the various functions should be mutually supportive, for example, IT should support a marketing strategy that leads to a financial advantage for the firm.

In conclusion, successful implementation of strategy will depend upon there being congruence in planning, implementation and control at each level within the organisation's strategic hierarchy.

49 Market size, share and growth

Text references. Market size, share and growth are covered in chapter 13 of your BBP Study Text.

Top tips. In addition to describing the concepts, to score highly it is important that you relate your answer back to the scenario given.

Easy marks. A number of knowledge marks are available here for describing the concepts of market size, market share and market growth.

Examiner's comments. Main weaknesses were due to candidates discussing the process of competitor analysis in a very general sense, without reference to the key concepts referenced in the question requirement. Some candidates used the BCG matrix, but described the four quadrants without application to the context of the scenario.

Marking scheme

	Marks
Market size explained	3
Market share explained	3
Market growth explained	4
Maximum marks awarded	10

A **market** comprises the customers or potential customers who have needs which are satisfied by a product or service.

In order for CP Company to determine what strategic approach to take in response to the increased competition and reduced prices it is important to understand the total size of the market, CP Company's own share of that market and the extent to which the market is growing. The reasons for this are discussed below.

Market size

It is useful to get an idea of the size of the market based on total sales volume or sales value of all competitors. However, it can be difficult to determine how to actually define the market. In this instance, CP Company will need to decide if it believes it competes in the ready-made dessert market as a whole, or in the more specific market of chocolate desserts. This will need to be determined before the size of that market can be estimated.

An understanding of the market size will provide CP Company with an indication as to the total value of the market that CP and its competitors are competing for.

Market share

CP Company's market share is the proportion of the market defined above that is being serviced by CP Company. CP Company has grown rapidly over the past year, however, this does not necessarily mean that its share of the market has increased. It is noted that there is now increased competition which would indicate that the market is growing. Therefore it is possible that, despite the increased size of CP Company, its market share could have decreased.

It would be a strategic advantage for CP Company to have a larger market share as this would allow it to benefit from economies of scale, leverage over suppliers and have greater influence over price.

By understanding CP Company's market share, JF can make a more informed strategic decision over the most suitable response to competition and pressure on prices.

Market growth

Market growth involves estimating how much bigger the market has got in recent years, particularly over the last year. Higher growth tends to be associated with newer markets, while more mature markets tend to experience very little growth.

If the market has a higher growth rate then it represents potential opportunities for CP Company to make more sales and increase their revenue. However, it has been seen that there is now increased competition in the market and so the likely response of competitors will need to be taken into consideration. This is because profits are greatly reduced when there is high competition in a quickly growing market.

If the rate of growth is low, fewer new competitors will be attracted to the market. If there are also high barriers to entry then this can be very profitable, however, this is unlikely in the ready-made chocolate desserts market.

50 PV Company

Text references. Mission is covered in Chapter 11.

Top tips. Do not confuse mission with vision. Vision would be the overall aspiration for the future.

Easy marks. The question is fairly general, so you should not have had too much difficulty making valid points.

Examiner's comment. Many candidates confused the broad nature of mission statements with the more specific nature of objectives. Rather than confining discussion to the justifiable claim that a mission statement is useful because objectives can be derived from such statements, some candidates went on to argue that the mission/objectives should be specific, time bound and measurable. There was a similar tendency for candidates to claim too much for mission statements when when they came to discuss the relationship between mission statements, values, culture and strategic planning.

Marking scheme

	Marks
1 mark per valid, explained point (½ if not explained) to a maximum of 2 each for each of:	
Explanation of mission	
Help to give direction where there is a range of views	
Clarifies why the company exists	
Sets goals clearly	
Future strategies and competencies	
Goals and ethics	
Culture	10
	10

What is a mission?

A **mission** can be defined as a business's basic function in society. It is often visionary, open-ended and has no time limit for achievement. It is its reason for being. Mission is concerned with the overriding purpose and core values of PV Company based on the values and expectations of its stakeholders. It should be distinguished from vision. Vision represents the overall aspiration for the future of PV Company whereas PV Company's mission is what business it is in, in other words why it exists.

The mission will also state the basic function of PV Company in society in terms of the services it provides. It will also be concerned with the scope and boundaries of the organisation.

Benefits of developing a mission for PV Company

There are many good reasons for PV Company developing a mission especially given the lack of direction and range of views that currently exist. The staff have no common agreement on what the **priorities and objectives** of the company should be.

A mission will help PV Company clarify why it exists and the **scope and boundaries** of PV Company's activities. Knowing its reason for existence and its range of influence will help PV Company decide on its purpose.

PV Company needs to set goals, aims and objectives to achieve its mission. Goals flesh out the mission in concrete terms. Objectives are quantified and aims are unquantifed goals. A clear mission will enable PV Company to set goals more clearly as these should support the mission. It will assist PV Company in providing a basis for consistent planning decisions and in translating the organisation's purposes and direction into objectives suitable for assessment and control.

A mission would also act as a yardstick by which plans are judged and help to **make decisions more consistent**. It could be used to evaluate possible future strategies. It should cover elements of strategy, for example the competence and competitive advantages by which it hopes to prosper.

The mission would help PV Company frame its **goals and ethics**. For example, should the company be opposed to animal testing of products or excessive packaging?

The **values** stated in the mission should relate to the culture and should capture the basic, often un-stated beliefs of the people who work for PV Company.

A clear mission would **help key stakeholders** understand what PV Company is doing especially those outside the organisation. This could help to provide a consistent understanding and purpose between the different interest groups and stakeholders connected to PV Company.

Many organisations write their missions down in a **mission statement** and this would help PV Company to communicate its mission in wider society and reinforce the key elements of the mission.

51 Levels

> **Text references.** Levels of strategy are covered in Chapter 11.
>
> **Top tips.** Start with an explanation of what functional strategy is, and where it fits into the hierarchy of strategies. It is important that you mention that there is both top down and bottom up communication.
>
> **Easy marks.** The explanation of functional strategy will get you three easy marks.
>
> **Examiner's comment.** Many candidates appeared not to have an understanding of the 'other layers of strategy' referred to in the question and a significant number of candidates confused operational strategy and functional strategy even suggesting they operated at different levels. As a result, they were unable to offer a coherent answer to the question.

There is a hierarchy of strategies within an organisation. These strategies may be divided into three distinct levels:

(a)   **Corporate strategy** is the most general level of strategy in an organisation. Corporate strategy is ' concerned with what types of business the company as a whole should be in and is therefore concerned with divisions of scope' (Johnson and Scholes).

(b)   **Business strategy** defines how an organisation approaches a particular market or the activity of a particular business unit.

(c)   **Functional strategy** (also called operational strategy) involves decisions of strategic importance but which are made or determined at operational levels.

Functional strategies

Functional strategies are **also called operational strategies**. These decisions include product pricing, investment in plant, personnel policy, and so on. It is important that these strategies link to the strategic business unit strategies and through those strategies, in turn, to the corporate strategy, as the successful implementation of these is necessary for the fulfilment of both corporate and business objectives.

Functional strategies are the **detailed strategies of departments** such as finance, sales, IT marketing, production and human resources management. Functional strategies must support the overall corporate strategy of an organisation.

Functional strategies must ensure that finance, IT, marketing, production and other functions are pursuing courses of action that contribute to the realisation of business goals, rather than 'empire building' or 'doing his own thing'. In addition, the various functions should be mutually supportive, for example:

(a)   IT should support a marketing strategy that leads to a financial advantage for the firm.

(b)   Human resources need to ensure that new production staff recruited have the right skills.

In the development of functional strategies the communication process is both top down and bottom up. This ensures that people at all levels are aware of the plan and have a stake in implementing it.

In conclusion, successful implementation of strategy will depend upon there being **congruence** in planning, implementation and control at each level within the organisation's strategic hierarchy.

52   Levels of strategy

Text references. Levels of strategy are covered in chapter 11

Top tips. As well as describing the levels of strategy, strong answers will illustrate how the levels are linked and will explain each layer in the context of the scenario given.

Easy marks. Some easy knowledge marks are available for explaining the three levels of strategy.

Examiner's comment. Some sound answers but a significant number of candidates explained growth strategies in BRIC economies without any reference to the different levels of strategy, and hence did not end up answering the question posed.

Marking scheme

	Marks
Explanation of multi-levels of strategy	Max 2
Explanation of corporate strategy	1
Corporate strategy related to J plc	Max 3
Explanation of functional strategy	1
Business strategy related to J plc	Max 3
Explanation of business strategy	1
Functional strategy related to J plc	Max 3
Maximum marks awarded	10

Strategy exists at three main levels: corporate strategy at the top, followed by business strategy which then cascades down to functional strategy. These three levels of strategy are inter-linked and, to be successful, there should be goal congruence; the lower levels should support the higher level strategic objectives, which in turn influence the lower levels.

Corporate strategy

Corporate strategy is concerned with the overall vision of the organisation. The purpose, scope, strategy and principles of J company will be set out at this level. The expectations of J Company's stakeholders should be considered here as the corporate strategy should deliver value to key stakeholders who can both support or oppose a strategy.

Top level decisions such as acquisitions or the closing down of areas of the organisation will be made at this level. J Company is currently considering entering the new markets in the BRIC economies and the corporate objective of delivering 5% profit over the next two years has also been set. A market that can deliver this will need to be chosen at this level and the framework for achieving this will cascade down to the lower levels of strategy.

A further element of corporate strategy is the development of corporate policies, such as corporate social responsibility. J Company's official stance on such issues will be determined and documented at this level.

Business strategy

Business strategy defines how an organisation or a particular business unit approaches a particular market. This level of strategy looks at how competitive advantage can be obtained.

J Company's management at the business level are responsible for beating competition and winning customers and will need to formulate strategies to allow them to do this in the emerging markets. They will therefore be concerned with decisions such as what range of cars to offer in these markets, how to segment the markets and which segments to target.

The objectives cascaded down from the corporate level will provide a framework within which the business strategy should be formulated. This will ensure every area of the business is working towards achieving the objective of 5% profit growth in two years.

Functional strategy

Functional, or operational, strategy involves decisions of strategic importance, but which are made at operational level, eg product pricing. It is these decisions that determine the success of the strategy as, effectively, strategy is only implemented at this level.

These decisions are made by functions across J Company such as finance, human resources (HR) and marketing. The higher level strategy is filtered down to the functional units which then translate the strategy into specific targets, objectives and action plans. They ensure the specific resources are in place for the strategies to be successful. For example, J Company's HR function will need to establish what skills and knowledge are needed to deliver the strategy and where it should be sourced from.

For J Company's strategy to be successfully implemented, these functional strategies must be consistent with the business and corporate objectives of the company. If there are conflicts between the strategies that are implemented and the overriding strategy of the organisation, then it will inevitably fail.

53 Fast food culture

> **Text references.** Chapter 5 (on culture) and 1 (on cross-cultural leadership)
>
> **Top tips.** This is a very simple question based on culture in its widest sense, though management culture also rears its ugly head. Note the three problems mentioned in the question. How might these be analysed using *Hofstede's* model? Make sure you **tailor** your answer so that you address these particular problems. You would be equipped to produce a pretty good answer to this question if you merely read a decent newspaper regularly. Indeed, look at our advice in the front pages on how to develop business awareness.
>
> **Easy marks.** Differences of national culture and *Hofstede's* model of management cultures are obvious bases to build an answer on. There is no need to go into great detail about the latter in particular, however.

The problems experienced by FFC reflect common points of difference between national (and organisational) cultures.

One of the key models used to categorise these points of difference is the **Hofstede model**, which identifies **four key 'dimensions'** on which national cultures (and the corporate cultures modelled on them) differ.

(a)   **Power distance** describes the extent to which unequal distribution of power is accepted in a culture. **This may be a source of the complaints from country C employees about the style and practices of the country S managers**. It may be that country C is a low-PD culture, in which subordinates expect involvement and participation in decision-making, while country S is a high-PD culture, which favours top-down command and closer supervision: there will be an inevitable clash between managerial norms and assumptions, and the expectations of employees.

(b)   **Uncertainty avoidance** describes the extent to which security, order and control are preferred to ambiguity uncertainty and change. **This may also be causing stress and frustration for the country C employees**: either because (as a high-UA culture) they are given *insufficiently* clear task structure and rules by the country S managers, or because (as a low-UA culture) they feel restricted by excessive structure, rules and regulations. **Given the high degree of complaint by locals**, country C may be on the low-UA (dissent-tolerating) side of the scale.

(c) **Individualism** describes the extent to which people prefer to live and work in individualist (focusing on 'I') rather than collectivist (focusing on 'we') ways. Again, we don't know where the two countries fall on the scale, but the **complaints about seating arrangements and music, for example, may be due to their interference with social interaction**, if country C is a collectivist culture.

(d) **Masculinity** refers to the extent to which gender roles are distinct, and the extent to which masculine values (assertiveness, competition, material success etc) are dominant over feminine values (relationship, consensus, modesty etc). Again, we can only surmise that **there may be a clash of management styles**, in this respect, between **country S managers and country C employees**.

We might also note, more generally, that **two of the key elements of culture** (according to *Trompenaars*) are **rituals** and **artefacts**. There are **cultural differences in the values attached to food and rituals and customs around eating**, and these may account for some of country C's resistance to the food culture (and menus) introduced by the country S chain. There are, similarly, **cultural differences in 'taste' in artefacts such as music and architecture**: country C people may simply dislike country S's music, or have their sense of heritage outraged by incompatible architecture in their cities.

FFC's management have presumably decided to standardise as much of their operation as possible in order to enhance control and brand image and to achieve economies of scale. It seems likely that they will have to make some adjustments to this ethnocentric approach to their operation in country C if it is to be adapted more appropriately to the needs and wants of its new market.

54 T Venture

Text references. Chapter 11.

Top tips. The trick to part (a) is an understanding of the potential role of CSFs in strategy development and how the possession of core competences enables the CSFs to be achieved. **Unless you can distinguish between CSFs and core competences, you will not be able to answer this question**. The examiner noted that a significant number of candidates were unable to distinguish between CSFs and core competences and were unable to apply these concepts to the scenario.

Easy marks. A small number of easy marks will be available in part (a) for accurate definitions of CSFs and core competences. Linking CSFs and core competences in the context of strategy development will be more difficult and will generate the bulk of the marks. In part (b), full marks were available for simply stating, in bullet point format, four factors that would be critical to competitive success in relation to a business operation with which most students would be familiar.

(a) <u>Using Critical Success Factors</u>

Critical Success Factors (CSFs) are a **small number of areas in which (a) satisfactory results will enable successful competitive performance** and (b) an **organisation *must* excel in order to outperform competition**. *Johnson & Scholes* recommend six or fewer CSFs. T must attempt to determine the CSFs for his new venture for a number of reasons.

(i) **It is the only way he can present potential investors with a sound business case for his venture.** He is convinced he can succeed with his fast-food concept, but he needs to show he can define what success is, and what is necessary to achieve it, within the business sector he has chosen.

(ii) **CSFs provide a basis for strategy formulation**, as they focus on the strategic goals that must be pursued in order to compete successfully: the features of T's product/service that will be most highly valued by customers, and which will be a potential source of competitive advantage. The fast food market is highly competitive, so outperforming competitors will be a helpful priority.

(iii) **CSFs offer an alternative to a more comprehensive goal structure or hierarchy of objectives, which may be too rigid for a small start-up venture** in a new market: they will enable T to focus on competitive essentials and remain flexible in how he (and individual outlets within his chain) will pursue them at the tactical and operational level. This will allow for variations in local markets, infrastructure, produce availability, outlet manager ability and so on.

(iv) **CSFs provide a useful framework for identifying the business processes and activities which will yield each CSF**; defining the Key Performance Indicators (KPIs) which will be used to evaluate performance in delivering them; and monitoring competitor activity for its effect on the CSF structure.

Distinguishing CSFs from core competences

Competences are 'the activities or processes through which the organisation deploys its resources effectively.' (*Johnson & Scholes*). Core competences are competences which both outperform competitors and are unique or difficult for competitors to imitate.

Core competences represent the distinctive abilities that T's venture must develop and display if its CSFs are to be achieved. The two concepts are related, in that CSFs should focus attention on whether the venture has or can develop the core competences to compete successfully: both concepts take a competitive view of strategy. However, the emphasis has shifted from what must be achieved (CSFs) to the special skills and processes that will enable the required achievement (core competences).

(b)   Possible CSFs for T's chain of fast food restaurants

The CSFs for T's chain of fast food restaurants could include the following.

(i)   **Right restaurant locations.** Proximity to significant centres of population, easy access and adequate parking facilities

(ii)   **Distinctive brand identity.** Recognisable and distinctive brand with a good reputation for quality of service and diversity and freshness of produce

(iii) **Speed of service.** Must meet customer expectations based on benchmark standards set by competitors

(iv) **Child friendly facilities.** Needs of children and families must be catered for successfully

55 AT Company

> **Text references.** The positioning approach to strategy is covered in chapter 11.
>
> **Top tips.** The first part of the question is very application focused and as such you will need to make specific reference to the scenario to score well.
>
> **Easy marks** Some marks are available for theoretical knowledge of the problems that are associated with the positioning approach.
>
> **Examiner's comments.** The answers ranged from very good to very poor. A large proportion of candidates were able to provide an explanation of the positioning approach and some of its problems, though a minority were unable to define the approach and thus unable to complete an answer that gained any marks at all.
>
> Some candidates did not have an adequate appreciation of the positioning approach to the achievement of competitive advantage to do justice in developing a full answer to both parts of the question.

Marking scheme

		Marks
(a)	1 mark per valid point for explanation of the positioning approach up to a maximum of 6 marks	6
(b)	1 mark per valid point for potential problems with the positioning approach up to a maximum of 4 marks	4
	Maximum marks awarded	10

(a)   The **positioning approach** to strategy suggests that the main source of competitive advantage lies in how the organisation fits strategy to its external environment. Strategic objectives are set by researching the opportunities and threats that exist in the environment and developing organisational resources to exploit these conditions and get the organisation to where it wants to be. Increasing market share and reducing costs to a low level are also important strategic objectives.

Using this approach will require AT Company to constantly scan the environment and predict changes that are likely to occur. To do this the company will make use of tools such as Porter's five forces and the PESTEL model.

AT Company has used the information from the environment to develop a differentiated product that is aimed at a specific segment of the population. It is this differentiation which has created AT's competitive advantage.

(b)   The market in which AT Company operates has now become highly competitive which may cause it to lose its competitive advantage as more similar products come into the market. By continuing to rely on the positioning approach, AT Company may experience a number of potential problems:

Quickly becomes outdated

The rate of environmental change is too great for effective positioning strategies to be developed. Due to factors such as globalisation, technological change, and shifts in customer tastes and preferences, strategies developed in this way can be outdated before they can even take effect.

Not sustainable in the long term

Positioning advantages cannot be sustained in the long term as advantageous product-market positions are easily copied. This shortens the lifecycle of the product and the competitive advantage is lost.

Difficult to achieve

The positioning approach may require significant change within the firm which is difficult to achieve. It may be easier to move to a market environment that suits existing arrangements, skills, culture and capabilities.

56   MT

> **Text references**. Chapter 10 covers the rational model and emergent strategy. Chapter 11 covers strategy and the approaches to making strategy.
>
> **Top tips.** This is a Section A question, and the scenario is brief, but if you mention the contrasting approaches of MT and ZF rather than just launch straight into the arguments for and against, you will demonstrate that you have more than rote learning.
>
> **Easy marks**. The arguments for and against formal planning can come straight out of the Study Text.

ZF's proposed approach to strategy is the **rational planning approach**. The rational planning approach has three stages: strategic analysis, strategic choice and strategic implementation. The model represents a formal, planned approach to strategy development. This approach is typically rigid; strategies feed down in a top-down approach. MT, perhaps because he is an entrepreneur, prefers strategies that 'emerge' to those that are planned. **Emergent strategies develop out of patterns of behaviour**. They are unconscious patterns which eventually have long-tem strategic effects. However they do need to be grasped by management and used for the benefit of the organisation. So adhoc responses can be turned into strategies in time if they are successful. They are also **flexible** and **reactive** rather than **proactive**.

Advantages of formal, rational approach to strategy

(a)   A fundamental element of the formal approach is continuing **environmental analysis.** This would be important for S Software Development Company, as software development is a fast-moving , competitive environment.

(b)   Formal or planned strategy helps the organisation to take a **long view** and avoid short-termism while at the same time providing a sensible approach to the uncertainty of the future.

(c)   It guides the allocation of resources.

(d)   It **co-ordinates the activities** of the various parts of the organisation, ensuring the integration of operational management decisions into the higher strategy, the wider organisational context and longer term goals.

(e)   It sets a standard by which the actual performance of the organisation is **measured and controlled**.

(f)   It comforts providers of finance in particular and encourages **suppliers and employees** to think in terms of a long-term relationship.

(g)   The process of forming strategy requires wide and complex input so it can have a beneficial effect on managers' **personal development** and awareness and can assist with management succession planning. This will be particularly important in ensuring that when MT retires the company will not lack direction.

Drawbacks of formal approach

The concept of formal processes for strategy generation and their limited success in practice has led to criticisms of both the rational model and the very idea of strategic planning as a separate business activity.

(a)   The formal approach encourages a sense of **omniscience and control** among planners: this is dangerous because of the **inherent unpredictability of the business environment**, as an entrepreneur, MT has already had experience of.

(b)   There is an associated problem of **detachment**: planners' tendency to assume that strategy can be divorced from operations is inappropriate. Planners rarely have to implement the strategies they devise and feedback occurs too late or is badly filtered. Similarly, more junior managers, not directly involved in the planning process may misunderstand or resist the plans they are required to implement.

(c)   The idea of the **learning organisation** has been applied to strategy on the basis that an organisation's strengths and weaknesses can be in constant flux and strategy should reflect current developments as a kind of learning process itself.

(d)   The **expense and complexity** of the formal approach are inappropriate for smaller businesses.

(e)   **Goal congruence** between different business stakeholders is one of the aims of formal strategic planning. However, this advantage is **not applicable** in the case of S Software Development Company. The goals of the company are likely to be the same as those of the owners, MT and ZF. Indeed it could be argued that the rational approach does not work for small businesses because the success of the business depends on MT's ideas. MT may not be interested in growth, which the rational approach assumes to be a strategic aim.

57   N Airline

Text references. Chapter 11.

Top tips. This is a simple question on a very basic topic in strategic management and should be easy for you to answer well. The terminology used here is widely standardised, so there should be no confusion in your mind. Look back at the advice given in the front pages on **key skills**. Remember to make a point using theory, explain that point and finally illustrate it using the example of N Airline.

Easy marks. A question like part (a) revolves around definitions: you do not have to quote *Mintzberg* verbatim, as we do, so long as you can produce a clear and succinct version of your own.

(a)   Mission and objectives

Mintzberg says that **mission** 'defines the organisation's basic function in society, in terms of the products and services it produces for its clients'. A wider definition of mission would include reference to four elements.

(i)   **Purpose** would differ among types of organisations, but would define why the organisation was created.

(ii)   **Strategy** would define the nature of the organisation's activities and would therefore cover Mintzberg's definition quoted above.

(iii) **Policies and performance standards** as overall imperatives can be included in mission to emphasise their importance.

(iv)   **Values** are the pervasive beliefs and attitudes that underpin the organisation's culture.

Mission is therefore the overall definition of what the organisation exists to do.

Objectives are specific, well, defined targets whose attainment will support progress towards achieving the mission. They translate the generalised aspirations of mission into more specific, measurable and concrete terms that can be used to organise the organisation's work and provide specific targets to measure its success against. They therefore flow from and support mission.

While an organisation generally has only one mission, it is likely to have many objectives. These will be arranged in a hierarchy, with a relatively small number of high level objectives directly derived from and supporting the mission, and each of these being broken down into a cascade of supporting departmental, functional and even individual supporting objectives.

(b)   Strategic objectives for the airline

> **Top tips**. This question is unusual in its use of the instruction verb 'illustrate'. 'Illustrate' means 'use an example to describe or explain something'. The Examiner reminds you to use examples, so there is really no excuse for failing to link your answer to the setting in very concrete terms.
>
> Notice also the phrase 'strategic objectives'. **Try to focus on objectives that are truly strategic; that is, objectives that directly support N Airline's mission**. A good test of a possible objective would be to ask if it could be part of something with a wider scope. For example, 'minimise check-in delays' might be part of a wider objective to 'provide the best ground-based customer service'.
>
> This part of the question is worth six marks. The scenario is very short. You should therefore be aiming to find three, or possibly four, strategic objectives.
>
> Finally, do not forget the **SMART** mnemonic.
>
> **Easy marks**. The setting uses the word 'service' three times, which is an indication of a major priority for N Airline.

It is commonly considered that objectives should be specific, measurable, attainable, realistic and time bounded, **that is SMART**. The last quality in the list is probably inappropriate for many strategic objectives, since they will have continuing applicability.

Highest level of customer service

A **high level of customer service** is clearly a major part of N Airline's strategic vision and is intended to constitute its chief point of differentiation from its competitors. This might give rise to an objective such as the one below.

'To provide the highest level of customer service on the ground and in the air as measured by customer survey, unsolicited feedback and competitor benchmarking.'

The quality of customer service achieved will depend largely on **the people who deliver it**. HRM objectives might therefore be regarded as subordinate to the overall customer service objective. However, N Airline may wish to elevate its HRM objective to the strategic level in order to underscore its commitment to and dependence on its staff.

'To optimise recruitment, selection, training, development and remuneration practices so that all staff have the ability and motivation to deliver the highest level of customer service.'

Careful management of costs and revenues

N Airline's business model will inevitably involve a level of costs higher than those incurred by its rivals. This must imply higher revenues from higher ticket prices, which, in turn, will limit its market. **Careful management of costs and revenues** will be required if the company is to avoid cash flow crises. This is quantifiable in terms of gross and net margin, but the problem will be to set targets that are both adequate and attainable. An objective might be defined in terms such as those below.

'To manage the company's costs and revenues so as to facilitate the attainment of its objectives for customers and staff while generating a gross margin of X% and a net margin of Y%.'

58 Outsourcing costs

Text references. Transaction costs and asset specificity are covered in Chapter 11.

Top tips. This is a fairly straight forward question provided you are familiar with the concepts of transaction costs and asset specificity. However, make sure that you apply your knowledge to the scenario.

Easy marks. This question is very knowledge focused and, as such, if you have a strong understanding of transaction costs you should be easily able to gain marks for this knowledge.

Examiner's comments. The overall performance on this question was poor with only a very small minority able to produce a good answer.

In part (a) of the question many candidates described costs other than transaction costs in response to the question and in part (b) few candidates were able to define asset specificity and its role in transaction cost theory.

Marking scheme

		Marks
(a)	Types of transaction cost described e.g. (Max 4):	
	Negotiating and drafting legal contract	1
	Monitoring compliance	1
	Pursuing legal action	1
	Penalty payments	1
(b)	Explanation of asset specificity concept	Up to 3
	Examples explained (max 3):	
	Site	1
	Physical	1
	Human	1
	Dedicated	1
	Brand name	1
	Temporal	Max 3
		10

(a) When an organisation uses an outside supplier for an input or service, a transaction will take place between the two organisations. The price charged for the service or input will include a number of transaction costs. These transaction costs might include:

- Contract drafting and negotiation costs, including the time staff spend on these tasks.

- Costs of monitoring the supplier's compliance with the contract. Factors considered will include reliability, quality and invoicing.

- Legal costs, if action needs to be taken against the supplier in the case of non-performance.

- Cancellation and penalty payments should problems or disputes arise.

(b) Asset specificity relates to the extent to which an asset can be used in operations. If an asset can be used for only one range of operations then it is **specific** to that range of operations. For example, if an asset is used to supply only one client, and that asset can not be used elsewhere, then the level of asset specificity is high. If the client withdraws their contract, the supplier is left with an asset that cannot be redeployed and are no longer able to recoup the cost of investing in that asset. As a result, suppliers will only be willing to take this risk if there is a longer term guarantee of orders. Transactions involving assets with higher specificity therefore typically incur higher transaction costs.

Examples of types of asset specificity include:

Physical asset specificity: an asset with unique physical properties, such as rare mineral deposits.

Dedicated asset specificity: a man-made asset which has only one application, eg the 'Guppy' aircraft build to ferry Airbus wings from the UK to France.

Site specificity: the asset is specific to the location, eg a kitchen built on site at an airport for the airline to use as its main operational base

---

Alternative solutions

Other types of asset specificity you may have suggested, and would score marks for, are:

Human asset specificity: skills or knowledge that are relevant to the requirements of a single organisation.

Temporal specificity: This arises from an ability that is constrained to a specific time, eg a landing slot at an airport.

Brand name specificity: this arises if the brand's value will deteriorate if it is spread over too many products, eg the brand of any well known motor manufacturer.

---

59 OD

Text references. Chapter 12.

Top tips. Although this is a Section A question, it requires more than just reproducing learned material. You must apply your understanding of stakeholders and stakeholder mapping to the scenario given in the question. Note that you would not be expected to draw the grid; it is included for completeness only. The use, in the question, of 'power' and 'interest' should have alerted you to the fact that Mendelow's matrix should be used.

Easy marks. Identifying the most important stakeholders should be quite easy, and you will get some easy marks for general knowledge of types of stakeholder and their power.

Power and interest of stakeholders

In considering whether to accept the takeover bid, J must identify the key stakeholder groups and weigh up their respective levels of power and interest.

Mendelow classifies stakeholders on a matrix whose axes are **power held** and the **level of interest** in the organisation's activities. This is not an exact science, but a useful tool.

Level of interest

	Low	High
Low Power	A	B
High	C	D

This analysis could be usefully employed by OD Company when considering how to deal with its stakeholders.

Key players are found in segment D: **the takeover must be acceptable** to them, at least. J, the owner, falls into this category. He has significant power in making the decision, and significant interest. His interest will be in the money he stands to make from the takeover bid, but this may well not be the only consideration. Assuming he is a good employer, he will be aware of the responsibility he has towards other stakeholders, such as his employees and the wider community.

The **Board of ZZ Company,** which is making the takeover bid, **probably belong in Segment D**. They naturally have a high interest in the outcome, which would give them access to the brand and design capability of OD Company, and it is likely that they have a lot of power in terms of the money they can offer.

Stakeholders in segment B do not have great ability to influence strategy, but their views can be important in **influencing more powerful stakeholders**, perhaps by lobbying. **Employees in the manufacturing function** fall into this category: they clearly have a high interest in whether the bid is accepted since they stand to lose their jobs.

As individuals they have little power to influence the decision, but collectively they may well do, since they could lobby the local council of LM town and draw negative publicity.

In conjunction **with the trades union, manufacturing employees begin to move into Segment D** (high interest, high power). Trades unions have a strong interest in the outcome of the bid, to which they are opposed, and could organise employees into taking industrial action. This would have a damaging effect on production and goodwill, and could even put the bidder off.

Employees in the design or retail function have high levels of interest, although not quite as high as those in manufacturing, because their jobs are not necessarily at stake. Nevertheless, they will have a new owner, ZZ, which is based in another country, and could well bring in different working practices and a different style of management. As they have relatively little power to influence the decision, they belong in **Segment B.** In conjunction with the trades union, who would likely protest any detrimental changes to working arrangements, they would acquire more power.

Another **Segment B category** (high interest, low power) consists of the **current domestic suppliers of OD Company.** If the bid goes ahead, they will lose business to overseas suppliers. How strong an interest they have depends on whether OD is a major customer. A well diversified supplier might belong in Segment A of the matrix (low interest, low power).

Finally, OD Company is a major employer in LM town, and the local community is therefore a stakeholder in Segment B (high interest, low power). The local community includes families of those losing their jobs. Since members of the community can influence the reputation of OD Company by causing negative publicity, lobbying the media and politicians, their views should not be discounted.

The final decision is with J, but he should not make it without due consideration to all the stakeholder groups.

60   DPW

Text references. Models for assessing the external environment are covered in Chapter 12 of your Study Text.

Top tips. This question asks for an appropriate framework or model, and because the scenario is light on information, a general framework such as PEST is probably the most suitable. You could have used Porter's Five Forces too. Our answer uses PEST.

Easy marks. There are some easy marks for explaining the PEST model.

Examiner's comment. This question was generally well answered, especially by those candidates who chose to use the PEST framework for their answer. Those applying Porter's Diamond model also tended to score well.

Candidates choosing Porter's Five Forces model did less well because this model only covers the more immediate competitive environment and neglects the influence of the broader macro environmental factors.

Marking scheme

	Marks
1 mark per valid, explained point (½ if not explained)	
to a maximum of 2 each for each of:	
Explanation of reasons for motivation	
Inappropriate management style	
Need for participatory style	
Empowerment and delayering	
Feedback (appraisals)	
Learning and development	10
	___
	10

Assessing the external environment using a model/framework

PEST is a model for analysing the wider environment in which an organisation operates. PEST covers four headings: political-legal, economic, social and technological and is sometimes expanded to include legal, environmental and ethical matters.

DPW should use PEST to look at the wider environment in F Country to consider factors such as the political environment, economy and available technology that would affect any investment before making a decision to invest. So DPW needs to ask what information should be collected as part of the PEST analysis.

Political-legal environment. This includes any laws in F Country such as contract law, employee law, customer protection legislation and regulation of industry via competition law. Customers in F Country may be poorer and have less to spend on home furniture relative to P Country. **Competition regulation or tariffs** may inhibit overseas imports or conversely positively encourage them. This heading also consists of the political environment of F Country which includes internal stability, international relations and state involvement in the economy.

Economy. DPW needs to consider the rate of growth of the economy in F Country and internal demand for goods and services that would help or hinder its brand. If the economy is entering recession, DPW may still wish to enter the F market but will have to keep an eye on margins and heightened competition. In times of boom, S Company must try to identify the level of demand and plan to meet this. **Inflation, unemployment, taxation** and the **availability of credit** are all factors DPW must consider carefully.

Social and cultural environment. Typical social and cultural trends that DPW may wish to consider include the number of women entering the workforce, rising standards of living, values and beliefs held and the population **split between the sexes.** These trends affect the type and availability of customers and their potential spending power. In general, men have most spending power, particularly in less developed countries, but if the attitudes within a country change, there is increased potential for an untapped market of economically active women. And in more traditional countries, women may have the primary say in how the home is decorated.

Attitudes such as **patriotism** may affect consumers' willingness to buy from foreign companies. Will the consumers of F country wish to buy furniture from a foreign country? Will they prefer their own styles – in which case DPW might find it easier to invest in local businesses, or alternatively will they see foreign furniture as exotic and fashionable? If DPW currently sells self-assembly or flat-pack furniture, it would need to consider whether P country has a culture of DIY.

Technological. T for "technological" is relevant here. If it chooses to manufacture in P Country, labour costs are a factor, and the availability of technology may influence this. DPW needs to find out how developed the country is in terms of technology to determine **whether there is a market for its goods**. How widespread is internet use? Can sales be made over the internet or would a bricks and mortar presence be required? What is the transport infrastructure like, and how would the goods get to the customer or point of sale?

61 SM

Text references. This topic is covered in Chapter 13 of the BPP Study Text.

Top tips. Part (a) of this question tests your understanding of reasons for undertaking competitor analysis and their ability to discuss the important key competitor analysis concepts. It is best to start with a brief explanation of what is meant by a competitor and then go on to explain the reasons why FX should undertake competitor analysis. In Part (b) it is best to start by explaining what is meant by the terms market growth and market share and then explaining why it is important. A weak answer will only explain the key concepts. Good answers will explain the concepts in terms of understanding the importance of high/low market growth and high market share. The BCG matrix (part b) is not specifically mentioned in the E2 syllabus, but was covered at E1.

Easy marks. Part (a) is a good source of easy marks, with 1 mark available for every valid point and considerable flexibility in the points that can be made

Examiner's comments. Most answers were good, but there were some mediocre ones. Weaker scripts did not evidence an understanding of the key concepts, or differentiate between market growth and market penetration.

Marking scheme

		Marks
(a)	1 mark per valid point up to a maximum of 4 marks: Explanation of competitor Important to understand characteristics of competitors Understand strengths, weaknesses, strategies, objectives of competitors Helps to predict how FX could react to competitor actions Insights into past, present and future competitor strategies Informs FX how to develop future strategies	4
(b)	Market growth (max 3 marks) Market growth explained Why understanding high/low market growth is important Market share explained Why understanding concept of high/low market share is important	3 3 6 10

(a)   Competitor analysis

Competitor analysis can be defined as 'the identification of **the relative strengths and weaknesses** (compared with competitors or potential competitors) which could be of significance in the development of a successful competitive strategy' *(CIMA Official Terminology)*.

All companies must be on the lookout for potential competitors, who could have **an impact on their profits**, and they need to be able to **respond to any threats**. Examples of such threats include aggressive advertising campaigns, price cuts or the launch of a new product.

It is important **to identify competitors correctly**. In the case of FX, competitors would include other family businesses producing 'home-made' ice cream, but also larger producers of cheaper ice-cream or producers of 'home made' cakes and high quality confectionary.

FX would undertake competition analysis in order to

(i)   Assess the impact of the competition on FX's future profits
(ii)   Predict competitors' likely responses to FX's strategic initiatives. For example, if FX cuts prices, they may do the same – can FX meet that response?
(iii)   Copy profitable strategies used by competitors
(iv)   Identify and respond to aggressive actions by competitors

The following are just some of the questions that competitor analysis aims to answer:

(i)   How big are the competitors? What is their market share?
(ii)   What are their goals and strategies?
(iii)   What are their strengths and weaknesses in terms of advertising and marketing?
(iv)   How profitable are they, and what is their debt and gearing position?

(b)   Market growth

An important consideration when analysing competitors is how fast the market has grown in recent years, particularly over the last year. FX's strategy will affect its decision to get involved in a fast growing or more gradually developing market. Specifically, FX will need to estimate **how much the demand for home-made ice cream has grown and is likely to grow.** This may be based on sales volume or sales value.

Market growth can be influenced by factors not within FX's control. If there is a recession, or bad weather, demand for luxury ice cream is not likely to increase.

High or low growth?

The rate of growth is an important consideration for FX. Whether the rate of growth is high or low depends on the conditions of the market. The most important of these conditions is its size. A new, **smaller market can grow very rapidly**, but a **mature market may grow only slowly**. A small, fast growing market is a good source of opportunities for FX, but also for its competitors, who can penetrate such a market relatively easily. By contrast, a mature market has barriers to entry, although there is not the potential for growth.

Market share.

Market share is the **proportion of a market that is being serviced by an organisation**. For example, FX may have 20% of the UK market in 'home made' ice cream, but only 5% of the UK ice cream market overall. Increased market share is not necessarily the same as market growth: a market can grow as more competitors come into it, so that an organisation's market share declines even if the organisation itself is growing. It is generally considered to be of strategic advantage to have a large and growing share of a particular market for a number of reasons:

(i)   Economies of scale
(ii)   Leverage over suppliers
(iii)   Greater influence over prices

Market share is a useful tool for FX in **analysing its performance against that of its competitors**. In the short term profitability may be sacrificed for market share as margins are squeezed to increase sales. However, once a high market share is achieved, FX may well be able to influence prices and reduce costs through economies of scale. This will increase profitability in the long run.

Another way of looking at market share is using the Boston Consulting Group (BCG) matrix. This matrix assesses a company's products in terms of potential cash generation and cash expenditure requirements. Products or strategic business units (SBUs) are categorised in terms of **market growth rate** and **relative market share**.

Relative market share is assessed as a ratio: it is market share compared with the market share of the **largest competitor**. Thus a relative market share greater than unity indicates that the product or SBU is the market leader. BGG settled on market share as a way of estimating the costs associated with given products. This was chosen because both costs and market share are connected with **production experience**: as experience in satisfying a particular market demand for value increases, market share can be expected to increase also, and costs to fall. The connection between lower costs and higher market share was independently confirmed.

BCG concluded that **market dominance is essential for low costs.** Higher relative market share would result in:

(a)   **Lower unit costs,** and therefore higher profit margins than those of competitors

(b)   The power to be a **price leader.** If FX cutsprices, other firms must do so, even if they are thereby forced to sell at below unit cost.

(c)   FX's products would become the **'benchmark'**, against which competitors' products must be measured.

62 Digital media products

Text references. The resource-based approach is covered in Chapter 10 of your Study Text.

Top tips. To earn good marks for this question, it is important to explain the resource-based approach in sufficient detail. A brief discussion of its main features is insufficient. An answer might begin by explaining how a resource-based approach to strategy development differs from any other approach (such as developing strategy to meet changes in the business environment and exploit emerging opportunities). Since the question is about developing strategy, it will be helpful to mention to objective of sustainable competitive advantage. The resource-based approach should be described, with particular reference to the nature of resources and key resources in particular. Answers should also explain how key resources enable an organisation to develop core competences and how strategies should be developed to make the greatest use possible of these competences.

The question gives some useful items of information that you should ideally include in your answer. The company develops innovative products (one competence) at a fast pace (another competence). The Chief Executive states that there is a desire for the company to challenge itself and constantly stretch its capabilities. This is a feature of the resource-based approach: repeating this in your answer will earn one or two marks.

> **Easy marks.** Some marks can be earned simply by providing a description of the resource-based approach, so make sure that your explanation is clear.
>
> **Examiner's comment.** This question was generally poorly answered, mainly because candidates did not know enough about the resource-based approach.

Marking scheme

	Marks
Main features of resource-based approach, explained by comparison with an alternative approach to strategy development	2
Exploiting key resources to create competences that in turn are used to achieve sustainable competitive advantage	2
Nature of resources	2
Qualities of key resources: adding value, rarity, not imitable, not substitutable	2
Nature of core competences, with reference to Z Company	2
Continual challenge to stretch capabilities	2
Maximum marks available	12
Maximum attainable	10

A **resource-based approach** to developing business strategy focuses on the **resources within the organisation and the competences that they provide.** This approach differs from focusing initially on opportunities and threats in the business environment, and developing business strategies in response to environmental conditions.

With a resource-based approach, an organisation seeks to **gain competitive advantage by making use of its key resources and the competences** that those resources provide. Resources may be tangible, such as ownership of vital assets such as mineral resource, but they may also be intangible. Intangible resources may be the strength of a brand or reputation, intangible assets such as patent rights, or the skills and abilities of the work force.

The approach is based on the view that **key resources enable an organisation to develop competences that provide the foundation for gaining competitive advantage in the market.** In the case of Z Company, core competences exist in the development of innovative new products, and also the ability to develop them quickly. These competences presumably come from the existence of skilled and innovative employees, and a productive working environment that may be stimulated by a strong innovative culture and supportive management. Z Company may also continue to benefit from patent rights.

It has been suggested that for a resource-based approach to succeed in providing sustainable competitive advantage, the **resources must add value, be rare, must be difficult or impossible to imitate and also difficult or impossible to replace with a substitute.** These qualities are normally achievable more easily by intangible resources rather than tangible resources, which competitors are often able to buy or create through investment. In the case of Z Company a skilled and experienced team of product designers, working within an innovative culture and settled in their jobs, can provide a valuable and rare resource: competitors would find it difficult to establish a similar work force and culture of their own and human design skills are difficult to substitute with automation. Similarly, patent rights may possess the four key qualities.

To achieve sustainable competitive advantage with a resource-based approach, **key resources must be exploited to their full potential**, so that the organisation is able to offer desirable goods or services in a way that customers want and that is superior to the goods and services offered by competitors. The strategy is therefore concerned with identifying the best ways of making use of the key resources and core competencies.

The need for the company to challenge itself and constantly stretch its capabilities, as mentioned by the Chief Executive of Z Company, is therefore a critical aspect of the resource-based approach.

63 Competitor intelligence

Text references. Competitor intelligence is discussed in Chapter 13 of your BPP Study text.

Top tips. There are two main elements in the question: the type of competitor intelligence information required and the possible sources where it might be obtained. It would also be useful to introduce your answer by explaining briefly the reason for wanting to have this information, making reference to K Company in the question.

By taking an organised approach to the answer, and making sure that you deal with both parts of the question, it should be possible to construct an answer on the basis of general business awareness and common sense.

Easy marks. It should be a fairly simple task to identify the information about competitors that might be useful and possible sources. Make sure that you describe these in sufficient detail in your answer, and do not simply present a list in a brief bullet point style. The question, remember, is asking for a description, not simply identification.

Examiner's comment. Some candidates did very well on this question. However, a surprising number interpreted this question very broadly to mean not only the types of competitive intelligence information as the question intended but also to the broader environmental context , and so spent much unproductive time applying PEST and Five Forces analysis in a discussion of the general environmental context. Another weakness was that some candidates only described the types of information or the sources, but not both as required by the question.

Marking scheme

	Marks
Purpose of gathering customer intelligence information	1
Types of information: for each type of information, sufficiently described 1 mark	5
Sources of information: for each source, sufficiently described 1 mark	5
Maximum marks available	11
Maximum attainable	10

Information about competitors is very helpful for making strategic decisions, because business strategy should be directed towards the objective of achieving competitive advantage. This means being able to offer products or services in a way that customers find better (more attractive) than those offered by competitors. K Company requires information about competitors to decide whether to take the risk of entering the market in other regions of the country. The strength (or weaknesses) of existing competition will affect the decision.

The type of information that might be useful is as follows.

(a) K Company should establish the **identity of the competitors** in each region, and the size and resources of each of them (including trade names and reputation). If a regional market is dominated by one or two suppliers, it may be more difficult for K Company to establish a business than if there are many smaller competitors.

(b) It would also be useful to have information about the **nature of the products** and services offered by each of these competitors. This will help K to identify whether it can offer distinctive products or services that might be more attractive to customers.

(c) K Company designs and installs kitchens and also operates showrooms. Not all competitors may operate in the same way. For example, kitchenware designers may not act as installer or have their own showrooms. **Offering all services** may be a useful advantage for K over potential competitors.

(d) Information about the **apparent business strategies** of each competitor would be useful. For example, some companies may offer low prices, whereas others might offer differentiated products or services. K Company should be interested in whether there are any apparent gaps in the market that it can try to exploit.

(e)   Where possible, information should be obtained about the **profitability of competitors**. This might be easier to obtain for national companies than for small regional companies. Competitor profitability would help to indicate the financial strength of the competition, as well as the potential for profit for K Company.

(f)   It might be useful to find out **how competitors market their products and services**, and how much they appear to spend on marketing. This will help K to assess whether a carefully-planned marketing campaign might help it to gain a foothold in another region.

K Company might try to obtain the information itself, or might hire the services of an agency to do the work. The potential sources of information are as follows:

(a)   The **web sites** of competitor businesses. Competitors may be identified through use of a search engine and their web sites may provide useful information about products, services, prices and showroom locations and sizes.

(b)   **Annual report and accounts.** Some competitors may be required to publish or file financial accounts, which would be a useful source of information about sales and profitability.

(c)   There **may** be a **market research report** in existence about conditions in the kitchenware or home products industry. If so, this would be a source of much detail.

(d)   Searching through **national newspapers and magazines** and local newspapers and trade magazines might all produce some information of interest.

(e)   There may be a **business directory** that would provide the identities of other firms in the industry, and some information about them.

(f)   **Observation** can be a valuable source of market information. Researchers might visit a region and the showrooms of firms in the main towns of the region. Visits would help them to gain first-hand experience of the types of products on display, the quality of customer service and other aspects of competitors' business operations.

Most businesses selling consumer goods produce informative **product catalogues** and **price lists,** perhaps with details of discounts.

64 Y Corporation

> **Text references**. Porter's diamond is discussed in Chapter 12 of your BPP Study text.
>
> **Top tips**. The scenario here appears to be based on the Disney Corporation, and if you recognised this, it could have prompted some real-world insights you could have included in your answer. The question tested knowledge of a standard model, Porter's Diamond, but as usual you needed to apply it sensibly and consider the limitations to its use.

General

In the context of global competition, certain environmental influences are especially important. Porter's diamond suggests that there are inherent reasons why nations are competitive, and why specific industries within these nations achieve competitive success and profitability.

The national home base plays a big role in **securing competitive advantage** abroad. The home market contains environmental factors that the company operating overseas can build upon. In the case of the Y Corporation (Y), the home base is the USA. This is one of the strongest and most self sufficient economies in the world, and its cultural influences are spread globally.

Y has itself contributed to this influence with its particular brand of family entertainment. Whether or not this is an influence to be universally welcomed, the dominance of US culture nevertheless paves the way for companies like Y to enter overseas markets with relative ease and with huge resources to back them up.

Taking each of the elements of the diamond in turn:

Factor conditions

As referred to already above, the USA has vast resources. These include labour and skills, physical resources, a strong knowledge base and education system, and sophisticated capital markets. Its infrastructure is highly developed. The availability of resources (particularly labour) in the Far East must be confirmed.

Home demand

The demand for family entertainment at home in the US has developed into a huge market that is transferring overseas. The levels of customer service that are demanded in the US are very high, and the target market of children and their parents has become ever more sophisticated. Y will benefit from success in such a demanding environment, but it needs to be sure that customers in the home environment are representative of customers in the Far East.

Y has not just followed market demand however, but has helped to create it. The range of characters that it has developed, along with its theme parks, has helped to boost those demand levels. It has a unique product, brand image and reputation. This development will continue in the future.

Related and supporting industries

Ranging from catering and construction to film making and the application of technology, Y has a sound base of supporting industries in the US that could support it in any overseas ventures. However, the host government should also help to support the company with a suitable infrastructure.

Firm strategy, structure and rivalry

The market for theme parks in the US is a large and competitive one, with many parks for children and parents to choose from. Y, however, has a strong and unique brand image, and has become a household name to the extent that it dominates the family entertainment market. It has economies of scale in its operations that will help it to keep costs down. The presence of competition in the Far Eastern location must however be considered. The host government may be able to give information about the development of other attractions in the future.

Further information

Porter's diamond is a useful model when examining why Y Corporation has been successful in its home county. However, it is not a model which should be used to predict whether a company will be successful if it expands overseas. To make such a decision the directors should analyse the environmental conditions (political, economic, social, technological) in their target market and use them to decide what the opportunities and risks of establishing Y-land FE are, and therefore whether they should pursue the overseas expansion. Porter's diamond cannot provide this 'external' information.

65 XTX

Chapter reference. Chapter 12 for transaction costs and the theory behind this.

Top tips. You must be precise in your answer as transaction cost theory is quite specific. It looks at why firms exist and whether they should keep activities in house or outsource them. Any activity that is not a core competence should be looked at in case it could be outsourced.

Easy marks. This question relies on specific knowledge of transaction costing so you can get good marks if you know the theory but you won't otherwise.

Examiner comments. Overall performance was poor. Weaker answers did not refer to transaction cost theory and therefore couldn't address the requirements of the question.

Transaction cost theory looks at why businesses organise their activities in-house rather than contracting them out. The decision is made based on transaction costs. For instance, the costs of employing someone to write software (**the hierarchical approach**) against contracting for their services (**the market approach**) would be compared. The decision to contract out is complicated by the problems of uncertainty and bounded rationality. What this means is, contracts become too complicated to manage over time and so they would be brought in-house. Asset specificity needs to be considered as some assets are only useful in a particular organisation setting. These are specialised assets such as skills and site-related assets e.g. Airline kitchens.

XTX Company (XTX) faces increasing manufacturing overhead costs, and is considering outsourcing manufacturing activities to L where costs are lower.

XTX can use transaction cost theory to make the decision on whether or not to continue to manufacture sportswear and training shoes.

XTX needs to review its resources for manufacturing sportswear and training shoes, with a focus on how the best economic efficiency can be gained. The company needs to weigh up the advantages of asset specificity keeping activities in-house against the cost advantages of outsourcing activities that are not core.

XTX can choose between a hierarchy approach, and a markets approach.

The hierarchy approach would see XTX keeping assets in-house or employing staff directly, in other words internalising transactions. The policies and procedures of the company are used to control resources and their performance. XTX currently adopts the hierarchy approach in that it is currently organised as a vertically integrated organisation, doing as much as possible in-house, for instance, the design, manufacturing and retailing of its sportswear and training shoes.

XTX could choose the markets approach. Under this approach it would buy in the use of assets or contract for staff from outside. This involves an increased dependency on the market and as such the organisation will incur transaction costs. The Managing Director's consideration to outsource manufacturing reveals he is looking at a market solution. This assumes lower transaction costs by taking a markets approach.

The Managing Director must take into account the **costs of control** in addition to the unit cost of manufacturing sportswear. Therefore, he needs to include the transaction costs associated with performing a transaction with the companies to which the manufacturing is being outsourced. These costs of control arise out of the increased reliance on outside manufacturers and are costs connected with managing the transactions and operating under the terms of the contract.

XTX may benefit from having access to cheaper manufacturing by outsourcing, but there are some potential problems in outsourcing of which XTX should be aware of. The managing director must establish if there are likely to be any problems of, for example, control, security and asset specificity. He should guard against exposing the company to a single supplier where possible. D should also consider XTX's corporate reputation in dealing with manufacturers in L country. There may be a danger of counterfeiting when XTX loses control over the production of the licensed football and rugby strips. D should also consider the impact of possible currency fluctuations on the cost.

66 JKL Bank

> **Text reference.** Transaction cost theory is covered in Chapter 11 of your Study Text.
>
> **Top tips.** This is a fairly straightforward question presuming you are familiar with transaction cost theory, but make sure you do apply this to the scenario you are provided with.
>
> **Easy marks.** Describing what transaction cost is can earn you some easy marks here.

Transaction cost theory states that when an outsourcing decision is to be made the following two solutions must be compared:

- The hierarchy (in-house) solution
- The market (outsourced) solution

To apply this theory the Head of Insurance at JKL bank will therefore need to prepare a costing for both the in-house provision of the Customer Contact Centre (CCC) and the market cost of the provision of this service (ie outsourcing). The relative costs can then be compared and taken into account when deciding whether or not to outsource.

To calculate the cost of the existing internal CCC the Head of Insurance will have to consider all of the internal costs that are associated with running the CCC. This will include:

- The direct costs involved with employing the staff of the CCC
- Overheads associated with the employees (office space, utilities, human resources and so on)
- Cost of the assets used by the CCC (desks, telephones, computers and so on)
- Other internal costs (IT support, training and so on)

The market cost, ie the cost of outsourcing, consists of the transaction cost which is the amount that JKL bank will pay to the outsourcer for the provision of the service, and the external control costs associated with this.

For JKL Bank, the overall transaction cost is likely to be fairly low, as it is usually cheaper to outsource standard, generic processes such as customer service. Other factors that point to a relatively low transaction cost are as follows.

- The equipment required for a CCC is standard office equipment and so the level of asset specificity is low.

- The work of the CCC is carried out by telephone and as such could be provided from anywhere. The level of location specificity is therefore low.

- The human asset specificity will be high initially as the outsource provider will have to accumulate knowledge relating to the JKL bank such as the insurance policies they offer, processes related to making claims, changes to policies and renewals as well as understanding the systems used by JKL. This will however reduce as the outsourcer becomes more familiar with the work.

- Finally, the temporal specificity is likely to be quite high as in the CCC the telephone calls from customers will have to be answered, presumably with a certain number of rings. A switch to email would reduce this but it may not be feasible to ask customers to contact the department in this way.

The other element of the market cost is the external control costs that will be incurred. This could be large and must be carefully controlled. These costs include:

- Costs of negotiating the contract

- Legal costs in drafting the contract

- Enforcing costs, such as setting up service level agreements and managing the relationship between JKL and the outsource provider on an ongoing basis.

Once these two costings have been prepared, the Head of Insurance at JKL Bank can use this information to provide a financial basis on which he can make his decision.

However, he must remember that financial viability is only part of the picture. Other factors such as reputational damage if customers are not happy with the service provided by the outsource partner and the effect of related redundancies on the morale and motivation of the remaining staff at the bank must also be taken into account.

67 CN

Text reference. Chapter 13 covers Porter's five forces.

Top tips. *Michael Porter's* five competitive forces should be well known to students. It is very important to understand their purpose, to be able to apply them to a situation and to know how the results of any analysis should be interpreted.

Easy marks. Easy marks could be gained by identifying the five forces. To gain the bulk of the marks however it was necessary to set out how, in general terms, they could be used to assess industry competition and then to set out in relation to each force the market circumstances which would tend to increase or reduce the strength of that force, with intelligent application to the confectionery industry.

The level of competition and therefore rate of profit which CN Company and its joint venture partner will face in Country K will depend on the strength of the competitive forces at work in that country.

Michael Porter identified **five market factors**, or forces, that will drive the competitive position of a given supplier in a given industry.

These five forces, taken together, will provide an overall assessment of CN Company's competitive position in Country K and its long-term profitability. Entry into Country K would be suggested if, overall, the five forces were found to be weak and the prospective returns high.

Taking each force in turn:

(a)   Threat of market entry

CN is considering **entry to the market** via a joint venture with a partner established in the confectionery business in Country K. This approach may facilitate its entry and enable it to overcome barriers to entry (for example, access to distribution channels, how easy it is for other firms to enter and erode profits) and commence operations relatively quickly.

(b)   Substitutes

Substitutes are products that differ from the product in question but provide similar satisfactions. In the case of confectionery, substitutes might include savoury snacks, light food snacks, fruit, cereal bars and other healthy options. CN Company could use the experience of its partner to assess the importance of such substitutes.

(c)   Customers' bargaining power

Customers will be looking to achieve lower prices or to obtain a higher quality confectionery product. If they have the power, through number or relative size, to get what they want they will force down the profitability of the firms in the confectionery industry.

The strength of the threat from the **bargaining power of customers** will depend on a number of factors.

(i)   **The level of differentiation amongst confectionery manufacturers.** If they all produce the same product, customers have less choice and therefore less power.

(ii)   **The cost to the customer of switching from one supplier to another** – Since CN Company is a manufacturer, its customers are likely to be retailers in which case they will exercise considerable power via their ability to switch easily between suppliers.

(iii)   **Whether a customer's purchases from the industry represent a large or small proportion of the customer's total purchases**. In this case retailers could represent a material threat if – as in the UK – a small number of very large retailers account for a substantial proportion of confectionery sales and are in a position to drive a very hard bargain in relation to the prices paid to the manufacturers. CN Company could seek to counter such a threat by investment in their brands.

(d)   Suppliers' bargaining power

Suppliers can influence the profitability of a firm by exerting pressure for higher prices .

The **bargaining power of the supplier** depends on a number of factors.

(i)   The number of suppliers in the industry
(ii)   The importance of the supplier's product to the firm
(iii)   The cost to the firm of switching from one supplier to another.

Given the widely available nature of the ingredients needed for confectionery production it is unlikely that suppliers to CN Company will be limited and hence the power of suppliers is likely to be modest.

(e)   Competitive rivalry

The intensity of competitive rivalry within the confectionery industry will be driven by the number of companies operating in this sector, the anticipated industry growth rates and the profitability of the industry as a whole. If the market is dominated by multinationals with strong brands and there is modest growth and profitability levels this market will not be attractive to CN Company. If at the other extreme a large number of small local suppliers dominate the market place, the margins being achieved are substantial and there are no well established brands the market opportunities for CN Company could be significant.

68 Corporate appraisal

Text references. Chapter 13.

Top tips. This question is fairly general, and there is not a great deal of information about the specific strengths and weaknesses of the company or the opportunities and threats facing it. Do not neglect the second part of the question, on what such a corporate appraisal would involve.

Easy marks. These are available for knowing what SWOT means and for a definition of corporate appraisal.

Examiner's comment. This question was generally well answered, but some candidates repeated points in their answers.

Marking scheme

	Marks
Definition of corporate appraisal	1
1 mark per aspect of corporate appraisal (½ if not explained) to a maximum of 4:	4
Strengths	
Weaknesses	
Opportunities	
Threats	
Why undertaken (1 mark per valid point, maximum 2)	2
What it involves (1 mark per valid point, maximum 3):	
Internal data	
External data	
Match strengths to opportunities	$\underline{3}$
	$\underline{\underline{10}}$

Purpose of corporate appraisal (SWOT)

A corporate appraisal is 'a critical assessment of the strengths and weaknesses, opportunities and threats in relation to the internal and environmental factors affecting an entity in order to establish its condition prior to the preparation of the long term plan' (CIMA). PRC Company is adopting a more formal approach to developing strategy, and a corporate appraisal is a first step. It is part of the strategic analysis of the organisation's strategic position – the first part of a rational planned approach.

Internal appraisal: strengths and weaknesses

A strengths and weaknesses analysis will identify two things.

(a)   The areas of the business that have **strengths** that should be exploited by suitable strategies
(b)   The areas of the business that have **weaknesses** which need strategies to improve them.

The strengths and weaknesses analysis is internal to the company and intended to shape its approach to the external world. For instance, the identification of shortcomings in skills or resources could lead to a planned acquisition programme or staff recruitment and training.

External appraisal: opportunities and threats

An **external appraisal** is required to identify profit-making opportunities that can be exploited by the company's strengths and also to anticipate environmental threats against which the company must protect itself. The external appraisal is the **opportunities and threats** part of SWOT analysis.

PRC Company would need to identify opportunities and threats in order to:

(a)   Develop strategies to deal with them

(b)   Assess the feasibility of any strategies proposed

(c)   Check the appropriateness of the firm's current strategies

What would be involved?

To carry out a SWOT analysis, PRC Company would need to **collect data,** both internal (strengths and weaknesses) and external (opportunities and threats).

Internal data might include production reports, staff appraisals, customer feedback, quality control issues and management accounts.

External data about customers and competitors includes published accounts and annual reports, market research reviews and reports (eg *Economist Intelligence Unit);* investment analysts' notes; industry experts and consultants; suppliers, shared customers, the competitor's marketing strategy; public communications (magazines, journals and newsletters) and the internet.

A great deal can be gleaned from using one's own company as a model, and adjusting it for significant differences in competitors' businesses. For example, a firm might make some sub-components in-house, whereas a competitor might buy them on the open market.

The ultimate aim is to **match strengths to opportunities**. Specifically, in the case of PRC Company, its strength is the fact that it is an established firm (twenty years) with products that, we assume, are trusted. A potential threat might be online retailers aggressively cutting price. This presents an opportunity for PRC Company to develop an online presence, but capitalise on its established brand.

69   FF Supermarket 5/11 qu 1

Text references. Porter's five forces are covered in Chapter 13 of your Study Text.

Top tips. Answers should demonstrate an understanding of the five forces in Porter's model, but a simple description of these is insufficient. The question asks about the contribution of the model for the assessment of the attractiveness of the industry to firms operating within it, and an overall explanation of the purpose or use of the model should be provided. The question also clearly invites answers to comment on the application of the model – and each of the five forces – to the supermarket business.

Easy marks. Make sure that your answer demonstrates an understanding of the five forces in the model.

Examiner's comment. Answers were of mixed quality. Errors fell into two main categories; candidates who lacked an understanding of the Five Forces model and those who demonstrated an understanding of the model but did not apply it adequately to the supermarket industry.

Marking scheme

	Marks
Explanation of the usefulness of the model in assessing the strength of industry competition and profitability for industry participants	2
Discussion of each of the five forces, with some reference to the supermarket industry in each case: up to 2 marks for each of the forces	10
Maximum marks available	12
Maximum attainable	10

Nature of the Five Forces model

Porter's Five Forces model identifies five factors or forces that operate within any industry, and the strength (or weakness) of these forces affects the nature of competition, profitability and therefore the attractiveness of the industry to participants or potential new entrants. The model can therefore be used by the Board of FF to assess the attractiveness (and potential profitability) of operating in the supermarket industry.

Assessing the attractiveness of the supermarket industry using the model

Each of the five forces contributes to the strength of competition and potential for profit in the industry.

Existing competition. The rivalry between existing direct competitors in the industry affects the strength of competition. In the supermarket industry, it is probable that rivalry between the major companies is very strong. If so, the supermarkets will compete strongly on price and profit margins will be low. It may also be difficult to increase market share due to the actions of competitors.

Threat of new entrants. Profit margins in an industry may also be affected by the threat that new entrants will come into the industry, attracted by the profit potential. If barriers to entry are low and firms can enter the market fairly easily and for relatively small cost, new entrants would be attracted by high profits margins. As more firms enter the market, prices and profit margins would fall. If barriers to entry are high, the threat from new competitors is low. In the supermarket industry, the threat from new entrants may be low, due to the high cost of establishing a new chain of supermarkets.

Bargaining power of suppliers. When suppliers to firms in the industry are powerful and have strong bargaining power, they are able to demand high prices for their products. Firms within the industry may not be able to pass on high prices of supply to their customers, and profit margins would therefore be limited. If suppliers have weak bargaining power, firms in the industry should be able to negotiate attractive prices for their purchases, thereby increasing profitability. In the supermarket industry, suppliers probably have weak bargaining power, because supermarkets are major customers and are able to switch to different suppliers if they do not like the prices that any supplier is asking for.

Bargaining power of customers. In a similar way, the bargaining power of customers can be an important force in an industry. Powerful customers are able to demand lower prices or better terms of supply, and profit margins would be low. When customers are weak, because they rely on the supplier for their goods, firms are able to charge higher prices and earn a higher profit margin. In the supermarket industry, the strength of the bargaining power of customers lies in their ability to switch to an alternative supermarket company for their purchases.

Availability of substitutes. When there are readily-available substitutes to the products or services provided by an industry, profitability is restricted because customers can switch to buying gods in the different industry. In the case of supermarkets, substitutes may be local small convenience stores or an independent on-line supplier. If supermarkets raise their prices there may be a risk that more customers will use a local store rather than travel to the supermarket.

Conclusion

The analysis of industry competition for the Board of FF will help the Board to assess the strength of competition in the industry and the potential for profitability. This should assist the Board in preparing its strategic plans for the future.

70 F Company

Text references. Chapter 10.

Top tips. This question is rather puzzlingly worded. The requirements of either part (a) or part (b), if taken in isolation, are clear enough. However, when they are combined it is difficult to see where one ends and the other begins: part (a) asks, effectively for the benefits and drawbacks of the policy suggested by G, while part (b) asks for a comparison of the views of G and P. The problem would appear to be avoiding in the answer to part (b) repetition of much that was said in the answer to part (a).

We think the best way to resolve this conundrum is to note carefully the last sentence of paragraph three of the scenario and to build an answer to part (b) around a comparison between the positioning and resource-based approaches to strategy. We can then relegate the formal, top-down model to a minor role as just one approach to a positioning-based strategy. **This confusion shows the importance of planning your answers carefully**. Read our advice on how to approach questions in the 'Passing P5' section in front pages to help you here.

You may care to note the way we have made reference to theorists in our answer: this sort of thing adds authority, but you have to get the names right! There were up to two marks for each benefit and each drawback in part (a). In part (b), there were a maximum of six marks each for key points on the positioning approach, and the resource based approach.

We have included more points in our answer than you need for a good answer. Extra material is identified as alternative answers which you can use for revision.

Easy marks. Candidates who have a basic knowledge of the rational model should find part (a) fairly easy to score a pass mark in.

(a)   <u>Benefits and drawbacks of a top-down approach to strategy</u>

The most comprehensive kind of formal, top down strategic planning is described by the **rational model** of strategic analysis, strategic choice and strategy implementation (the ACI model).

This is a logical and comprehensive approach, which attempts to consider all relevant information and options. It is primarily top-down, because of the need for high-level information and decision making: strategic decisions then 'cascade down' to lower levels of the organisation for implementation at a tactical and operational level.

<u>Benefits of top-down planning for F Company</u>

F Company seems to be particularly concerned about **developments in its immediate market environment**, having lost market share and to new entrants and failed to respond to customer demand for new products. Proper, continuing **environmental analysis** should be one of the most important features, therefore, of any system of planning introduced by the company. This would be a fundamental aspect of the rational model.

The rational model could bring other advantages to F Company.

(i)   It helps the organisation to take a **long view** and avoid short-termism while at the same time providing a sensible approach to the uncertainty of the future.

(ii)   It guides the **allocation of resources**.

(iii)   It **co-ordinates the activities** of the various parts of the organisation, ensuring the integration of operational management decisions into the higher strategy, the wider organisational context and longer term goals. This is another particular concern G has about F Company.

<u>Alternative answers</u>

(iv)   It sets a standard by which the actual performance of the organisation is **measured and controlled**.

(v)   It comforts providers of finance in particular and encourages **suppliers and employees** to think in terms of a long-term relationship.

(vi)   The process of forming strategy requires wide and complex input so it can have a beneficial effect on managers' **personal development** and awareness and can assist with management succession planning.

<u>Drawbacks of top-down planning methods</u>

The concept of formal processes for strategy generation and their limited success in practice has led to criticisms of both the rational model and the very idea of strategic planning as a separate business activity.

(i)   The formal approach encourages a sense of **omniscience and control** among planners: this is dangerous because of the **inherent unpredictability of the business environment**, which F Company has already had experience of. In practice, strategic thinking tends to be iterative and even muddled, with the various processes and stages being undertaken on an *ad hoc* basis. Moreover, many developments of strategic significance, or information about them, occur at **operational** level. Environmental uncertainty also tends to lead managers to adopt an approach of **bounded rationality**, satisfying themselves with solutions that are acceptable rather than ideal.

(ii)   There is an associated problem of **detachment**: planners' tendency to assume that strategy can be divorced from operations is inappropriate. Planners rarely have to implement the strategies they devise and feedback occurs too late or is badly filtered. Similarly, more junior managers, not directly involved in the planning process may misunderstand or resist the plans they are required to implement.

(iii)   The idea of the **learning organisation** has been applied to strategy on the basis that an organisation's strengths and weaknesses can be in constant flux and strategy should reflect current developments as a kind of learning process itself.

> #### Alternative answers
>
> (iv)   The formal approach is usually couched in terms of a **planning cycle** and this may extend for up to five years. Even a one year cycle is not responsive enough to changing circumstances.
>
> (v)   The **expense and complexity** of the formal approach are inappropriate for smaller businesses. Cost control is important for any organization and F Company, as an under-performing medium-sized business, must be particularly wary about spending on functions that do not have an immediate impact on the bottom line.
>
> (vi)   There has been much comment on the place of **strategic objectives**. A sociological perspective, such as that of *Cyert and March*, views the emergence of strategic objectives as the result of a **political** or **bargaining process** involving a variety of priorities and interest groups. Here we may remark that today the capitalist, free market philosophy seems more strongly established than ever and most Western business organisations acknowledge the creation of shareholder value as their primary objective.
>
> (vii) There is a view that great strategies should not really be rational at all, but should emerge from **inspiration and entrepreneurial talent**. *Brunsson* argues for the selection of a reasonable course of action from among a small number of choices, while *Ohmae* finds that good strategy is made by practical people who 'have an intuitive grasp of the basic elements of strategy'. The criticisms are directed less at planning in principle, than at the assumption that **planning can create strategies** as opposed to supporting strategic decisions, co-ordinating them and mobilising resources.

(b)   Alternative views of competitive advantage

Positioning approach

The views of G and P represent opposite sides in a current debate about the best way to approach strategy. The rational model is only the most formal of several approaches to a strategic method that is based the process of **adapting the organisation to its environment**. This adaptive or **positioning-based strategy** approach, which pays great attention to markets, consumers and competitors, may be contrasted with the **resource-based approach**.

(i)   In many modern industries, the **rate of environmental change is too great** for effective positioning strategies to be developed. F Company's experience seems to bear this out. The rate of economic and social change brought about by globalisation; shorter product lifecycles; rapid technological innovation; and changing consumer taste all make a measured response out of date before it can take effect.

(ii)   **Positioning advantages cannot be sustained in the long term**. Advantageous product market positions are **too easy to copy** to last long and more rapid product lifecycles erode initial advantage. F Company is suffering from the efforts of agile new entrants to its industry.

(iii)   It is more difficult to **adapt the organisation** than to **adopt a new environment**. The positioning approach may require significant change within the firm, which is difficult to achieve. It may be easier to move to a market environment that suits existing arrangements, skills, culture and capabilities.

Resource based approach

The resource based approach to strategy emphasises the **possession of scarce resources** and **core competences** by the organisation. Strategy, it is suggested, consists of exploiting such resources and core competences in order to gain competitive advantage. This approach lies behind the growing practice of **outsourcing**: the organisation concentrates its efforts on those parts of its operations that no other organisation can perform for it.

Resources may be obvious things such as favoured access to a particular **raw material** or a piece of legally protected **intellectual property**; they may also take less tangible forms, such as a well–known **brand**. F Company may be able to utilize these ideas by emphasizing **quality** or **innovation** in its future operations.

It is important to realise that it is possible to acquire or develop new competences, but this takes time. The possession of a particular advantage thus constitutes a competitive advantage but its validity may decline if other firms develop equivalent capabilities.

Competences must therefore be developed and kept up to date on a continuing basis. *Johnson and Scholes* define core competences as those that both **outperform competitors** and are **difficult to imitate**.

The resource-based approach is not without its difficulties.

(i)   Core competences are **difficult to identify and assess**: a wrong appraisal could lead to the loss of wider competence or source of advantage by misdirected outsourcing.

(ii)   Attempts to apply core competences (or other resources) widely across a range of markets and operations may make the firm **vulnerable to more focused, single market operations**.

(iii)   The emphasis on unique resources is reminiscent of the 'product orientation' decried by marketing experts: competitors who are more in touch with **market requirements** may be more successful. On the other hand, a strategy based on a sequence of unique products, as in the pharmaceutical industry, can be successful.

(iv)   **Investors** may or may not be convinced by the resource based view. Where there is a clear, identifiable and credible strategy, they may well maintain their support. However, a strategy based on exploiting existing markets may be more intuitively acceptable.

(v)   The competence approach seems to support ideas such as cross-functional, activity based management, team working and the use of network structures both within the organization and in its relations with suppliers and customers. However, the need to safeguard core competence capability against erosion by staff turnover and direct sharing of know-how may lead to a **perceived need for close control of activities** and narrow limits on outsourcing.

71   Porter's diamond and PEST

Text references. Chapter 12 covers Porter's Diamond and PEST.

Top tips. You need a good knowledge of Porter's Diamond for Part (a), and you need to apply common sense, because there is not much information given in the scenario. Don't just pluck arguments out of nowhere – if they are based on assumptions, however, hypothetical, explain and justify them.

Part (b) is more straightforward. It asks for an appropriate framework or model, and because the scenario is light on information, a general framework such as PEST is probably the most suitable. You could have used Porter's Five Forces too.

Easy marks. In Part (b) you can earn some easy marks for explaining the components of PEST.

Examiner's comment. Generally there was a strong performance in Part (a). Weaker answers tended to know the dimensions of Porter's Diamond but were not then able to develop their answers to explain the various dimensions in the context of the scenario. A few candidates used Porter's five forces as the basis for their answers, hence did not score any marks. Other candidates did not read the question or scenario sufficiently carefully and referred to companies in the wrong country. In Part (b) candidates who used Porter's Five Forces rather than PEST did not score as highly.

Marking scheme

		Marks
(a)	Listing the key determinants in Porter's diamond, ½ mark each -2	
	Factor conditions:	
	Basic factors less relevant – 1	
	Advanced factors – relate to 'new' industry – 4	
	Demand conditions – nature of market – 2	
	Strategy, structure and rivalry – 1 mark per valid point, maximum 3	
	Supporting industries, clusters – 1 mark per valid point, maximum 2	
	Other valid (1 mark)	
	Maximum	15
(b)	3 marks per PEST factor explained point (1 if not explained) to a maximum of 10	10
		25

(a)   Sources of competitive advantage

S Company could usefully use Porter's Diamond to assess the potential advantages that its competitors from PP Country enjoy. There are four key determinants which might give PP Country an edge:

- Factor conditions
- Demand conditions
- Related and supporting industries
- Firm strategy, structure and rivalry

Factor conditions

Resource factors can be split into two categories: basic factors and advanced factors.

Basic factors – Basic factors include natural resources, climate and the availability of cheap semiskilled or unskilled labour.

These basic factors are usually inherent in a country, but they cannot create a sustainable competitive advantage for a nation because they are widely available. In the context of the consumer electronics industry in which S Company operates, basic factors will not play a significant role. The demand will be mostly for skilled labour, and the need for natural resources is not great.

Advanced factors – Whereas basic factors are usually inherent in country, advanced factors have to be developed. They are associated with the scientific and technological infrastructure of a country and include a **highly educated workforce** who can use the modern production technology an investor may require, as well as good communications links. These communication links may be **digital communications** (such as internet and broadband), as well as **physical links** such as the road network.

The fact that companies in PP Country have already made inroads into the markets in D Country suggests that PP Country has some of these advanced factors. Unlike basic factors they can help a nation create a **sustainable competitive advantage**. Therefore, education and communication factors are two key factors for S Company to consider in its analysis of the competition.

Capital can also be an important advanced factor. For example, it is possible that the Government of PP Country is providing capital to improve its infrastructures and communications networks. Private investors from other countries may also see PP Country as a promising market.

Demand conditions

A **tough domestic market** is an important element in producing competitiveness. If customers in PP Country demand high standards in the goods they purchase, producer firms in PP are likely to produce **high quality, innovative goods** in order to meet domestic customer demand. This is likely to help these firms be competitive on the international market.

However, because the market for consumer electronic components is global, the domestic demand conditions may not be as important in this industry as some others.

Firm strategy, structure and rivalry

Firm strategy and structure – The **way in which firms are created, organised and managed** in PP Country could have a significant impact on its companies' competitiveness. For example, if the business environment encourages small, local business (for example, through beneficial tax regimes) the companies may be less able to adapt to a less friendly business environment in another country such as D Country.

Another factor that is sometimes important when a company wishes to break into an overseas market is **cultural aspects** of business. **Management structures, management styles** and **work ethics** vary significantly between countries. While some purchasers in D Country may not be concerned who they buy their components or products from, others, conscious of their image, may wish to source only from reputable suppliers with responsible attitudes to the workforce.

Workers' attitudes to the consumer electronics industry, and to multinational companies, could be important here. PP Country's firms are likely to be competitive if they are considered prestigious, and is therefore attractive to the better-educated people in the country.

Rivalry among existing firms – The nature and extent of any existing rivalry in the consumer electronics industry in PP Country is also important. Porter argues that a strong domestic rivalry and the quest for competitive advantage within a nation can help organisations become more competitive on a global scale.

One particularly important aspect of this is that **rivalry and competition spurs innovation**. If PP Country provides an environment which encourages innovation, this could be a potential threat to S Company in such a fast moving industry.

<u>Related and supporting industries</u>

Supporting clusters – The existence of a set of strong **related** and **supporting industries** is important to the competitiveness of firms.

For example, if some companies in PP Country can produce the component parts more cheaply than D Country, other PP Country companies may be able concentrate on the end products (mobile phones, laptops) which they can in turn produce and sell more cheaply.

<u>Government's role</u>

Many governments are looking to **encourage the development of key clusters**, where a region becomes associated with a particular industry. If PP Country has already started to develop a consumer electronics industry cluster this could be a very important factor in giving it a competitive edge

The Government in PP Country can also play a more general role in encouraging growth of new industries, either indirectly (for example, by **investing in infrastructure**, or **higher education**) or directly (for example, by offering **subsidies to foreign investors**).

<u>The diamond as a whole</u>

Although the diamond highlights four key determinants which could affect the competitiveness of companies in PP Country, it is important that S Company looks at all four of them together. All four of the determinants need to be present, because it is the combination of all of them which develops competitive advantage. The diamond does not guarantee success for any organisation in this industry operating in the country.

(b)   <u>Assessing the external environment using a model/framework</u>

PEST is a model for analysing the wider environment in which an organisation operates. PEST covers four headings: political-legal, economic, social and technological and is sometimes expanded to include legal, environmental and ethical matters.

GR should use PEST to look at the wider environment in NN Country to consider factors such as the political environment, economy and available technology that would affect any investment before making a decision to invest. So GR needs to ask what information should be collected as part of the PEST analysis.

Political-legal environment. This includes any laws in NN Country such as contract law, employee law, customer protection legislation and regulation of industry via competition law. Customers in NN Country may be poorer and have less to spend on electronic goods relative to DD Country. **Competition regulation or tariffs** may inhibit overseas imports or conversely positively encourage them. This heading also consists of the political environment of NN Country which includes internal stability, international relations and state involvement in the economy.

Economy. GR needs to consider the rate of growth of the economy in NN Country and internal demand for goods and services that would help or hinder its brand. If the economy is entering recession, GR may still wish to enter the NN market but will have to keep an eye on margins and heightened competition. In times of boom, S Company must try to identify the level of demand and plan to meet this. **Inflation, unemployment, taxation** and the **availability of credit** are all factors GR must consider carefully.

Social and cultural environment. Typical social and cultural trends that GR may wish to consider include the number of women entering the workforce, rising standards of living, values and beliefs held and the population **split between the sexes.** These trends affect the type and availability of customers and their potential spending power. In general, most consumers of electronic gadgets are men, particularly in less developed countries, but if the attitudes within a country change, there is increased potential for an untapped market of economically active women.

Attitudes such as **patriotism** may affect consumers' willingness to buy from foreign companies.

Technological. Although last in the acronym T for technological is the most important factor. GR needs to find out how developed the country is in terms of technology to determine **whether there is a market for its goods**. This is particularly true of laptops and MP 3 players. In the case of mobile phones, however, an undeveloped country may not have the infrastructure for landlines, so that mobile phones are a necessity.

How widespread is internet use? Can sales be made over the internet or would a bricks and mortar presence be required? What is the transport infrastructure like, and how would the goods get to the customer or point of sale?

72 Strategic models

Text references. Chapter 12 has good material to help you answer part (a) of this question. Part (b) refers to national culture which is explained in Chapter 5.

Top tips. The second paragraph in the question explains what you need to do in part (a). Whatever models you choose must provide data on the **external environment and competition** in L country. An obvious choice is PEST to analyse the environment and one of the models looking at competition such as Porter's Five Forces should cover that aspect of the question. You need to explain briefly why you have chosen the models to analyse W's strategy. There are lots of opportunities to earn marks here by explaining and applying the two models. As a rule of thumb, you should aim to earn two good points for each PEST factor and one or two for each of the Five forces. That means write a sentence or two but not a long paragraph on each! **Remember to explain and apply**.

Part (b) dwells on **cultural differences** which arise **between countries**. Thus this needs you to answer using theory that refers specifically to **national cultural differences** rather than theories of culture in organisations. A good model to use here is Hofstede's model of cultural differences between countries. Try to list each dimension of the model separately and explain why these may matter to W. Again there should up to two marks on offer for each dimension.

Easy marks. As is often the case, a little theoretical knowledge will earn you the easy marks in this question.

Examiner's comments. The main issue for a number of candidates was that they only used **one** strategic management framework rather than **two** as required. In part (b), common errors were to discuss culture in general terms without referring to *Hofstede* or applying it to the business. Some candidates wrote about organisational culture instead of international culture comparisons.

(a)   Evaluating strategy using models/frameworks to explain key external environmental and competitive factors

PEST is a model for analysing the wider environment in which an organisation operates. PEST covers four headings: political-legal, economic, social and technological and is sometimes expanded to include legal, environmental and ethical matters. *[The examiner mentioned these latter matters briefly]*.

W should use PEST to look at the wider environment in L country to consider factors such as the political environment, economy and available technology that would affect any investment before making a decision to invest. So W needs to ask what information should be collected as part of the PEST analysis.

Political-legal environment. This includes any laws in L such as contract law, employee law, customer protection legislation and regulation of industry via competition law. There may be **minimum wage laws** affecting the cost of labour relative to F country. **Competition regulation** may inhibit foreign investment or conversely positively encourage it. This heading also consists of the political environment of L country which includes internal stability, international relations and state involvement in the economy.

Economy. W needs to consider the rate of growth of the economy in L and internal demand for goods and services that would help or hinder its brand. If the economy is entering recession, W may still wish to invest but will have to keep an eye on margins and heightened competition. In times of boom, W must try to identify the level of demand and plan to meet this. **Inflation, unemployment, taxation** and the **availability of credit** are all factors W must consider carefully.

Social and cultural environment. Typical social and cultural trends that W may wish to consider include the number of women entering the workforce, rising standards of living, values and beliefs held and the population split between the sexes. These trends affect the type and availability of labour and the potential spending power of the customers for the clothing who are presumably women. **So there are two aspects to this analysis which are the composition of the workforce and the nature of consumers**. In turn these will be reflected in the attitude to working for foreign companies and buying from foreign companies.

Technological. W needs to find out what technology is available in L that would affect the manufacturing and sale of its clothing. If factories have suitable advanced manufacturing processes then W would be able to use these otherwise it would have to bring in its own technology and set up its own plant. Are sales done over the internet or would W have to sell the clothing through shops or catalogues? What transportation is needed and how would the clothes get to the point of sale?

Porter's Five Forces considers the specific market or industry for a business. The five forces are the threat of new entrants to the industry, the threat of substitute products or services, the bargaining power of customers, the bargaining power of suppliers and rivalry between current competitors in the industry. **W would use this analysis to review the clothing industry in L before it makes the decision to invest.** As W is seeking to escape a market with strong competition it would not wish to enter another market under the same conditions.

Threat of new entrants. If W looks at itself as a new entrant then it would consider how easy it is to break into the market. Factors to consider include the strength of competitive retaliation from existing firms and the technology it would need to compete in the market.

Threat of substitutes. Are there products which exist in another industry that would compete for disposable income with women's clothing in the industry W operates in? If there are strong threats from substitutes then W may wish to reconsider a decision to invest.

The bargaining power of customers. W needs to consider three main factors: how similar products are in its industry, the cost of customers going from one supplier to another and the proportion of total purchases by a customer that are spent on clothes. These all affect the bargaining power of customers relative to W.

The bargaining power of suppliers. Suppliers can influence the profitability of a firm by exerting pressure for higher prices or by reducing the quality of the goods and services they supply. W should investigate the number of suppliers in the industry, the importance of the products supplied to it and any costs of switching suppliers.

Current competitive rivalry in the industry. W needs to look at the number of competitors in L in the clothing market. Fierce competition will drive down profits if the market isn't growing and make it less of an attractive prospect especially if there are high costs of advertising and promotion and keen pricing.

(b)   <u>Why W needs to take account of cultural differences when managing the new operation in L</u>

Country culture can have a significant impact on how operations are run in L. W needs to be aware at least of cultural norms regarding women, religion and status in L that will affect how employees relate to each other, management of the business and relations with its customers and suppliers. Language is a possible barrier requiring language training by W's managers. W also needs to consider the educational standards of the local workforce and adapt its training to accommodate this.

Hofstede devised a model of organisational culture which explains **work-related cultural differences**. He used five dimensions on which cultures differ. These are power distance, uncertainty avoidance, individuality/collectivity, masculinity/femininity and time orientation.

Power distance measures the extent to which the unequal distribution of power is accepted. So in a high power distance culture, the sharing of power is more unequal and subordinates accept greater control and less say over what they do. In low power distance cultures there is more participation in decision-making by all employees. W clearly needs to find out where organisations in L fit into this continuum especially in relation to its current business model and possibly modify its local operation accordingly.

Uncertainty avoidance denotes the extent to which security, order and control are preferred over ambiguity, uncertainty and change. Low uncertainty avoidance cultures welcome creativity and tolerate risk, dissent, conflict and deviation from norms more than high uncertainty avoidance cultures. W may need to tailor its current operations to suit the way the local workforce makes decisions.

Individuality/collectivity reflects the extent to which people prefer to live and work as individualists focussing on themselves primarily or as collectivists emphasising more the group or society. Where there is a high degree of individualism in the organisation, individual success in achieving the task is seen as more important than individual relationships. The organisation is largely impersonal.

For W this means the local organisation would need to think about how important individual achievement, relationships in the organisation and achievement of the task is. For instance, W needs to consider how staff are paid and whether it chooses to recognise unions.

Masculinity/femininity measures the extent to which social gender roles are distinct. High masculinity denotes cultures where roles are clearly differentiated and masculine qualities such as assertiveness, competition and decisiveness are dominant. Low masculinity cultures value feminine values of consensus and focus on relationships. Again W needs to understand how local norms would affect its management of the local business and educate its managers to expect possible differences.

Time orientation. This is the extent to which people expect rapid feedback on decisions, evaluation and promotion. Again, W need to look at how their existing ways of working would suit those in L country and modify them if necessary. For instance, time orientation may have an impact on the level of urgency expected from the management team.

In conclusion, Hofstede's model emphasises the importance of cultural and human factors. Many new developments fail because they fail to understand how cultures and organisations operate in a particular country.

73 VCR

Text references. Chapter 10 of your Study Text covers approaches to strategy.

Top tips. You need a good knowledge of the rational and emergent approaches to strategy to answer part (a). You should not have too much trouble with this if you are clear on the two approaches. Make sure that as well as describing the approaches you clearly state the difference between the two and how this would affect the development of strategy at VRC.

Part (b) asks you to discuss the strategic management models/frameworks that R could use in order to undertake an analysis of the strategic position of the VRC company. This will involve discussing mission and objectives, PESTEL, SWOT analysis and Porter's Value Chain and Five Forces models are all relevant.

Easy marks. In Part (a) a number of easy marks can be gained from describing the rational model. In Part (b) you can earn some easy marks for explaining the components of the various models that are used in strategic anlaysis.

(a)   Current approach

The current approach used to develop the strategy of VRC is described as 'unplanned, ad hoc and opportunistic'. This suggests that the organisation has been following an **emergent approach** to strategy development. This is where strategies emerge in an organisation without formal, deliberate prior planning. They develop out of the day to day routine activities of the organisation, and these strategies are not drawn up as separate activity.

For an organisation using an emergent approach to strategy the task of the strategic management will be to control these emergent strategies in the light of a broader insight into the business' capabilities.

Suggested approach

The business consultant is recommending a more formal, **rational approach** to strategy.

The rational approach is a planned and methodical way of looking at strategy and is significantly different from the ad-hoc method being used at present within VRC. The rational approach is a top-down approach involves three main steps: strategic analysis, strategic choice and strategy implementation and control.

An **analysis of current position** makes up the first step of the rational planning model. This involves considering the current mission and objectives of the organisation and carrying out a **strategic analysis** of the organisation (see part (b)). This provide an understanding of the organisation's internal strengths and weaknesses along with the external opportunities and threats in the wider environment.

The second stage, **strategic choice**, begins with the **generation of strategic options**. The analysis from stage 1 can be used to generate a variety of different options for consideration. The aim is to use the organisation's internal strengths to take advantage of market opportunities. Each option is then assessed to determine whether it would be feasible, suitable in light of the organisation's current position and acceptable to stakeholders of the organisation.

In light of this evaluation **strategy selection** will then take place to determine the best strategy for the organisation to follow. This will be heavily influenced by the values of the managers involved in this process.

The final stage of the rational model is the **implementation and control of strategies**. Implementation means that the strategy chosen will be embodied in a corporate plan and adopted by the organisation. From the corporate plan, the plans for the operations will be developed and the strategy will filter down from the top to the bottom of the organisation.

Although the implementation and control of strategy is listed as the final step, this is not quite true as the rational approach is an ongoing method where the control of the strategy will feed back into the strategic appraisal stage. This means that the newly implemented strategy will regularly be reviewed and the strategic position analysed to ensure that the strategy is working and that the objectives methods and plans are still relevant to the organisation.

Summary of differences in approach

The proposed rational method of developing strategy is therefore significantly different to the emergent approach that has traditionally been used to develop strategy within VRC. The main differences can be summarised as follows.

The proposed rational method is much **more formal and prescriptive** than the existing emergent approach.

The existing emergent approach involves taking small steps and as such has a fairly short-term emphasis compared to the rational model which has a much **longer-term approach** to strategy.

Emergent strategies come from the operations of the organisation and are developed as a reaction to the conditions faced by the organisation. This approach to strategy places operational managers at the heart of its development, in contract with the **top-down approach** taken by rational strategic planning. As a result, the rational approach can also be much **less innovative**.

These changes are clearly significant and not only will there be a fundamental change in approach to strategy, there is also likely to be a significant change to the entire culture of the organisation as a result.

(b)   Strategic analysis makes up part of the first stage of the rational planning model and is concerned with understanding the broad strategic position of the organisation. It involves analysing both the internal position of the organisation and the wider environment in which the organisation operates.

To carry out a strategic analysis of VRC, R should begin by carrying out an **internal appraisal** of the organisation. This should be followed by an analysis of the **external environment** in which the organisation operates. Then the internal appraisal and the external appraisal should be combined to form an overall **corporate appraisal** of VRC. A number of strategic models/frameworks can be used by R to help him achieve this. They are discussed below in context the stage of the strategic analysis where they would be used.

Internal appraisal

Internal appraisal involves looking at the internal processes and capabilities of the organisation. The following models can be used by R to help him carry out this analysis.

A **resource audit** allows the organisation to begin the process of determining its competencies by looking at the resources that is has available. Resources are classified into two key headings:

Basic resources, which are those resources which are similar to those held by the completion. Basic resources are easy to copy and so are unlikely to be a source of competitive advantage.

Unique resources are those which are not held by the competition and would be difficult to obtain or recreate. These resources are a key source of competitive advantage and the more of these an organisation possesses the stronger its competitive position is likely to be.

Porter's Value Chain can then be used to determine how well those resources are being used by the organisation, and how much value is being added after those resources have been acquired. The value chain is a model of value activities and the relationship between them. It consists of primary activities (inbound logistics, operations, outbound logistics, marketing and sales, and service) and support activities (firm infrastructure, human resource management, technology development, and procurement). Linkages occur between the elements of the value change and one element can affect the costs or effectiveness of other elements in that chain. The sum of the value added by these activities is shown in the value chain as the 'margin'. The greater the value added, the greater the margin. Value chain analysis can help the organisation to see where more value could be added if better use was made of the organisation's resources.

The findings from these models can be used to form a summary list of **strengths and weaknesses** which will be used later as part of the corporate appraisal section of strategic analysis.

External appraisal

The organisation operates within its external environment. This is made up of a number of factors that impact upon the organisation but cannot be directly affected by the organisation itself. Several models can be used to help R to analyse the external environment.

PEST/PESTEL analysis can be used to analyse the environment using a number of headings which summarise the main environmental factors that affect the organisation, namely Political; Economical; Social and Technical. The additional E and L have been added in more recent years to reflect the increased awareness for the Environment and to recognise Legal factors as a separate influence from those discussed under Political. The categories of PESTEL are interlinked in reality and any one development in the external environment could be analysed under several of the PESTEL headings to recognise the different influences it can have on an organisation.

Porter's Five Forces is a model which can be used to determine the profitability of the wider industry in which the organisation operates. This model summarises the level of threats faced by an organisation from the five key forces that influence the industry in which they operate. The five forces are: threat of new entrants; threat of substitute products; bargaining power of customers; bargaining power of suppliers; and the intensity of existing competition. The greater the threat posed by each of these forces, the more difficult it will be for an organisation to compete in that industry.

The Five Forces model can help an organisation to determine its strategy as it establishes the key drivers of profitability in the industry. So, to increase profitability, an organisation will need to develop a strategy that deals with these forces and, wherever possible, finds ways to reduce their impact.

The findings from these models can be used to form a summary list of **opportunities and threats** which will be used later as part of the corporate appraisal section of strategic analysis.

Corporate appraisal

The overall corporate appraisal takes the findings of the internal and external analysis and combines them to produce an overall picture of the strategic position of the organisation.

Anoher model that is often useful this stage is the **SWOT analysis**. The model enables the internal strengths and weaknesses and external opportunities and threats that have been identified in the previous stages to be considered and appraised to gain an understanding of the current strategic position of the organisation.

The SWOT analysis can help establish appropriate strategies, for example to see how weaknesses can be converted into strengths, how threats can be converted into opportunities, and how the strengths of the organisation can be used to take advantage of opportunities in the environment.

74 WFH Trading Company

Text references. The rational model is covered in Chapter 10.

Top tips. Part (a) tests your knowledge of the rational model. To score the highest marks you need to provide a detailed explanation of each of the stages, and in the correct sequence.

Part (b) requires you to discuss the benefits and disadvantages of the formal/rational approach. Make sure you relate your answer back to the given scenario to improve your chances of scoring well.

Easy marks. Up to two easy marks are available in part a) for providing a diagram of the formal/rational approach. This will then also provide you with a framework on which to develop the rest of your answer.

Examiner's comment. Part (a) of this question was generally well answered though there were a few poor answers. The main error stemmed from a lack of preparation and showed up in those candidates' answers that sought to bluff their way through with a series of broad generalisations that had little to do with the stages involved in the formal/rational approach to strategy. This kind of approach only wastes time and gains few, if any, marks. Future candidates are advised to avoid this approach.

The answer to part (b) of this question was generally well done. There were few significant errors with most candidates able to recall and explain a sensible set of both benefits and disadvantages of the formal/rational approach to strategy.

Marking scheme

		Marks
(a)	Diagram of formal/rational approach	Up to 2
	Determining mission	1
	Setting goals and objectives	1
	Internal analysis	Up to 2
	External analysis	Up to 2
	Corporate appraisal	Up to 2
	Strategic options	Up to 2
	Evaluation and choice	Up to 2
	Implementation and monitoring	Up to 2
	Maximum	<u>13</u>
(b)	Up to 2 marks for an explanation of formal/rational approach	
	1 mark per benefit up to a maximum of 6	
	1 mark per disadvantage up to a maximum of 6	
	Maximum available	<u>12</u>
	Maximum marks awarded	<u>25</u>

(a) The rational model is a planned and methodical way of looking at strategy in an organisation. The main stages involved in this are as follows:

Mission

The first step for WFH Trading Company (WFH) is to determine their mission. This is the overall purpose of the organisation; the reason why it exists. WFH must consider the expectations of stakeholder groups when setting the mission.

Goals and objectives

WFH will then need to break the mission down into more specific goals and objectives. It is important that the goals and objectives set are consistent with both the internal and external environment in which WFH operates. Therefore the next two steps involved detailed analysis of the organisation and its environment.

Position audit

WFH will need to assess the capabilities (ie strengths and weaknesses) of the company and its resources. A resource audit is a useful tool at this stage.

Environmental analysis

The competitive environment and the threats and opportunities that exist in the wider environment will be considered using tools such as Porter's Five Forces and the PESTEL model.

Corporate appraisal

The corporate appraisal brings together the results of the position audit and the environmental analysis. At this stage WFH will assess the overall importance of strengths, weaknesses, opportunities and threats (SWOT) in light of their mission and objectives.

Strategic option generation

At this stage WFH will use all the information they have obtained so far to generate a variety of options for consideration. The aim is to build on the capabilities of the business to exploit market opportunities.

Strategic options evaluation

WFH will next evaluate each of the options identified above to determine if it is feasible, suitable given the existing position of the firm, and acceptable to stakeholders. Techniques to assess and value options include financial criteria such as net present value (NPV) and scenario building for less certain environments. The fit of the option with WFH's mission and objectives also need to be considered.

Strategy selection

WFH will then choose a strategy according to the evaluation criteria above. The values of the managers involved in this decision will greatly influence which strategy is chosen.

Strategy implementation

WFH will next have to embed the chosen strategy into a corporate plan. This is then used to develop more specific plans for operations. Supporting policies and procedures will also be put into place.

Review and control

The suitability of the strategy will then be constantly monitored and evaluated to determine its likely success in helping WFH achieve its strategic objectives. The external environment also needs to be monitored for changes or for any unforeseen events. This information is fed back to the start of the rational model planning process and changes are made where necessary.

(b) The rational model represents the planned approach to strategy development. Strategies are developed using a logical process to make deliberate decisions. Employing this approach would have a number of benefits for WFH:

Identifies risk

Formal strategic planning would help WFH identify risks. They can then implement procedures to manage those risks to reduce their impact or likelihood of occurring or both.

Encourages creativity and initiative

Formal planning can encourages the management team to come up with new and fresh ideas.

Forces decision making

Formal planning links the strategy very closely to the environment therefore encouraging WFH to become more dynamic in responding to changes in their environment. It highlights the need to change and adapt, not to just stand still and survive.

Proactive approach

Linking WFH's strategy to its capabilities and the wider environment will encourage WFH to take a more proactive approach and avoid short term, reactive decisions. This should help WFH to become a cutting edge organisation.

Improved control

By using the rational model, WFH will break down their mission into specific operational targets. Explicit targets leads to better management control.

Consistency

Long-term, medium-term and short-term objectives, plans and controls can be made consistent with one another. They will all directly support the mission of WFH. This will greatly assist in the co-ordination of activities and will ensure any investment decisions fit the mission and support the long-term business needs.

Supports succession planning

Developing and communicating a formal strategy ensures everyone in the organisation knows what they are working towards. The whole management team will have a strong understanding of the strategy of WHF. Therefore, if a key member of this team, such as RF or JT, were to leave WFH the plans for the business will not be lost with them and the strategy can continue.

However, WFH may also experience a number of problems with implementing such a system of strategy development. These include:

Opportunity cost

Formal planning is a complex, costly and time consuming process. RF and JT will therefore need to consider the opportunity cost involved in spending time and resources on planning rather than on main business operations.

Too rigid

Formal planning can be viewed as a rigid and infrequent process. Given that environments are dynamic and subject to constant change, this may mean that the strategies developed using the rational model become quickly outdated and as such may fail. Environmental uncertainty also tends to lead managers to adopt an approach of bounded rationality, settling for solutions that are acceptable rather than ideal.

Loss of creativity and entrepreneurial spirit

The focus on systems, targets and plans has the potential to create a very bureaucratic process which can stifle creativity and hinder risk taking.

Goal congruence may not be achieved

A benefit of formal planning is to align all goals and objectives of the overall business, the different operational areas and the company's stakeholders. However, this may not happen in practice as it may not be possible to separate the goals of the company from the individual goals of the two owner managers.

MOCK EXAMS

CIMA – Managerial Level

Paper E2

Enterprise management

Mock Examination 1

You are allowed **three hours** to answer this question paper.
You are allowed 20 minutes reading time before the examination begins during which you should read the question paper, and if you wish, make annotations on the question paper. However, you are **not** allowed, **under any circumstances**, to open the answer book and start writing or use your calculator during this reading time.
You are strongly advised to carefully read the question requirements before attempting the question concerned.
Answer ALL FIVE compulsory question in Section A.
Answer the TWO compulsory questions in Section B.

DO NOT OPEN THIS PAPER UNTIL YOU ARE READY TO START UNDER EXAMINATION CONDITIONS

SECTION A – 50 marks

Answer ALL FIVE questions – 10 marks each

Question 1

Because of its failure to serve a sufficient number of clients and/or to provide a service of the required quality, Company J, a state-owned business has had its funding cut for three consecutive years. This is putting pressure on people throughout the organisation. Departments and individuals have been set more demanding targets and large-scale redundancies have recently been announced. This has resulted in considerable conflict. The service professionals are convinced that the marketing and sales department is responsible for the troubles of the organisation. This view is not shared by the marketing and sales people. They believe that the poor quality of service offered is the real reason for the decline in demand for services and for the resulting cuts in government funding. The effect of these differences between departments is one of declining co-operation between the direct service providers and the personnel in marketing and sales.

Of the more immediate concern to senior management, however, is the threat of industrial action by the trades unions determined to protect their members' jobs. Even individuals like the management accountant are finding themselves in conflict with departmental managers with whom they have previously enjoyed good relations. Requests for information on the costs of providing services are being met with hostility and the management accountant's job becomes more difficult by the day.

Required

Discuss the potential consequences arising from the conflict between the various departments and groups within SOB. **(10 marks)**

Question 2

Company Z is not working efficiently. The Board have decided that a new information system is required and have entered discussions with contractors. The management accountant has been appointed project manager. She is concerned about several problems that she can foresee arising during the lifetime of the project.

First, she is worried about the CEO's habit of vagueness and lack of precision in speech and writing. She fears that her responsibilities will be confused and the aims of the project unclear. She is also concerned about her personal working relationships, in that neither the Finance Director nor the Operations Director appears to be taking much interest in the project. She is not sure who she should report to, with what frequency and about what. Finally, she worries that proper control over the external contractors will not be exercised since she has had no contact with them: all discussions have been at Board level.

Required

Explain how the PRINCE2 system of project management could help the management accountant solve these specific problems. **(10 marks)**

Question 3

The CityGo Bus Company, formerly a regional operating division of a public corporation, has been acquired through a management buy out led by the general manger, Jim Ryan.

Competition will be intense as soon as the routes become fully competitive in January 20X3. The company has a number of weaknesses that have to be attended to immediately.

The most important of these is that its computing systems are totally integrated into the previous owner's systems. Internal management accounts are almost non-existent and most management reports were directed at the corporation's management team not at CityGo's management. It had never been possible to devolve budget responsibility down to key line managers in operations and maintenance.

The privatisation timetable means that CityGo has only a few months to set up new computer based systems.

The requirement will be for a project management process that can deal with tight timescales involving a complicated set of interrelated decisions and actions. CityGo management must realise that effective project planning and control need different management skills than those required to run operational processes.

This is the immediate requirement but in the longer term CityGo must put in place a strategy for managing information resources in ways which enable it to achieve a competitive advantage or at least competitive parity with other bus operators.

Required

Examine the attributes of a project management process and assess the range of project management tools and techniques which are available to CityGo to help achieve an efficient changeover to new financial systems.

(10 marks)

Question 4

NYO.com was established in February 2000. Since then, the company, which provides on-line financial advice, has experienced rapid growth and the management has not really had the time to get all management systems and procedures into place.

The company has asked you to look at the way in which the company deals with its disciplinary problems and procedures.

Required

Explain why NYO.com should have a formal disciplinary procedure.

(10 marks)

Question 5

It has been stated that an industry or a market segment within an industry goes through four basic phases of development. These four phases – introduction, growth, maturity and decline – each has an implication for an organisation's development of growth and divestment strategies.

The following brief profiles relate to four commercial organisations, each of which operate in different industries.

- **Company A.** Established in the last year and manufactures state of the art door locks which replace the need for a key with computer image recognition of fingerprint patterns.

- **Company B.** A biotechnological product manufacturer established for three years and engaged in the rapidly expanding animal feedstuffs market.

- **Company C.** A confectionery manufacturer which has been established for many years and is now experiencing low sales growth but high market share in a long established industry.

- **Company D.** A retailing organisation which has been very profitable but is now experiencing a loss of market share with a consequent overall reduction in turnover.

Required

Explain:

(a)   The concept of the industry life cycle.
(b)   The phase of development in which each of the industries served by the four companies is positioned.

(10 marks)

Total marks for Section A = 50

SECTION B – 50 marks

Answer BOTH questions

Question 6

Don Mac is the world's largest and best-known foodservice retailing group with more then 30,000 'fast-food' outlets in over 120 countries. Currently half of its restaurants are in the USA, where it first began fifty years ago, but up to 1,000 new restaurants are opened every year worldwide. Restaurants are wholly owned by the group (it has previously considered, but rejected, the idea of a franchising of operations and collaborative partnerships).

As market leader in a fiercely competitive industry, Don Mac has strategic strengths of instant global brand recognition, experienced management, site development expertise and advanced technological systems. Don Mac's basic approach works as well in Kandy or Kuala Lumpur as it does in Kansas; although the products are broadly similar, the menus are modified to reflect local tastes. Analysts agree that it continues to be profitable because it is both efficient and innovative. The group's vision is to be the worlds favourite through service, cleanliness and value, and it is following three main strategies:

- To achieve profitable growth by building on key strengths
- To 'delight' every customer in every restaurant
- To be good employer in each community in which it has a restaurant. (Despite this, some critics claim staff are mainly unskilled and lowly paid.)

Don Mac's future plans are to maximise global opportunities and continue to expand markets. Don Mac has long recognised that the external environment can be very uncertain and consequently does not move into new locations or countries without first undertaking a full investigation.

You are part of a strategy steering tem responsible for investigating key factors concerning Don Mac's entry for the first time into the restaurant industry in the Republic of Borderland.

Required

Prepare an environmental analysis using

(a)	The PEST framework	**(7 marks)**
(b)	One other model	**(11 marks)**
(c)	Indicate what further information on Borderland is needed for Don Mac.	**(7 marks)**

(Total = 25 marks)

Question 7

Project background

Southern Regional Health Authority (SRHA)

The SRHA manages the provision of medical care to the public within its local area. It is responsible for 50 medical centres and 10 hospitals.

You are a senior management accountant working for one of the southern region hospitals.

The 'Healthweb' national information network is a central government-led initiative which aims to provide a secure and dedicated network environment for all medical practitioners and managers, to share and access healthcare information. Other regions within the country have already connected to the network, with 95% of medical centres and hospitals within these regions utilising the facilities.

The SRHA has been sent a target by the central government to have 80% of all medical centres and 90% of all hospitals within the region connected to the Healthweb one year from now. Prior to the project commencement, most information within the hospitals and medical centres was kept by a manual, paper-based system, and all data exchange was done by means of telephone or by post. The senior management team of the SRHA set a project board in January 2002 to oversee the progress of the project and so specify the project objectives.

Project management

The central government has contracted a large telecommunications company, T, to manage and control the network and to project-manage the regional connection projects. T was contracted to provide all hardware and software systems support, training and maintenance.

The SRHA project team was mainly made up of managers and technicians from T, but also included three doctors and three senior managers.

Project progress

Each medical centre and hospital within the southern region was allowed to discuss terms of usage, (that is, the hardware and software requirements, which aspects of the Healthweb to utilise and the timing of the implementation) separately with the GPC project team.

Financing within the SRHA

Many doctors and senior managers were concerned about the limited resources of the hospitals and medical centres being spent on unnecessary technology and that the disruption of the project might affect the quality of service to patients. Other regions had reported large costs in computer upgrades and facilities, which could have been better spent on direct patient care.

Although the central government has set up a 'Technology Fund', some of which has been set aside for this project, obtaining the funds has proved difficult in other regions. In addition, there has been no previous consistency in financing connection to the network, with some regional health authorities paying all of the costs. Other regions have invested only in the initial technology, with all on-going operational costs being paid by the individual hospitals and medical centres.

The hospital executives at the hospital in which you are a senior management accountant are concerned that the senior managers not involved directly in the GPC project are unaware of its nature and importance.

Required

You have been asked by the executives of your own hospital to prepare a memorandum to the other senior managers in the hospital which should:

(a)   **Discuss** the relationship of the project manager to:

    (i)   The project sponsor (that is, the central government).
    (ii)   The project board.
    (iii)   The medical and administrative users (in medical centres and hospitals).

    Include in your answer a discussion of the potential conflicting project objectives of the above stakeholders.   **(15 marks)**

(b)   **Explain** the potential project management problems which might arise from allowing each hospital and medical centre to discuss individual terms of usage of the Healthweb separately with the GPC project team.   **(10 marks)**

(Total = 25 marks)

Total marks for Section B = 50

Answers

DO NOT TURN THIS PAGE UNTIL YOU HAVE
COMPLETED THE MOCK EXAM

CIMA – Managerial Level

Paper E2

Enterprise Management

Mock Examination 2

You are allowed **three hours** to answer this question paper.
In the real exam, you are allowed 20 minutes reading time before the examination begins during which you should read the question paper, and if you wish, make annotations on the question paper. However, you are **not** allowed, **under any circumstances**, to open the answer book and start writing or use your calculator during this reading time.
You are strongly advised to carefully read the question requirements before attempting the question concerned.
Answer ALL FIVE compulsory question in Section A.
Answer the TWO compulsory questions in Section B.

DO NOT OPEN THIS PAPER UNTIL YOU ARE READY TO START UNDER EXAMINATION CONDITIONS

SECTION A – 50 marks

Answer ALL FIVE questions – 10 marks each

1 Product portfolio

R Company produces a range of hair and beauty products. T, the Finance Director, and P, the Marketing Director, are reviewing the outcome of some product portfolio analysis which has recently been undertaken. They are keen to gain a better understanding of how the company's products are performing, specifically in terms of market share and market growth.

The analysis has revealed the following:

- Product A had a high market share but is in a market where there is low growth
- Product B has a low market share but is in a high growth industry
- Product C is a market leader with high market share in a high market growth industry
- Product D has a low market share and is in a low growth industry

Required

Describe what the analysis shows about R Company's current product portfolio and the implications for the future development of its products. **(10 marks)**

2 Strategy in multi-business organisation

Strategy is developed at different levels in large organisations. The process starts with the corporate strategy which is then translated into the strategy for the business divisions and business functions.

Required

(a) **Explain** what the corporate strategy of a multi-business organisation is typically concerned with.**(6 marks)**

(b) **Describe** the important role that the corporate level strategy has in relation to the development of the business and functional strategy in a multi-business organisation. **(4 marks)**

(Total = 10 marks)

3 Competitive advantage and rivalry

DF Company, a relatively new company, is in the business of designing and building farm equipment and machinery. Whilst it has been successful in its first few years of operation, sales are now in decline as competition in the industry has intensified and there is greater rivalry between competitor organisations.

A review undertaken by consultants has recommended that, in order to gain sustained competitive advantage, the company needs to establish the basis on which it can compete more effectively against its rivals in the future.

Required

(a) **Describe** the concept of competitive advantage and include reference to the different bases DF Company could use to achieve competitive advantage. **(5 marks)**

(b) **Describe** the factors that can create competitive rivalry between organisations. **(5 marks)**

(Total = 10 marks)

4 X Company project stakeholders

X Company, a private security firm, has signed a contract to fund the design, construction and running of a local police station. This arrangement is a public private partnership agreement whereby the local police authority will pay X Company revenue to run the support services of the local police station.

The local police authority has made a statement saying 'this will mean the support services provided by the police will now be delivered externally by specialists who can deliver greater savings and improve efficiency and effectiveness'. X Company has a 10 year deal to provide a range of support services including human resources, finance and IT. X Company has set up a project board (effectively the project sponsor) to oversee the progress of the project and has appointed one of its senior management accountants as project manager.

Required

(a) **Distinguish** between the role of the project owner and project sponsor, with reference to X Company's project.   **(4 marks)**

(b) **Explain**, with a view to successfully completing X Company's project, the relationship required between the project manager and

(i)   the project owner;
(ii)   the project sponsor;
(iii)   the project team.   **(6 marks)**

                                                                                (Total = 10 marks)

5 Influences on culture

Organisational culture is an important concept since it impacts on most aspects of organisational life and the way in which work is performed. Every organisation will have its own unique culture which will be determined by a wide range of factors and will develop over time.

Required

Explain the factors which can influence the development of an organisation's culture.   **(10 marks)**

Total marks for Section A = 50

Section B – 50 marks

Answer BOTH questions from this section

6 PRINCE2 methodology

L Company, a manufacturer of family cars, has invested in a robotic painting system for its cars. Ensuring the right quality of paintwork on each car is a critical success factor for the company.

However, the project to deliver the robotic painting system has experienced a number of problems. At the end of the project, expenditure was over budget and the level of reliability specified in the project quality document has not been met. The company is now facing major quality issues with the robotic system not delivering the standard of paintwork required by the customer. This is resulting in cars being delivered late to the customer and this is creating reputational issues for L Company.

A meeting between the project manager and the project board has ended up with everyone blaming each other, saying it was not their responsibility. It is clear that the project board did not use a project management methodology and did not have control systems in place in order to identify the problems that have occurred. The need for a methodology and the importance of project reviews were recognised in the meeting as important for future projects.

Required

(a)   **Explain** how using the elements of a PRINCE2 methodology could have helped to prevent the failures of the robotic painting system project. **(13 marks)**

(b)   **Discuss** the importance of undertaking a project completion review and provide examples of what would be involved in such a review for the robotic painting system project. **(12 marks)**

(Total = 25 marks)

7 GBF Group

GBF Group is a leading food and beverage manufacturer with an international presence in over 50 countries worldwide. The group has seven strategic business units (SBUs) and each has responsibility for one of the group's key business segments. The business segments comprise:

* Frozen foods
* Dairy products
* Pet food
* Biscuits
* Confectionery
* Breakfast cereals
* Soft drinks

Each of the strategic business units operates autonomously and currently each one has its own finance function. However GBF Group does require each SBU to have a multi-disciplinary management team, made up of representatives from all of the different functional specialisms. GBF Group's Chief Executive believes that these management teams are crucial to the group's success in developing strategy and improving the performance of individual SBUs.

A new Finance Director has recently been appointed to GBF Group and one of his key priorities is to review the effectiveness of the current structure in place for providing the finance function for each of the different SBUs. He has also made it known that he is considering alternative models for delivering the finance function across the group, based on his experience in other organisations where he has previously worked.

Required

(a)   (i)   **Explain** the advantages and disadvantages of each of GBF Group's strategic business units (SBUs) having its own finance function. **(9 marks)**

      (ii)   **Discuss** TWO alternative models that the GBF Group could use to deliver the finance function other than the one it currently uses.   **(6 marks)**

  (b)   **Explain** the factors that will contribute to the effectiveness of a high performing multi-disciplinary management team for the GBF Group.   **(10 marks)**

(Total = 25 marks)

Total marks for Section B = 50

Answers

DO NOT TURN THIS PAGE UNTIL YOU HAVE
COMPLETED THE MOCK EXAM

A plan of attack

Plan to avoid panic

All questions are compulsory, but they don't need to be tackled in the order they appear. Spend the 20 minutes reading time planning. Think of what you know (for the Section A questions, which test knowledge) and get an overview of the scenario questions (Section B). Start planning these if you have time.

Section A

Remember that the first five marks of the question are easy to get than the last five, so don't spend too much time struggling to think of finer points. Question 5 is a good one to do first as plenty of fairly easy marks can be earned by describing the factors that affect culture. Question 2 would be a good second choice as you can gain a number of marks for your knowledge of corporate strategy and levels of strategy without too much application. Question 1 would be a good one to do next you have strong knowledge of the BCG matrix. If not, you may be better leaving this question until you have answered the questions covering areas of the syllabus that you know more about. Question 3 requires you to apply knowledge to a given environment, although it is not a detailed scenario. Question 4 should be left till last (for Section A). It is more difficult as it requires you to apply your knowledge to the specific situation.

Section B

You **must do answer plans** if you have not already done so. Make sure that you look at the requirements first as this will structure your answer. Then read through the scenario carefully, underlining the key points – clues that the examiner has helpfully planted.

Question 6 shouldn't cause you too many problems if you are familiar with the PRINCE2 methodology, as there are straightforward marks available in part b for knowledge. However, be careful to relate your answer to both question parts specifically to the scenario in the question. This is particularly important in part (a).

Question 7 requires solid knowledge of embedded finance functions, shared servicing and outsourcing. If you have this knowledge, you should find this question reasonably straight forward. In both question parts there are plenty of marks available just for demonstrating your knowledge in this area.

Allocating your time

Always **allocate your time** according to the marks for the question in total and for the parts of the questions. Unless, that is, you haven't studied or revised a topic at all, when you could earn marks elsewhere. But you should have studied all topics. And always, always **follow the requirements exactly**.

You've got free time at the end of the exam.....?

If you have allocated your time properly then you **shouldn't have time on your hands** at the end of the exam. If you find yourself with five or ten minutes spare, however, go back to **any parts of questions that you didn't finish** because you ran out of time.

Forget about it!

And don't worry if you found the paper difficult. More than likely other students would too. Don't be tempted to do a 'post mortem'. If this were the real thing you would need to forget the exam the minute you leave the exam hall and think about the next one. Or, if it's the last one, celebrate!

Section A

1 Product portfolio

Text references. Product portfolios and the BCG matrix are covered in chapter 13

Top tips. To score highly on this question you will need to ensure you explain both the position of each of the products and clearly describe the implications for the future. Structuring your answer well will help you here.

Easy marks. If you have strong understanding of the BCG matrix you should quickly be able to identify what category each of the products would fall under and gain some easy marks. Make sure you develop your answer from here to indicate appropriate strategies for each of the products to ensure you address all the requirements of this question.

Examiner's comments. This question was generally well answered, however, many candidates simply repeated sections of the scenario without reference to the implications of the analysis for the development of R Company's products.

Marking scheme

	Marks
1 mark per valid, explained point (½ if not explained) to a maximum of 3 for each of the four products :	
Maximum marks for the question	10

The product portfolio of R Company and the implications for the future development of its products can be considered using the BCG matrix.

The BCG matrix classifies products in terms of their capacity for growth within the market and the market's capacity for growth as a whole. Products are categorised in terms of market growth and relative market share. Ideally, an organisation should have a balanced portfolio of products.

Product A has a high market share in a low growth market and is classified as a cash cow. This type of product needs very little expenditure and can generate high levels of cash income which can be used to invest in new products that are at the development stage. The low market growth suggests that this product is unlikely to experience much growth, so a suitable strategy would be a hold strategy in which the market share of the product is maintained. However, if this product is weak, a harvest strategy may be more appropriate.

Product B is operating in a high growth industry but has only a low market share and is therefore classified as a question mark. R Company will need to determine whether product B will require significant expenditure in the hope of increasing its market or if it is more likely that rival products will squeeze it out of the market. If it is worth the expenditure then a build strategy would be appropriate, if not then a harvest strategy would be better.

Product C can be classified as a star as it is a market leader in a high growth area. In the short term this kind of product requires more capital expenditure than the cash they generate in order to maintain their market position, however, they promise high returns in the future. Investing in this product via a build strategy would therefore be appropriate.

Product D has both a low market share and is operating in a low growth industry and therefore is classified as a dog. This product could be a cash trap which ties up funds and provides a poor return on investment in which case divesting of this product would be the most sensible option. However, product D may have a useful role, either in completing a product range or keeping competitors out. If this is the case, a hold strategy would be more appropriate for this product.

2   Strategy in multi-business organisation

Text references. Levels of strategy are covered in chapter 11

Top tips. As well as describing what is meant by corporate strategy, a strong answer should also include some examples of the type of decisions that would be made at this level.

In part b) you will need to discuss the relationship corporate strategy has to the other levels of strategy and demonstrate the importance of this framework.

Examiner's comment. Most candidates achieved a pass mark on this question. Many candidates lost marks because of poor performance in part (b). It was evident that many candidates were unable to distinguish between the three levels of strategy and therefore unable to spell out the role that corporate strategy played in relation to business and functional strategy.

Marking scheme

	Marks

(a)   1 mark per valid, explained point (½ if not explained)
to a maximum of 6 for each of:
Role of strategy – strategic direction for growth
Acquisitions, mergers etc.
Balanced portfolio of strategic business units
Overall aim and purpose – mission statement
Stakeholders
Example of a stakeholder
Corporate social responsibility
Other

     6

(b)   1 mark per valid, explained point (½ if not explained)
to a maximum of 4 for each of:
Explanation of business/functional strategy
Constrain lower levels
Reduce any reputational issues
Guidance when levels of autonomy at lower levels are high
Ensure control and goal congruence

     $\frac{4}{\overline{10}}$

(a)   Corporate strategy is the most general level of strategy in an organisation. It is concerned with what types of business the company as a whole should be in and is therefore concerned with decisions of scope. An example would be choosing between diversifying or limiting the activities of the business.

Corporate strategy is concerned with the overall vision of the organisation and will involve setting the mission statement of the organisation. This is a generalised statement of the overriding purpose of the organisation and will cover the purpose, scope, strategy and principles of the organisation.

The corporate strategy of a multi-business organisation will also consider the balance of business and possible synergies across different business units.

The expectations of stakeholders should be considered here as corporate strategy should deliver value to key stakeholders, who can both support or oppose a strategy. For example, customers can boycott the company by removing their custom and shareholders can sell their shares. Such actions can significantly disrupt strategy.

A further element of corporate strategy is the development of corporate policies, such as corporate social responsibility. The ethical position of the company, and the extent to which this is to be used as a basis for strategic differentiation, are determined at the corporate level.

(b)   Corporate strategy guides decisions and strategies delivered at lower levels.

Business strategy defines how an organisation, or a particular business unit, approaches a particular market. This involves decisions such as whether to offer a wide range of products or to specialise. Management are responsible for beating the competition and winning customers.

Functional, or operational, strategy involves decisions of strategic importance, but which are made or determined at operational level, for example pricing policies or investment in plant. It is these decisions that determine the success of the strategy as, effectively, strategy is only implemented at this level.

The levels of strategy must be consistent with each other. The corporate strategy sets the overall direction which then guides and constrains decisions made at lower levels. Objectives set at the business and functional levels should be clearly linked to the overall strategic aims. Failure to do so could lead to reputational damage and reduced profitability.

The lower levels are given autonomy for decision making, therefore it is very important that the direction provided by the corporate level is clear. Any misunderstandings could lead to conflict which will reduce the efficiency and effectiveness with which strategic objectives are achieved. Clear guidelines are therefore necessary to achieve goal congruence and control.

3 Competitive advantage and rivalry

Text references. The competitive environment is covered in chapter 13

Top tips. As always, make sure you relate your answer back to the scenario in order to gain the full amount of marks on offer.

Easy marks. Some marks can be earned in part (a) simply by providing an explanation of competitive advantage and the three generic strategies.

Examiner's comments. Few candidates answered this question well. For part (a) many candidates rightly noted the two main approaches to securing competitive advantage; either by the positioning approach or via the resource based approach. This represents a good start to answering the question but to complete the answer it is necessary to go beyond this and spell out the actual bases for advantage which include Porter's generic strategies of cost leadership, differentiation and focus as the outcome of a positioning analysis and/or to make reference to the kinds of unique, hard to imitate core competences that resource based theorists argue are the real bases of sustainable competitive advantage.

For part (b) many candidates simply presented Porter's Five Forces model and argued that each of these forces created competitive rivalry, an answer which is only partially correct. What was required was to consider other factors that form part of the detailed analysis of competitive rivalry.

Marking scheme

		Marks
(a)	1 mark per valid, explained point (½ if not explained) to a maximum of 5 for: Explanation of competitive advantage Reference to low price Reference to differentiation/added value Too hierarchical and rigid	5
(b)	1 mark for explanation of competitive rivalry Up to 2 marks per factor for description of factors, eg: Low rate of growth High fixed costs High exit barriers Low differentiation Other	5
		10

(a) Competitive advantage refers to any activity or factor which gives one organisation an edge over its rivals. Organisations should adopt a strategy which is intended to achieve some form of competitive advantage. Doing something better, or more efficiently than competitors should ultimately lead to profitability. If this can be done long term, despite the efforts of competition, then the organisation possesses a sustainable competitive advantage.

There are three bases on which DF company could use to achieve competitive advantage.

Cost leadership

This means being the lowest cost producer in the industry as a whole. By producing at the lowest cost, the manufacturer can compete on price with every other producer in the industry and earn higher unit prices.

Differentiation

This is the exploitation of a product or service which the industry as a whole believes to be unique. This can be achieved via brand image, product special features, marketing techniques etc.

Focus

This involves restricting activities to only part of the market (a segment). This is also known as a niche strategy. There are two ways to achieve this:

- Providing goods/services at a lower cost to that segment (cost focus)
- Providing a differentiated product/service to that segment (differentiation focus)

The basis on which DF company chooses to compete will be determined by its own core competences, its strengths and weaknesses as well as those of its competitors. The critical success factors of its customer base and the wider environment in which the company operates also must be clearly understood before an appropriate basis for competition can be set.

(b) Organisations that provide a similar product/service aimed at the same target market will experience a certain degree of competitive rivalry. The intensity of competitive rivalry within an industry will affect the profitability of the industry as a whole as price wars and advertising fees reduce the profits of the rivals.

Factors that can create competitive rivalry include:

Low barriers to entry

Low barriers to entry to the industry increase the number of organisations in that industry and so rivalry is created.

Market growth

Rivalry is intensified when firms are competing for a greater market share in a total market where growth is slow or stagnant.

Cost structure

If fixed costs are high, there is short-term temptation to compete on price as any contribution from sales is better than none at all.

Switching costs

If switching costs are low, ie customers can easily change suppliers, then the suppliers will compete. In some industries, the Internet has increased both the number of suppliers and the ease of switching supplier, for example switching to an online bank.

Uncertainty

Uncertainty in the environment will increase rivalry. If one firm is unsure what another is up to there is a tendency to respond by developing a more competitive strategy.

High exit barriers

Exit barriers make it difficult for an existing supplier to leave the industry and as such will fight to maintain market share until they are forced out.

Strategic importance

If success in a particular market is a prime objective for a number of firms, these firms will be likely to act more competitively to succeed in that market.

4 X Company project stakeholders

> **Text references.** The roles and management of project stakeholders is covered in chapter 7
>
> **Top tips.** Although some marks will be available for identifying the general responsibilities of the various stakeholders, to ensure success in this question you will need to discuss the more specific responsibilities of each of these stakeholders in the given scenario.
>
> **Examiner's comment.** This question was generally well answered. Some candidates did not read the scenario carefully enough and mixed up the identification of project sponsor and project owner despite the fact that this information was provided in the scenario.

Marking scheme

		Marks
(a)	1 mark per valid, explained point (½ if not explained) to a maximum of 2 for: Definition of owner Recognition of local authority Recognition of needs 1 mark per valid, explained point (½ if not explained) to a maximum of 2 for f: Definition of sponsor Recognition of project board Recognition of concerns	
		4
(b)	1 mark per valid, explained point (½ if not explained) to a maximum of 2 each up to a total maximum of 6: Relationship with owner – eg resources not wasted, management of expenses Relationship with sponsor/board – eg project progress on objectives, decisions on corrective action Relationship with team	
		6
		10

(a) **Project owner**

The project owner is the person for whom the project is being carried out and is primarily interested in the deliverables achieved. The project owner of the X Company project is the local police authority. The deliverables that need to be met are the 'greater savings' and 'improved effectiveness and efficiency' referenced in the statement made by the police authority.

Project sponsor

The project sponsor provides and is accountable for the resources invested into the project and is responsible for the achievement of the project's business objectives. In the case of the X Company project, the project board set up by the X Company is also acting as the project sponsor, and the chair of that board will have overall responsibility for delivering the business needs.

(b) **Project manager and project owner**

The project owner, the local police authority, has defined its requirements for the project. The funds for the project, however, are being provided by X Company. The project manager will therefore need to ensure that the owner's requirements are reasonable, given the funds available, and to ensure that this does not create conflict.

Progress of the project will be reported by the project manager directly to the project board and therefore it is unlikely that there will be much direct communication between the project manager and the project owner. However, it will be necessary for the project manager to manage the expectations of the police authority (the owner) in terms of the savings and improved efficiency the project can deliver.

Project manager and project sponsor

The project board is acting as the project sponsor and is responsible for the overall success of the project. It will have to ensure the objectives of the police authority are met without compromising its own business objectives.

The project manager is responsible for ensuring the objectives set by the project board are met. To achieve this there should be regular communication between the project manager and the project board relating to project progress and the completion of project milestones. Timely action will need to be taken should any deviation from the project objectives arise.

Project manager and the project team

The project manager is responsible for ensuring project tasks are completed and as such will have to co-ordinate and motivate the project team. Tasks and responsibilities consistent with project objectives will be allocated to each member of the team. The project manager retains ultimate responsibility for the achievement of this work. Any changes to the project that have been approved by the project board must be clearly communicated to the project team by the project manager.

5   Influences on culture

> **Text references.** Culture is covered in Chapter 5 of your BPP Study Text
>
> **Top tips.** To score highly on this question you will need to provide a wide range of factors rather than just a few.
>
> **Easy marks.** Some easy marks are available for briefly explaining what is meant by organisation culture. You may be able to generate some ideas as to what may affect culture even if you don't have strong technical knowledge in this area.
>
> **Examiner's comment.** Most candidates gained a pass mark for this question. Weaker answers included those that simply presented cultural typologies such as Harrison's role, task, power and people cultures and/or McKinsey's 7S framework without any attempt at explaining how each type or element can actually influence the development of an organisation's culture.

Marking scheme

Marks

Up to 2 marks available for a brief explanation of organisational culture
Up to 1 mark for each factor that can influence culture, eg:
    Vision
    Management style
    Nature of business
    Ownership
    Size
    History
    Structure
    Attitude to risk
    Reward system
    Diversity – product range
    Diversity – geographical spread
    Nationality
    Other
Maximum marks awarded   <u>10</u>

Culture can be defined as ways of behaving, and ways of understanding that are shared by a group of people. It is 'the way we do things around here'.

Organisational culture is determined by a wide range of factors and will develop over time. Factors that can influence its development include:

The organisation's founder

A strong set of values and assumptions is set up by the organisation's founder. This original culture can live on long after the founder has retired or left the organisation.

The organisation's history

The era when the organisation was founded is often reflected in the culture. This is often visible in the organisation by:

- Symbols: logos, corporate identity and things which take on symbolic value to people
- Rituals and routines: ceremonies and formal procedures and customs
- Stories: tales of success and failure, how things got to be the way they are

These factors legitimise behaviour an promote priorities.

Leadership style

Organisations with a strong culture recruit and develop managers who naturally conform to it and perpetuate the culture.

The organisation's environment

Nations, regions, occupations and business types all have their own distinctive cultures and these will therefore influence that of the organisation.

The size of the organisation

Number of employees, turnover, number of locations and so on will affect the way the organisation is run.

Ownership status

The culture of an organisation headed up by an owner manager will have a very different culture to one owned by many shareholders.

Organisational structures

The formal authority/communication channels, departments, teams and so on directly affect the culture of the organisation.

Control systems

Culture will be affected by the ways in which control is exercised: standards, monitoring, supervision and so on.

Overall, it can be seen that the culture of an organisation is affected by many different factors and, as such, is very difficult to change.

Section B

6 PRICE2 methodology

Text references. PRINCE2 is covered in chapter 6.

Top tips. PRINCE2 is specifically listed as a topic in the syllabus and as such it is important that you understand how it works. In particular, you must be able to explain the system's emphasis on outputs rather than processes.

It is important with this question that you do not just describe the various components of PRINCE2 but that you relate your answer back to the scenario to demonstrate how it could have helped prevent the specific failings that were encountered in the robotic painting project described in the scenario.

Easy marks. If you have a strong understanding of PRINCE2 you should be able to gain a number of easy marks in describing the system and its components in part (a).

Theoretical marks can also be gained in part (b) for discussing the process of a post completion review, but application to the scenario is required to bring your answer up to the standard required for a pass.

Examiner's comment. Part (a) produced many weak answers. The main weakness included the absence of any explanation of PRINCE2 methodology and even when candidates were able to outline the methodology there was often an absence of its application to the case in question.

Part (b) produced a few good answers but also many poor ones. Many candidates avoided the key focus of the question and simply detailed the need for the checking of cost, quality and time issues. Many also neglected to make reference to the lessons that could be learned for future projects, an important point in answer to this question

Marking scheme

		Marks
(a)	Introduction to PRINCE2	Up to 2
	Rectification earlier in the project	
	Components – organisational chart, work packages	Up to 2
	Responsibilities identified on L Company project	1 each
	Component – Business case	
	Reputational issues managed on L Company project	
	Setting plans/standards/control points	Up to 3
	Corrective action taken on L Company project	1 each
	Management products as check points	
	PRINCE2 forces the identification of potential problems	
	Maximum marks awarded	<u>13</u>
(b)	One mark for each of the below to a maximum of 12	
	Project involves:	
	Debriefing meetings with all parties involved	
	Assessment of all aspects of project performance (time, cost, quality)	
	Importance:	
	Understand successes and failures	
	Identify areas for improvement for L Company in future projects	
	Improvement on performance of team members	
	Improvement on client satisfaction	
	Understanding of CSFs for L Company	
	Review of business case	

Reinforces the need for L Company to use milestones and progress reporting
Company needs to assess quality achieved
L Company needs to analyse reasons for cost over-runs
Recommendations need to be circulated throughout the organisation
L Company will need to train everyone on the methodology to be used

$$\frac{12}{25}$$

(a) PRINCE2 is a project management methodology that encompasses the management, control and organisation of a project. It can be used for projects of any size and complexity and focuses on delivering results. A fundamental aspect of PRINCE2 is that a project is driven by its business case and its continuing viability is checked at regular intervals.

Using the elements of PRINCE2 methodology could have helped to prevent the failings of the robotic painting system project in the following ways:

Clear management structure, roles and responsibilities

Under PRINCE2 roles and responsibilities are clearly defined and a structure of authority and accountability is put in place. This would have been beneficial in the robotic painting system project as everyone involved in the project would have understood their own responsibilities which would have prevented the hostile meeting where no one would take responsibility for the problems. In addition, the problems would have been less likely to occur in the first place as the relevant people responsible for the areas where issues were encountered would have picked this up earlier and corrective action would have been taken. This would also have ensured that no gaps were left (ie no areas for which no one was responsible or accountable) as may have been the case here.

Business case and clear objectives

The quality issues that have arisen suggests that L company did not fully understand the objectives and scope of the project and the project has failed to meet the standard required by the client.

Had PRINCE2 been used a detailed business case would have been produced to justify the need for the project. This business case would clearly identify the objectives of the project, the scope of the project and what is to be achieved by it. This would act as the driving force behind the project ensuring that the project stay in line with the benefits and business objectives defined. The reputational issues that L company is experiencing would also have been avoided.

Controls and deliverables

Under PRINCE2 plans and standards are defined for everything that the project needs to deliver including the quality required, the timescale and the cost of delivery. This is then formally monitored throughout the duration of the project to ensure the standards and objectives are being met.

The project itself is broken down into stages and control points within the project are identified. Progress is formally documented and any issues identified at the control points will be quickly addressed via corrective action.

This has not happened during the robotic painting project which was both over budget and behind schedule, yet this was not identified until the end of the project.

The high degree of structure and documentation required under PRINCE2 would have increased the number of controls in place and forced potential problems to be quickly identified and addressed.

(b) A post-completion review is carried out once the project is finished and the outcomes have been delivered. It examines how well the project was run and the success of the project management process. It considers the problems that were encountered, why they were encountered, how they were dealt with, and the lessons that can be learnt. As such this review helps to determine how future projects can be managed more effectively. By making the project management process more efficient and effective, the costs associated with future projects can also be reduced.

The review also considers the successes of the project and the behaviours and skills that led to these successes are reinforced to ensure they are employed again in future projects.

The post-completion review should involve input from the project team and their feedback should be taken into consideration and action taken if necessary. This provides the opportunity for the project manager to discuss individual performance and objectives for the future.

The satisfaction of the client should also be obtained in order to determine whether the project has met their requirements and provide them with the opportunity to feedback any concerns or issues they may have. This is particularly relevant for L company as it would appear that the critical success factors have become confused. It will be necessary to understand why and take appropriate measures to ensure this problem is not repeated in future projects. Quality issues will need to be considered here to determine the causes of this.

The review will also involve revisiting the business case to ensure that the intended benefits of the project have in fact been realised. The L company project was delivered behind schedule, therefore the review should highlight the need for progress reports and milestones throughout the project. It was also over budget and so the reasons for this over-spend should be identified and the lessons learnt fed back in to the process to avoid making the same mistakes in future projects.

Overall it can be seen that a post-completion review is crucial in identifying the problems and issues in a project and determining ways the process can be improved. Circulation of the findings to those involved in other projects will allow them to learn from the mistakes and improve. The starting point for any new project should be a review of the documentation of any similar projects undertaken in the past.

The post-completion review documentation that is circulated with respect to the L company project must include the impact that the lack of project methodology has had on the outcome of this project and the effectiveness of establishing a methodology such as PRINCE2 should be considered.

7 GBF Group

Text references. Outsourcing and shared servicing is covered in chapter 3 and team development is covered in chapter 2

Top tips. To score highly in this question, you will need to provide a balanced discussion of the advantages and disadvantages, followed by a solid description of outsourcing and shared service centres.

Part (b) requires you to provide a detailed explanation of the factors that contribute towards an effective team. Strong answers will back their answer up with the relevant theory and specifically apply this answer to multi-disciplinary teams.

Examiner's comment. Part (a) was generally well answered. Several candidates did not make clear for whom a dedicated finance function for each SBU was advantageous or disadvantageous.

Part (b) was generally poorly answered. Many candidates misread the question and instead of considering the factors that can contribute to the effectiveness of a multi-disciplinary management team argued instead that such teams were effective because of the composition of the team. Other answers only made reference to the theories of Tuckman and Belbin and so gained relatively few marks.

Marking scheme

Marks

(a)　(i)　1 mark per valid, explained point (½ if not explained)
to a maximum of 5 each for each of:
Advantages, eg stronger connection with SBU, local knowledge, contribute to strategic decisions, information needs, stronger relationship and trust
Disadvantages eg cost, duplication of activities, finance staff feel isolated, no sharing of best practice, inconsistencies in financial reporting and systems across the company
Maximum marks available　　9

(a)	(ii)	Shared service model described	3
		Outsourcing model described	3
		Maximum for part a	15
(b)		1 mark per valid, explained point (½ if not explained) for each factor	
		Up to 3 marks for discussion of balance of roles referencing Belbin	
		Maximum for part b	10
		Maximum marks for question	25

(a) (i) Each business area (SBU) of GBF group operates autonomously and each has its own finance function.

Advantages for GBF group of each SBU having its own finance function include:

Better informed decisions

The local knowledge and improved relationships should enable members of the finance team to provide information that will assist in the making of strategic decisions for the SBU.

Local knowledge

The finance team will have increased knowledge and understanding of the day to day activities of the SBU. This will allow the finance function to better understand the needs of the SBU and make a more valuable contribution to its strategic decisions.

Improved relationships

There should be an increased level of trust and better relationships between the finance function and the management of other business areas.

However, there are also a number of disadvantages for GBF group of each SBU having its own finance function. These include:

Increased costs/duplication

As each SBU has a dedicated finance function yet all will carry out similar work it is likely that a number of activities are being duplicated. This may be considered to be a wasteful use of resources and is often the catalyst for moving towards a shared service model where one centralised finance function serves all the SBUs of the group.

Lack of consistency

The different finance functions may begin to develop their own ways of working. The isolating nature of this approach may mean the various finance functions have little or no contact with each other. This prevents the sharing of knowledge and best practice and leads to inconsistencies of approach.

(ii) Two alternative models that the GBF group could use to deliver the finance function are outsourcing and a central service unit (shared servicing). These are discussed below.

Outsourcing

Outsourcing the finance function would involve contracting it out to an external vendor. This has the potential to greatly reduce the cost of the function and remove any uncertainty around the cost that will be incurred. However, it would also require that the GBF group relinquish control over the function and open them up to the risk presented by an uncertain level of quality.

Outsourcing is best suited to basic transaction processing functions such as payroll and expense management and so may not be the most appropriate choice here given the complexity of providing ad-hoc financial information to support decision making specific to an SBU.

Shared servicing

A more appropriate alternative might be shared servicing, where a shared service centre would consolidate the transaction-processing activities of many operations with the GBF group. The aim of these centres is to achieve significant cost reductions whilst improving service levels through the use of standardised technology and processes and service level agreements. This approach would allow GBF group to retain full internal control of its finance function.

(b)   Multi-disciplinary teams are made up of individuals with different specialisms to facilitate the sharing of knowledge, skills and experience. The effectiveness of GBF group's multi-disciplinary team will be affected by the following factors.

Purpose and objectives

In order for the team to be successful it is crucial that each individual member has a strong understanding of the purpose and objectives of the team.

Roles and responsibilities

These must be clearly defined and each team member should know exactly what is required of them personally as well as understanding what will be contributed by others. To facilitate this it is necessary to have clear communication procedures and for regular team meetings and status reviews to take place.

Trust and commitment

Success of the team will be dependent on each team member being committed to both the team's purpose and achievement of its objectives. Trust and participation by all team members is necessary to achieve this.

Strong leadership

Given the diverse background of team members in a multi-disciplinary team strong leadership is particularly important. The leader will be responsible for ensuring the members communicate effectively and develop sufficient trust in each other.

Skill balance

A good balance of skills and personality types will contribute to the likely success of the team. Ideally, the nine team roles identified by Belbin should be adopted by members of the team, however two or more roles can be adopted by a single member of the team if necessary.

CIMA – Managerial Level

Paper E2

Enterprise Management

Mock Examination 3
November 2012

You are allowed **three hours** to answer this question paper.
In the real exam, you are allowed 20 minutes reading time before the examination begins during which you should read the question paper, and if you wish, make annotations on the question paper. However, you are **not** allowed, **under any circumstances**, to open the answer book and start writing or use your calculator during this reading time.
You are strongly advised to carefully read the question requirements before attempting the question concerned.
Answer ALL FIVE compulsory question in Section A.
Answer the TWO compulsory questions in Section B.

DO NOT OPEN THIS PAPER UNTIL YOU ARE READY TO START UNDER EXAMINATION CONDITIONS

SECTION A – 50 marks

Answer ALL FIVE questions – 10 marks each

Question 1

The Board of GG Supermarkets has been steadily increasing the company's visibility both on the high street and online. Although GG has a favourable market position it does not always attract favourable media attention. Some of the media often suggest that GG's growth has come at a price for farmers, customers, workers, town centres and the environment and that GG is ignoring its social responsibilities.

The Board feels that the adverse media comments are not its concern as it only has a duty to shareholders. Any consideration of the media issues would be in conflict with the benefit to shareholders which is its primary concern.

Required

Discuss why the Board of GG should recognise that being socially responsible does not necessarily conflict with GG's responsibility to its shareholders.

(Total for Question One = 10 marks)

Question 2

KS, the Finance Manager of TZY Company's Finance Department, is aware that it is approaching the time of year when he needs to conduct staff appraisals. However, he is conscious that, in the past, feedback has suggested that many members of his team feel that the appraisal process is a waste of time, and that they have better things to do. This year he wants to make sure that staff perceive it as a valued activity.

Required

Explain the points KS could make about the appraisal process to help staff appreciate its value both for themselves and for TZY Company.

(Total for Question Two = 10 marks)

Question 3

Cornbridge is a large region in T Country with a beautiful coastline and large areas of natural habitat, which include the nesting grounds of rare birds. However, the region is suffering from high unemployment and unsightly derelict buildings. D Company, an international mining company, has discovered substantial mineral reserves in Cornbridge. It is looking to obtain government permission to undertake a mining project in the area which would provide jobs and boost the economy.

There is pressure from the Cornbridge Protection Alliance (an organisation which includes wildlife protection representatives, residents worried about noise and pollution, environmentalists and anti-capitalist groups) to stop the Government from granting permission to D Company. The Alliance has also expressed concerns about the safety of workers given that there has been recent publicity about fatalities in the mining industry. The main union representing the workers of D Company has suggested that it has no concerns regarding this project as D Company has an exemplary record for health and safety.

Required

Recommend the different strategies that could be used by D Company to manage its various stakeholder groups with an interest in the mining project.

(Total for Question Three = 10 marks)

Question 4

R Company is in the business of manufacturing contemporary and traditional furniture for the home. When the previous sales director retired after working for more than 20 years for the company, his replacement, BG, was faced with the task of reversing the downward trend in sales. However, BG was disturbed to find a general lack of cohesion throughout the different departments. This was characterised by poor communications and widespread frustration, including hostility between staff in the various departments. Department heads blamed each other for the current financial performance of the company and its reduced sales. In addition, the departments appeared to have developed their own plans resulting in conflicting priorities.

BG recognises that for the company to prosper in the future, he needs to get everyone in the organisation to work together.

Required

Explain what BG could do to resolve the conflict that has developed in R Company.

(Total for Question Four = 10 marks)

Question 5

In the face of rising costs, the senior management in PT Company has decided that significant cuts will be needed in the budgets of some of its departments. The promotional budget was singled out to be hardest hit. However, YE, the Marketing Manager, considered that this was a soft target for making major savings and had not been thought through sufficiently. In particular, he feels that plans to launch a new product range would be severely hampered by a lack of promotional support and that this could threaten the future of the company. Unfortunately, his view is not shared by other department heads who feel that perhaps the current business climate is not ideal for such ambitious plans. A meeting has been arranged with senior executives where YE hopes he will be able to negotiate an increase in the promotional budget.

Required

Explain how YE should approach the negotiation, including reference to the different stages in the negotiation process.

(Total for Question Five = 10 marks)

(Total for Section A = 50 marks)

SECTION B – 50 marks

Answer BOTH questions

Question 6

The Board of S Company has agreed in principle a project for a large scale upgrade to its management accounting systems. The Finance Director has been asked to provide the detailed requirements for the project. So far, no one else in the business has been involved in the discussions about the project.

The Finance Director believes that the project process should proceed in the following way:

- No details of the functionality should be set; it is important that the system is allowed to grow in scale during the life of the project;

- Progress should be reported as and when the project manager feels it is appropriate;

- P, who is a member of the Finance Department, should be selected as project manager; the Finance Director believes it is a good opportunity for P, who has not previously managed a project.

The main activities and timescales are given in the table below.

Activity		Duration (weeks)	Preceding Activity
A	Document Requirements	8	-
B	Review and select package	6	-
C	Demonstration of package	2	A,B
D	Training	7	C
E	Test programs	5	C
F	Changeover	6	D
G	Completion	4	E,F

The Finance Director has heard that the Project Management Institute recommends a five stage process for managing projects. He is interested in understanding more about this process and how it helps to deliver a successful project.

Required

(a) **Discuss** how each of the Project Management Institute's five project management process areas could be used to address the potential problems that could occur in the Management Accounting System project.

(15 marks)

(b) (i) **Construct** a Critical Path Analysis (CPA) for the Management Accounting System project.

(6 marks)

(ii) **Explain** how information from the CPA could help to ensure that the project is delivered on time.

(4 marks)

(Total for Question Six = 25 marks)

Question 7

FF Company offers high quality perfumes, skin care products and home scents, including candles. Although the company opened its flagship store more than 10 years ago, it was the launch of its internet business shortly afterwards that has contributed to its current status as one of the leading brands in its industry. Indeed, as a result of its online sales success, the company has subsequently opened retail outlets in major cities and airports worldwide.

Much of the success of FF Company can be attributed to its abilities in combining different fragrances in order to create unique scents which are unlike anything produced by major competitors. The use of simple but elegant packaging perfectly complements the tasteful and subtle scents in the product line, as well as reinforcing the company's brand identity.

The company's marketing capability and use of IT in developing its website has enabled it to track and quickly spot any changes to consumer buying patterns. It is clear from the company's research information that to prosper in this industry constant product innovation is critical. A flexible technology based approach to new product development adopted by FF Company enables its skilled team of fragrance designers to come up with new scents that can be used alone or in combination with others in the collection. The company also has good relationships with its various suppliers, on whom it relies to provide the high quality materials needed to create FF's products.

Although FF Company has continued to be the market leader and innovator in the last two years, new competitors have entered the market attempting to imitate the company, but offering cheaper products. In response, the Marketing Department at FF Company is setting up a market analysis team. Its remit will be to undertake competitor analysis to enable the company to keep in touch with the developments of its competitors. This will involve the regular collection of competitor intelligence using qualitative and quantitative research techniques.

Required

(a)   **Explain** how FF Company could use the Porter's value chain framework to help it understand its internal capability.   **(15 marks)**

(b)   **Discuss** the techniques of undertaking qualitative and quantitative research and the types of data FF Company could collect to inform its competitor analysis.   **(10 marks)**

(Total for Question Seven = 25 marks)

(Total for Section B = 50 marks)

Answers

DO NOT TURN THIS PAGE UNTIL YOU HAVE
COMPLETED THE MOCK EXAM

A plan of attack

Plan to avoid panic

All questions are compulsory, but they don't need to be tackled in the order they appear. Spend the 20 minutes reading time planning. Think of what you know (for the Section A questions, which test knowledge) and get an overview of the scenario questions (Section B). Start planning these if you have time.

Section A

Remember that the first five marks of the question are easy to get than the last five, so don't spend too much time struggling to think of finer points. Question 2 is a good one to do first as plenty of fairly easy marks can be earned by explaining the benefits you have learned. Question 1 would be a good one to do next, because it is a straightforward test of book knowledge. Question 5 would be a good choice for a third question, if you are familiar with the negotiation process. If not, you may be better leaving this question until you have answered the questions covering areas of the syllabus that you know more about. Question 4 requires you to apply knowledge to a given situation, although it is not a detailed scenario. Question 3 should be left till last (for Section A). It is more difficult as it requires you to apply your knowledge to the specific situation.

Section B

You **must do answer plans** if you have not already done so. Make sure that you look at the requirements first as this will structure your answer. Then read through the scenario carefully, underlining the key points – clues that the examiner has helpfully planted.

Question 6 shouldn't cause you too many problems, as there are straightforward marks available in part b for knowledge. However, be careful to relate your answer to part a specifically to the scenario in the question.

Question 7 is a classic scenario question, with a clear narrative and a lot of useful information given to you. There will be a number of marks for demonstrating knowledge of Porter's value chain and competitor analysis, however, a large amount of your answer should be dedicated to application.

Allocating your time

Always **allocate your time** according to the marks for the question in total and for the parts of the questions. Unless, that is, you haven't studied or revised a topic at all, when you could earn marks elsewhere. But you should have studied all topics. And always, always **follow the requirements exactly**.

You've got free time at the end of the exam.....?

If you have allocated your time properly then you **shouldn't have time on your hands** at the end of the exam. If you find yourself with five or ten minutes spare, however, go back to **any parts of questions that you didn't finish** because you ran out of time.

Forget about it!

And don't worry if you found the paper difficult. More than likely other students would too. Don't be tempted to do a 'post mortem'. If this were the real thing you would need to forget the exam the minute you leave the exam hall and think about the next one. Or, if it's the last one, celebrate!

Question 1

The Board of GG believes that considering these issues would be in conflict with the benefit of shareholders. They are assuming that addressing the concerns would lead to increased costs and decreased revenues and therefore reducing the profitability of the company. GG may also perceive that spending shareholder funds on other objectives not directly related to shareholder wealth maximisation would be irresponsible as well as a waste of management time.

However, longer term, it is not necessarily true that being socially responsible would conflict with GG's responsibility to its shareholders. This is for a number of reasons.

Retention of public support

In order to survive and succeed, organisations must satisfy the needs, wants and values of customers and prospective customers. People are now very aware of issues such as environmental damage, worker exploitation, product safety and consumer rights. Therefore in order to retain public support for its products, GG Supermarkets may need to be seen to be responsible in these areas. If public support is lost, custom will decrease and profits will plummet. Being socially responsible would therefore complement the responsibility to shareholders as it would help to ensure that profitability is retained long term.

Quality employees

Employers must compete to attract and retain high quality employees. If an organisation gets a reputation as a socially responsible employer that treats the workers well it will find it easier to do this. This will greatly reduce the costs associated with recruitment and high labour turnover, directly impacting on profits and shareholder satisfaction.

Facilitate operations

GG Supermarkets is part of a social system. It will rely on the local communities of which it is a part for access to facilities, business relationships, media coverage, labour, supplies, customers and so on. By acknowledging their responsibilities as part of this community, GG may find that many areas of their operation are facilitated. Again, this would support the maximisation of wealth for shareholders.

Avoid penalties

Certain social responsibilities are imposed on organisations by law, regulations and Codes of Practice. GG Supermarkets could be affected by such legislation, particularly in relation to environmental care, employment protection, equal opportunities, health and safety, product labelling and consumer rights. If GG fails to comply with any such requirements it may face financial and operational penalties.

Adopting a more socially responsible approach would be in keeping with the stakeholder view of organisations. This view emphasises that organisations are not solely 'self interested' and acknowledges that other interested parties have a legitimate interest and may have influence over the organisation. For example, workers can withhold labour and customers can withhold business. Taking account of the needs and claims of influential stakeholders is therefore crucial to the long term existence and productivity of GG Supermarkets.

Question 2

> **Text references.** The appraisal process is covered in Chapter 2.
>
> **Top tips.** Note that this question asks you for the benefits to both the individuals and to the group. Make sure that you address both parts of this question by ensuring you look at the process from both perspectives.
>
> **Easy marks.** This question is very knowledge based and as such there should be plenty of marks available for simply re-producing 'book knowledge'.

There are a number of benefits of the appraisal process for both KS's staff and for TZY Company. To help staff understand the value of the appraisal process, KS could make the following points.

Feedback

A key benefit to the individual is that the appraisal system provides feedback about the performance and competence by comparison against agreed targets and established standards. This lets the individual know how they are doing.

This also allows any particularly strong work to be recognised, praise to be given, and any training or development needs to be identified and addressed. This is both a benefit for the individual and for the organisation.

Staff development

Appraisals allow future opportunities and career development to be discussed which can be very beneficial to the employees in helping them to further their career.

In addition, this is beneficial to the organisation as it will both provide a basis for general HR planning (including succession planning) and also assist in the identification of candidates for promotion.

Pay and rewards

Appraisal provides a basis for remuneration and ensures that all reward decisions are fair and based on abilities rather than personalities. This is highly beneficial to both the employees and the organisation, encouraging fairness, transparency and motivation.

Linked targets

A key benefit of appraisal to the organisation is that it allows individual targets to be linked to corporate objectives. This aides goal congruence as it helps to ensure that everyone in the organisation is working towards the same ultimate goal, therefore helping to ensure that corporate goals are met.

This is also of benefit to employees as it can help them to understand how their contribution affects the organisation as a whole and can therefore play a part in motivation and job satisfaction, encouraging team spirit.

Consistency

Appraisal provides a systems for assessing the competence of employees. The same process will be followed across the entire organisation helping to ensure the process is fair and consistent. This reassures employees that they would be assessed in the same way regardless of the area of business they work in. This feeling of fair treatment can enhance the way an employee feels about the organisation, knowing all employees are treated on merit.

Communication

The appraisal process improves communication between managers and subordinates. This is beneficial to both the individuals involved and the organisation as it provides the opportunity for issues to be raised and dealt with before they turn into more serious problems.

Question 3

Stakeholders are those persons and organisations that have an interest in the strategy of an organisation. The key stakeholder groups that have an interest in the D Company mining project include the government, the Cornbridge Protection Alliance (consisting of wildlife representatives, residents, environmentalists and anti-capitalist groups), workers and the workers union.

Stakeholder mapping would be a useful tool for D Company in helping to determine an appropriate strategy for managing the various stakeholder groups. This tool identifies a strategy for the stakeholder group by identifying the level of power and interest possessed by that group. This technique is applied to the D Company mining project below.

The Government

Given that Cornbridge is suffering from high unemployment and unsightly derelict buildings it is likely that the government would support a project which would provide jobs and boost the economy of the region. The government therefore has a high level of interest in this project.

In order for the project to go ahead, permission will need to be granted by the government, therefore, their level of power is also high.

This means that the government are key players. In order for this project to go ahead it must be at least acceptable to this stakeholder. D Company will need to produce a strong case for the project and work closely with this group to get them on side if the project is to be a success.

Cornbridge Protection Alliance

This stakeholder group consists of wildlife protection representatives, residents worried about noise and pollution, environmentalists and anti-capitalist groups. These stakeholders are likely to have a high level of interest in this project.

Residents will be directly affected due to the negative impacts of noise and pollution on their surroundings and quality of life. There may also be additional knock on effects such as a drop in the value of their homes.

Environmentalists, anti-capitalists and wildlife representatives will also have a high level of this impact as this project will industrialise the area, destroy the natural beauty of the area and potentially damage the nesting ground of rare birds.

The power of these stakeholders is relatively low individually as they do not have significant ability to influence strategy. However, collectively as the Alliance, their views could be important in influencing more powerful stakeholders – in this case, the government. The Alliance is currently putting pressure on the government to prevent this project from going ahead.

D Company should therefore manage this group by ensuring that they are kept informed at all times.

Workers and the worker's union

The Alliance has expressed concerns about the safety of workers in light of recent publicity about fatalities in the mining industry. The main union representing the workers, however, has suggested that it has no concerns regarding this project as D Company has an exemplary record for health and safety. It is therefore likely that, at the present time, the level of interest held by this stakeholder group in relation to the project is relatively low.

The level of power of this group is also reasonably low as it is unlikely that they have a great deal of influence on strategy.

D Company therefore needs to expend only minimal effort on managing this stakeholder group at present. However, it should continue to monitor this group for changes in levels of interes, power or both. For example, interest levels could rise if other mining fatalities are brought to light, particularly if they occur elsewhere in D Company. Power levels could also rise should the unions put pressure on the government or organise strike action. The approach D Company takes with this stakeholder group would then need to change accordingly.

Question 4

Text references. Conflict management is covered in Chapter 3.

Top tips. The kind of conflict that has arisen in the scenario is intergroup conflict. The involvement of the various heads of department provides a difficult situation that will need careful handling. Make sure you take this into consideration when describing the steps that could be taken by BG.

Easy marks. If you are not strong on this area of the syllabus it is unlikely that there will be any easy marks, however, there may be something to gain from applying a common sense approach.

The conflict that has developed in R Company involves a number of department heads and as such this situation can be described as intergroup conflict. BG could take the following steps to resolve it.

Integration devises

Forcing individuals from the different departments to work together, for example in a joint problem solving team, may help to encourage the team members develop a more co-operative attitude. BG would have to identify a suitable co-ordinator to help this team develop and learn to work together to meet the objectives it has been set up to achieve.

Confrontation and negotiation

BG could bring the various department heads that are involved in the conflict together and force them to confront the problem and negotiate a solution. BG will need to ensure he manages the situation carefully and presents the situation in a way that encourages a win-win strategy. To achieve this, BG would need to present the situation as a problem to be solved rather than a battle to be won.

Consultants

BG could attempt to resolve the conflict by bringing in external consultants or third party mediators/arbitrators. Their aim would be to improve communications, expose group think and stereotyping and acting as an 'honest broker'.

Job rotation

To improve the communication problems and negative stereotyping which appear to be at the heart of the R Company conflict, BG could consider seconding a number of personnel into other departments. These people would act as 'ambassadors' when conflict arises and would break down the barriers of communication.

Super-ordinate goals

In order to encourage the departments to work together rather than against each other, BG could set shared corporate objectives which over-arch the agendas of the individual departments.

Inter-group training

People from the conflicting departments could be sent on joint training courses to break down barriers, encourage communication and emphasise shared goals and working styles.

Organisational adjustments

Making improvements to the procedures' structure and workflow can minimise the frustrations of interdependence, role ambiguity and overlaps of authority that are being experienced by R Company.

Issue breakdown

BG could tackle specific issues by breaking them down into components that can be dealt with specifically and innovately.

Question 5

> **Text references.** The negotiation process is covered in Chapter 4
>
> **Top tips.** To gain a pass in this question you will need to relate your knowledge of the stages of negotiation to the given scenario and explain a range of tactics that can be used for effective negotiation.
>
> **Easy marks.** There are a few knowledge marks for demonstrating knowledge of the four stages of negotiation.

There are four main stages in the negotiation process: preparation, opening, bargaining and closing. The approach that YE should take for the negotiation with PT Company's senior executives at each of these stages is considered below.

Stage 1 – Preparation

This stage involves data gathering and analysis. YE will need to research the reasons behind the decision to heavily cut the promotional budget and the underlying trends and research this decision was based on. He suspects that the decision had not been sufficiently thought through so he will need to research this to determine the extent to which this is true.

In addition, YE will also need to prepare his own case by pulling together the evidence that demonstrates why he believes the new product range and the way it is promoted to be crucial for the success of the company. He will need to prepare analysis to demonstrate the impact the financial cuts would have on the new product range and what that actually means in terms of projected revenue. This should allow YE to demonstrate the strategic importance for PT Company of protecting the promotional budget from such severe cuts.

At this stage, YE will also need to determine the strategy and tactics he will employ during the negotiation. This will involve identifying what he wants to get out of the process; is he willing to take some cut to the budget, and how much is acceptable? YE will need to have a strong idea of what he is and is not willing to accept, and under what circumstances he would do so.

Potential areas of conflict, as well as potential areas of movement will need to be identified. YE will then need to decide how he will respond to these. What will his response be where conflict is encountered? Can this be turned around? How will he ensure that the possible areas of movement from the other side will lead to concessions being made? What concessions would YE himself be willing to make?

YE will need to use this information to formulate his negotiation strategy by establishing:

- The ideal outcome

- The realistic outcome

- An acceptable fall back position if he has to concede. This is the least favourable outcome that YE could accept without failing to meet his objectives.

Finally at this stage, YE will need to prepare for the meeting itself by considering the purpose of the meeting, where it is to be held, the pace at which the meeting should be run, and the personalities involved. An understanding of the skills and level of experience those individuals have in negotiation will help YE to be fully prepared before the meeting starts.

Stage 2 – Opening

The second stage of the negotiation process involves opening the meeting. The case of each side will be presented. YE will need to ensure his case is put forward clearly, concisely and without conflict or hostility.

Both parties should view this as an opportunity for fact finding rather than point scoring or unconsidered opposition. Both YE and the senior executives should gain an understanding of the other party's position and its strengths and weaknesses.

Stage 3 – Bargaining

YE and the senior executives will now need to try to establish some common ground. This allows them to explore areas where agreement might be reached on realistic and fall back positions. Negotiation strategy and bargaining power should then be used. YE will need to ensure that he doesn't give anything away without getting something in return. YE should be aware that we ill probably have to make some concessions in order to bring the two parties closer together.

If the senior managers make new proposals or counter proposals, YE should insist that the meeting is adjourned so that he can consider this without the other side knowing his thoughts before he is ready to tell them his decision.

YE should ensure that he adopts a suitable, business-like approach throughout the meeting. He should keep his points concise and use language that everyone will understand. While he should remain assertive he should avoid aggression and show respect for the other side.

Stage 4 – Closing

The final stage of a negotiation is similar to closing a sale. Both YE and the senior managers will need to be satisfied that all issues have been discussed and they clearly understand what has been agreed. The points should then be written up, circulated and checked by both sides. YE will need to read this carefully to ensure it is a true record of what was agreed and he is satisfied with the outcome. When both YE and the senior management have approved all clauses, the agreement can be formally printed, signed and circulated.

Question 6

Text references. Critical Path Analysis is covered in Chapter 8.

Top tips. While there are some marks available in part (a) for demonstrating your knowledge of the various stages involved in the project, most of the marks available are for applying this knowledge to the scenario and describing how problems specific to this situation could be avoided. Read the scenario carefully and avoid just listing out generic problems that could occur and how following this process would prevent them.

Take care with your presentation of your Critical Path Analysis diagram in part (b)(i). Present it clearly using a whole page and correctly labelled so that the critical path can be easily identified.

Easy marks. If you have practiced producing Critical Path Analysis diagrams, part (b)(i) should not cause you too many problems. If you have good knowledge of Critical Path Analysis you should also be able to earn a number of easy marks for demonstrating this knowledge by describing the technique in part (b)(ii).

(a)   The Project Management Institute's five project management process areas could be used to address the potential problems that could occur in the Management Accounting System (MAS) in a number of ways.

Process area 1: Initiating the project

Projects are initiated when a need or objective is defined. At this stage the requirements of the projects, its feasibility, the strengths, weaknesses, threats and opportunities (SWOT) of the project and a risk management plan will be defined. The more detailed the analysis carried out at this stage of the project, the more likely the project is to succeed.

An important consideration for S Company at this stage relates to the setting of the requirements of the project. A requirement is a statement of what is expected, or required, of a project. Project scope is all the things that have to be achieved if the project is to succeed. Requirements and scope must be clearly defined if the project is to have the best chance to succeed. This will also reduce the likelihood of re-work, continual changes, customer dissatisfaction and the associated escalation of costs. However, the Finance Director believes that no details of the functionality should be set, stating instead that it is important that the system is allowed to grow in scale during the life of the project. This approach is not recommended as it leaves the project open to the risk of scope creep (the scope of the project becoming increasingly bigger) which may cause costs to escalate out of control and the timeframe of the project to get longer and longer. If the requirements of the project are not set out at the outset, the project has nothing to work towards. There is also a risk the project will never be finished due to constantly changing requirements. The level of conflict and disagreement experienced over the life of the project is also likely to be greatly increased.

A further potential problem with this project is that only the Finance Director has had any input into the requirements and no one else in the business has been involved. This is inappropriate. If a project is to be successful, there should be consultation about the requirements with each of the key project stakeholders. Project stakeholders are the individuals and organisations who are involved in or may be affected by project activities; the end users, the project board, vendors of components that are to be bought in and so on. Consultation at the stages would help ensure all views are taken into account at an early stage and should lead to an improvement in the quality and suitability for purpose of the solution developed. Failing to do so can result in disagreements further down the line, rework, the development of an inappropriate solution and overruns in terms of budget and time.

Process area 2: Planning processes

The planning stage will involve determining and communicating what is to be done, by when and by whom. Responsibilities will be allocated and the measures of success for the project will be determined. The budget, timescale and resources (people and equipment) required will be set and committed to the project. The activities the resources need to undertake will also be identified.

The constraints of the project (time, cost and quality) will need to be formally set at this stage. This does not fit with the Finance Director's suggestion that the functionality should not be set. Allowing the project to grow is likely to cause overruns both in terms of time and money. To increase the likelihood of success of this project the constraints should be set in line with the requirements that have been set for this project. A critical path analysis or alternative tool can then be used to carefully plan the project to ensure it remains on track.

A further issue that could arise with the S Company MAS project relates to the setting of responsibilities. The Finance Director has suggested that P should be selected as the project manager, despite him never having managed a project before. This would not seem to be an ideal solution given that this is such a large scale project. This should be carefully considered at the planning stage as it would seem more appropriate for an experienced project manager to take overall responsibility for a project of this scale and nature.

Process areas 3 and 4: Executing and controlling processes

At the execution stage, the work on the project actually commences. The project manager will need to provide leadership and coordination to the project team and other stakeholders in order to successfully deliver the project. This is looked at here in conjunction with the controlling stage as the two should occur simultaneously. The project manager is responsible for monitoring and controlling the progress of the project towards its successful completion. This should be done by comparing the actual progress of the project to the plans that were established at the outset. This is crucial for ensuring the success of the project. There are two possible issues here for the MAS project.

First, if the functionality is not set, and the scale allowed to grow over the life of the project, then there will be nothing to compare actual progress against. This will make it very difficult for the project manager to monitor and control the project. He may not, therefore, know if progress is on track and will be unable to put suitable contingency plans in place.

Second, the Finance Director has suggested that progress of the project should be reported as and when the project manager feels it is appropriate. This is not sufficient to facilitate proper control of the project and may lead to problems being encountered. Progress reports show the current status of the project, usually in relation to the planned status. The report is an important control tool intended to highlight discrepancies. Given the large scale and importance of this project, a more regular progress reporting period would be appropriate. This would help to ensure that any problems encountered are addressed and contingency plans put quickly into place where any discrepancies are identified.

Process area 5: Closing processes

At the end of the project a completion report will be produced to summarise the results of the project, obtain client sign off, and identify any ongoing issues that will need to be addressed after completion. If the functionality of the MAS system is not properly defined at the beginning, it is possible that the project may never be viewed as complete. This is because it will be impossible to tell whether or not the objectives have been met. The extent to which there are ongoing issues is also likely to be higher.

A post-completion audit at the end of the process would be helpful for S Company. While this will not prevent problems being encountered in the MAS project, it will help the causes of these problems to be understood and reduce the likelihood of these problems being repeated in the future.

(b)   (i)

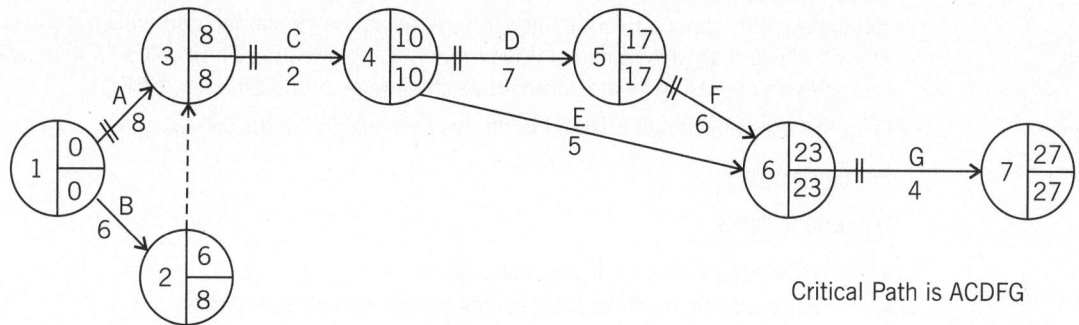

Critical Path is ACDFG

Key:

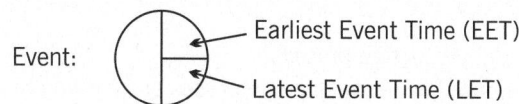

Event: Earliest Event Time (EET)
          Latest Event Time (LET)

Activity   ————————→

Dummy activity   - - - - - - - -→

Critical Path   ———⫫—→

(ii)   Critical Path Analysis (CPA) is a useful technique to help with planning and controlling large projects, such as the MAS project to be carried out at S Company.

By breaking down the project into tasks, arranging them in a logical sequence and estimating the duration of each, the total minimum duration of the project can be found. The duration of the whole project will be fixed by the longest path through the network, ie the critical path.

In order for the MAS project to be delivered on time, the activities on the critical path must be started and completed on time. By regularly monitoring and referring back to this analysis, S Company can ensure the project is running to schedule. Where any potential delays occur, they will be brought to light quickly and measures can be put in place to bring the project back into line.

As the sequence and timing of the tasks is determined at the outset and the tasks clearly defined, S Company will avoid time being lost due to poor scheduling, inappropriate order of tasks, confusion/disagreement over what is to be done next, and duplication or omission of key areas of work. These factors will all ensure the project is delivered on time.

Question 7

Text references. Porters value chain is covered in Chapter 11 and competitor analysis is covered in Chapter 13.

Top tips. As is often the case, the key with this question is to apply your knowledge to the situation you are given. This is particularly true in part b.

Easy marks. If you have a strong understanding of the value chain, you should gain a number of marks here for demonstrating this knowledge.

(a)   The value chain is the sequence of business activities by which, in the perception of the end user, value is added to the products or services created by the entity. Value chain analysis identifies the way the firm organises the business activities and how this then creates value.

The value chain consists of primary activities and support activities. Primary activities are directly related to production, sales, marketing, delivery and services. Support activities are the functions that support all of the primary activities.

Value chain analysis is a helpful tool which will allow FF to gain a better understanding of its internal capability. If FF can carry out its activities either more efficiently than its competitors, or combine them in such a way that will create a unique product, then the amount of value FF generates will be greater, and so therefore will generate competitive advantage, and ultimately, profit.

FF could use value chain analysis to do this by considering the following.

<u>Primary activities</u>

Inbound logistics

- How does it receive its raw materials?
- Are suppliers meeting or exceeding agreed quality standards?
- What kind of stock ordering system is used (eg JIT)?
- How much is spent on the storage of raw materials?

Operations

- How efficient is the production process?
- Could this be improved by rearranging processes or removing redundant activities?

Outbound logistics

- What levels of stock of the finished products are held?
- How are the goods transported to the various outlets and to customers direct?
- How quickly are goods ordered online dispatched?
- What delivery methods are used?

Marketing and sales

- Where are the goods sold?
- In what way are the products marketed?
- How successful is this?
- How easy is it for the customer to make a purchase, both online and instore?
- Which outlets or methods of sale generate the most revenue/number of transactions?

After sales services

- How is customer satisfaction measured?
- How many customer complaints are received?
- How are they dealt with?
- Is the returns policy communicated clearly?
- Percentage of products returned and reasons given for return
- What information is made available online (eg tips on getting the most out of the skincare products such which products complement each other and how they are best used)

<u>Support activities</u>

Procurement

- What purchasing policies are in place?
- How effective is the tendering process for large contracts?
- Can rates be negotiated with existing suppliers?
- What links could be made with suppliers to reduce costs?

Technology development

- What processes could be improved to enhance the efficiency and effectiveness of FF?
- How is IT used? Could it be used to better effect, for example an 'App' with e-commerce capability

Human resource management

- How is staff recruited?
- What is the level of staff turnover?
- To what extent are employees invested in (training and development etc)
- What reward policies are in place?
- Is the current level of staffing optimal?

Firm infrastructure

- Key activities such as finance, planning, quality control and management are crucially important to an organisation's strategy capacity in all primary activities. FF will need to review each of these areas to determine where any improvements could be made that would allow these activities to better support the primary activities.

By answering these questions, FF can identify where better deals could be negotiated, savings made or inefficiencies reduced, therefore improving the internal capacity of the firm.

(b) Qualitative research involves collecting and analysing non-numerical data and is useful for understanding behaviours and attitudes. For example, qualitative data that could inform FF''s competitor analysis might relate to brand awareness or why customers prefer one scent or product over another.

Qualitative research is by nature subjective and can be complex, time consuming and expensive. However, it can play a significant role in decision making. There are several ways in which qualitative research could be carried out at FF Company.

Observation. The way in which the product is sold by competitors, and/or the way customers use the product can be observed. This can be done either with our without the knowledge of the competitors or customers.

Interviews. FF could directly interview their customers about their perceptions of the products and their preferences. Interviewing past-employees of competitors may also be possible but confidentiality rules must not be breached.

Online surveys (feedback). Data could be collected from website visitors using online surveys and tools such as Google analytics.

Focus groups. This is particularly useful in relation to new products. It involves selecting and questioning a group of individuals that are representative of the target market in order to determine their preferences.

Analysis. The qualitative data obtained via the methods above must then be analysed to convert the data into meaningful information which can be used by FF to determine its strategy and to develop its products.

The types of qualitative data that FF could collect to inform its competitor analysis include:

- The products affected by the competitor including information such as the popularity, selling price and USP of each of the products. Any products which are in direct competition with specific FF products should also be identified.

- Marketing strategies and approaches used by competitors should be identified. Branding of competitive products should be considered along with details of customer awareness and perceptions of brands.

- Customer profiling can be determined. Who buys the competitors products? Are they the same people who purchase FF products? What factors make them choose which products to buy and from whom.

- Customer value analysis could be carried out. What it is about the products of FF and their competitors that customers value? Unique scents? Product design? Stylish packaging? And so on.

Quantitative research is based on facts and numbers and is objective. Ratios, trend analysis and other statistical methods can be used to convert the data into meaningful information.

The types of quantitative data that FF could collect to inform its competitor analysis includes:

- Financial information. FF could review the competitors' operating statements. Trend analysis of sales and profit margins should be reviewed and financial ratios such as EPS, ROI and liquidity could be calculated. This information can be compared to FF's own financial information and industry standards.

- Time taken to dispatch goods ordered on line, number of customer complaints, speed of resolution of complaints, and percentage of customers who re-order are all examples of quantitative data that FF could obtain to determine

Notes

Notes

Notes

Notes

Notes

Notes

Notes

Notes

Notes